This is a gift

from

the generous

collection

of

KAZUO SUGITANI

HOW TO SUCCEED IN EXPORTING AND DOING BUSINESS INTERNATIONALLY

HOW TO SUCCEED IN EXPORTING AND DOING BUSINESS INTERNATIONALLY

ERIC SLETTEN

JOHN WILEY & SONS, INC.

New York • Chichester • Brisbane • Toronto • Singapore

Copyright © 1994 by Eric Sletten
Published by John Wiley & Sons, Inc.

Library of Congress Cataloging-in-Publication Data

Sletten, Eric.
    How to succeed in exporting and doing business internationally/
  by Eric Sletten.
        p.   cm.
    Includes index.
    ISBN 0-471-31128-6 (cloth)–ISBN 0-471-31129-4 (paper)
    1. Export marketing–United States–Management. 2. International
business enterprises–United States–Management.   I. Title.
HF1416.5.S57   1993
658.8'48–dc20   93-23318

Printed in the United States of America
10 9 8 7 6 5 4 3 2 1

Throughout the writing and editing of this book, two groups of individuals continually came to mind: the men and women of the American Graduate School of International Management (Thunderbird) and the United States and Foreign Commercial Service. They share the common bond of working at the forefront of America's quest for economic prosperity and growth, although they are spread throughout the world and work in two distinct fields of endeavor. What I have learned about international business operations, or at least that part worth knowing, comes from them. I am proud to call both groups my colleagues, and I dedicate this book to them.

Preface

Perhaps you have received an inquiry from abroad and are wondering what to do about it. Or maybe you sense your company has some international potential. Possibly you are contemplating a need for your firm to institutionalize its international efforts, or you have a well-established international marketing effort underway and need to get the entire company behind the effort. For all of you, the problems are the same and, surprisingly, so are the solutions.

Most U.S. firms that are involved with the international marketplace started out when their interest was piqued by an international inquiry generated by attendance at a U.S. trade fair or perhaps by an advertisement placed in a U.S. publication. How you decide to proceed—to develop your international market or not—will likely set the tenor of your company's fortunes for a number of years to come.

There are two basic ideas from which this book flows. First, I will not teach you how to succeed with regard to international business. Rather, I will teach you how not to fail. I say this because there is an element of luck to all business. The only logical way to proceed is to develop a strategy and approach that minimizes luck as the only determining factor with your international efforts. There is nothing wrong with luck (I have had good fortune work for me more than any man has a right to expect in one lifetime), but it more often provides the occasional dessert rather than the bread and butter.

The second idea is that 90 percent of the means by which your firm conducts domestic operations are directly transferable to the international marketplace.

The sad fact is businesspeople who claim to be the most knowledgeable on the subject of international business generate income by making it seem dangerous, risky, difficult, and mysterious. I'm referring to some of the export management companies, bankers, freight forwarders, lawyers, and successful exporters who do not want to attract domestic competitors by virtue of acknowledging that the process just isn't that difficult. I know this is to be the case because I too have engaged in the same sort of subterfuge. At times, I did this to make money and in other cases so I would appear or feel more important. The unfortunate result of this deceptive information is that the audience eventually comes to believe it (after all, we are trained to credit the "experts"). Behind this lies the failure of U.S. business to learn how and when to use the "experts." The "experts" cannot really be blamed for adding to the mythology; they are only doing what any of us would in the same situation—attempting to make a living.

Nevertheless, there are many people who are knowledgeable and can be of great assistance in generating and managing international growth. Part of the key is knowing how and when to use their services, a subject covered in the book. These individuals are powerful and valuable allies when properly employed. If you take the time to understand who they are and what they do, they will not only generate additional revenue for your firm, but will become revenue sources themselves.

If 90 percent of your domestic operations are directly transferable to international operations, it follows that it is the other 10 percent that leads most companies to fail. It is this 10 percent that I will focus on. By doing this, I will demystify the process and provide you with the information and procedures that will allow you to gain control of your destiny—and proceed from a well-developed and organized base.

When I graduated from the American Graduate School of International Management (Thunderbird) and began my international career with a heavy equipment manufacturer, it was the start of a long road leading through a number of companies and a relentless search for information about my chosen profession. The quest continues even now, as I document the practicalities I have learned, mostly the hard way, over the last 15 years. What I learned will astound most U.S. businesspeople: There is very little about international business that is mysterious, and, for the most part, the information you need to be successful is free. What you really require to garner maximum advantage from this book, and for your company, is some time, an open mind, and a great deal of willingness to make it work. That's it.

Contents

Chapter 1

The Business Reasons for Exporting and Doing Business Internationally

Here is what many people think about doing business internationally:

- Only large companies can be international.
- You have to produce a product that no one else has ever made.
- It is expensive.
- It is dangerous, mysterious, and unknowable.
- You have to hire seasoned professionals at outrageous salaries.
- You need to speak many languages.
- You will run afoul foreign laws and tax codes.

These ideas are all myths, as the following facts show:

- According to the U.S. Small Business Administration, 25 percent of all exporters are firms with fewer than 100 employees.
- High-technology firms with new products are in the minority among exporters.
- The United States is in the midst of an export boom. The weak dollar, growth in consumer demand in foreign markets, and an opening of traditionally closed economies have all combined to make the time ripe for export efforts. In fact, the time has been ripe for some time. Exports accounted for 45 percent of the growth in the U.S. economy between 1966 and 1990. In 1990, exports accounted for 85 percent of this growth, and there are no indications of any change in direction.

1

- Half of all exporters sell in only one market, and fewer than 20 percent export to more than five markets. The conclusion drawn by most experts is that these numbers indicate that many U.S. firms are not actively pursuing overseas opportunities but rather respond to them when they arise.

- Approximately 100,000 U.S. firms export, and over 80 percent of them are small and medium sized. However, among leading U.S. firms, 95 percent export, 85 percent import, 80 percent operate foreign subsidiaries, and 65 percent operate foreign manufacturing facilities. Among medium-sized firms, 45 percent export, an increase of 9 percent over 1990, and 55 percent of these exporting companies increased their exports over the previous year. Among small firms exporting, 41 percent reported export sales growth above their domestic sales; 23 percent said their export sales increased by between 20 percent and 49 percent in the previous year.

- I have done business in over 60 countries and do not speak the languages of most of them, am not overpaid, and had very few legal and no tax problems with foreign governments in over 15 years of working and living abroad. When exporters have legal problems, most often they occur because of inadequate distribution contracts. Tax problems most often develop once you have left the traditional export role and entered the market via a sales office or hiring direct employees in that market. You are very unlikely to do the latter in the initial stages of your effort, and both problems can be avoided with a minimal amount of diligence.

WHY EXPORT?

Why export? There are hundreds of reasons, all of them valid, but the principal one is business survival.

The Competition

All of the opportunities to expand export markets are two way. The same influences that make the international marketplace a good place for you make it even better for your foreign competitors. One-third of the goods and services in the world are sold in the United States, so clearly the United States is the first place overseas competition will look for new markets. Your only defense to this invasion is a good offense. If you can keep your competitors fighting for market share in their markets, you can delay or dilute their efforts in your market.

As the marketplace becomes more competitive, the need to conduct effective international operations has been redefined as a cost of doing business. Many companies, however, fail to regard the initial expense of engaging in export as a necessary cost component to their business, not unlike having fire insurance against the day the factory burns down.

When I was in the heavy equipment industry in the 1970s, I witnessed the emergence of a titan, Komatsu of Japan. We battled them for market share throughout the world, but it was not until they hit us at home that management acknowledged a serious competitor. By then it was too late. My company had made the mistake of taking its overseas distribution efforts for granted and, as a result, hastened the entry of Komatsu into the United States. (There were, of course, a number of other circumstances, including a great deal of support that Komatsu received from the Japanese government.)

However, we have to deal with the competition on the playing ground we are given. In general terms, I attribute the success the Japanese (and others) have enjoyed in taking markets from U.S. companies to a lack of aggressiveness by U.S. management. I hope this experience has taught us something about the need to battle foreign competition on their soil, not ours.

Good ideas are not proprietary. The United States has the most-followed industry press in the world, and very few new products or other developments escape careful scrutiny and subsequent imitation by overseas competitors. Many U.S. firms delay the international marketing effort so long that foreign competition emerges. When the overseas marketplace demands the product and the U.S. company refuses to respond, foreign producers jump into the game.

If you have a good product but lack skillful and strong international distribution, you will engender foreign competition by virtue of surrendering overseas markets they can exploit at great profit, simply because you decline to compete. In many cases, these foreign firms are much larger than their American counterparts, well capitalized, and able to price aggressively to gain market share in the United States.

Profit

The most stated reason for exporting is profit. That's why you are in business. In fact, most discussions of this subject will lure you to the export game by pledging record returns in record time. Certainly many companies discover they have better markets overseas than in the United States and as a result do very well, but many more businesses have to grind it out and take the long view. For most companies, international investment is made to ensure survival and generate additional revenue.

Your Neglected Assets

Your overseas distribution system is an asset just like plant and equipment (P&E). In most cases, it is even more valuable than P&E and demands ongoing investment to ensure that this asset maintains its value. It's not uncommon for large companies to buy other companies solely to capture their distribution systems. For example, IBM has acquired an interest in Wang computer to gain Wang's client base (that is, the distribution system).

Another consideration has to do with what I call the "new value-added." In the past, it was fairly common for a company to control all production elements for its products, from raw materials to the finished good. Today, in part due to low labor cost and high-capacity component manufacture (in many cases abroad), most U.S. companies are adding value by design engineering components, final assembly of the product, and the after-sales service and support. A good example of this trend can be found in one of the fastest-growing industry sectors in America: IBM-compatible computer manufacturers. For the most part, there is nothing proprietary about the products of these manufacturers, and the vast majority of the components are imported from abroad and assembled in the United States. One look at any *Personal Computing* magazine will show that these companies attempt to differentiate the products more on a support basis than any other. This "standardization" of production components is exactly what leads to the new value-added, with less value placed on the unique properties of the product and more on service and support. This support function is the direct responsibility of overseas distributors, because they are on the front line with the client base. Hence, the value of the distribution network increasingly is eclipsing the value of the product itself.

There is another indication that distribution systems are becoming the value-added: A growing number of companies are recognizing that they can stimulate exponential growth by pushing more products down the same distribution system. They are striving to broaden their marketing base by making additional products available to their customers through the same channel of distribution. The growth of large warehouse shopping outlets is instructive. Stores like Sam's and Price Club now sell everything from automobiles to frozen chicken breasts.

Thus, another good reason to export, aside from the fact it helps ensure survival and increases revenue, is that it enhances the value of your assets.

Diversification of Revenue

Exporting provides a broader marketing base. When market conditions at home lead to a decrease in revenue, exports can help minimize the impact.

During a particularly nasty downturn in the late 1970s, the company I worked for was facing a grim outlook, one so severe that large layoffs were being considered at one of our southwestern plants. The chairman of the board summoned me to his office. In an effort to avoid the layoff and the costly dispute with the unions that would inevitably follow, he wanted to know if my export sales could keep the plant functioning at reasonable capacity for three months. My reply was that it could be done if I were given a bit more freedom with regard to pricing and deliveries. He agreed, and the layoff was avoided. The margins on this new export business were not large, but the goal was achieved because we had systematically created a global distribution system that could sop up idle capacity.

The lesson here is that you gain a great deal of flexibility by having a worldwide distribution system that can be motivated to purchase additional product when the necessity arises. This is beneficial for downturns and for excess production runs or inventory as well. An added advantage is that you can stimulate sales in foreign markets without imperiling your domestic pricing levels (which you probably worked years to achieve) by dropping the price of your product drastically in the United States in order to move it.

When sales in the United States begin to decline, due to the introduction of new technology or product lines, you can extend the older product's life span by exporting it in increasing volume to lesser-developed countries. A friend in the telecommunications business did just that. He began marketing the obsolete product through a distribution network in Latin America and Asia, contributing to the bottom line by continuing to sell a product produced in an already amortized plant (which had paid for itself time and again). The older product sold well in the new markets because it was more easily serviced than the advanced model and somewhat less expensive as well.

After eight years of peddling the product in Third World markets, he licensed its production in 11 countries, thus continuing a stream of income from a defunct product line, at no cost to his company. As part of the licensing agreement, the foreign licensees not only paid royalties for the number of units produced but were tied to supply contracts for the component parts—yet another source of income.

As a manufacturer, your firm has already incurred its greatest costs by developing the product, getting production up and running, and launching the product in the United States (the most competitive market in the world). It makes sense to milk all possible revenue from this large fixed investment through maximizing sales.

To ignore the international marketplace may well be to walk away from the margin that puts your company in the profit category where all sorts of other opportunities become accessible. If you are in a highly competitive business, this additional capacity can also be reflected in your pricing and serve to keep you ahead of the competition.

Intelligence

Many companies have found that innovations developed to meet a need overseas also have a U.S. application. If you are not the innovator, the producers overseas will look to the United States and your customers, with the intent of selling them a product that may be superior to yours.

One good example of overseas innovation benefitting the home market are products that need to be exceptionally durable and less service dependent. Many computers and communications devices sold to the military in the

United States were developed for use overseas, where conditions are harsher. These products are highly appealing to the U.S. military because they are more ruggedly designed than commercial use would dictate. Another example is water purification technologies, now marketed in the United States, that were developed for use in remote Third World locations.

You must have an overseas presence to ensure your company is getting all the information you need with regard to competition, new product development, and emerging opportunities. Being able to study the foreign competition's products before they get to the United States enables your company to deal with them once they arrive. You will have the benefit of better directing your product development in order to meet any technological advantages they may enjoy. This, in turn, will make it more difficult for them to recruit distributors or filch yours. Their competitive response to your market entry abroad will also tell you about their costs, financial strength, ability and willingness to use price cuts as a marketing tool, and how they manage their distribution systems.

I think it fair to say that most of what I have learned over the years, at least that portion which turned out to be serviceable for me, was gleaned from observing my competition with a keen eye.

WHEN THEORY MEETS REALITY

I remember the first export seminar I attended, shortly after I graduated from the American Graduate School of International Management. Freshly employed by a Fortune 500 company to manage its Latin American distribution, I was brimming with optimism. I knew basic Spanish, had some familiarity with Latin America, and had completed my educational requirements, but I possessed absolutely no experience in the real world of international operations.

As I sat through the seminar, which had to do with the basics of export marketing, it occurred to me that nobody would ever consider entering international operations after one of these seminars. I first heard about a U.S. company that had shipped $200,000 worth of goods to Taiwan and was subsequently beaten out of payment because it had improperly filled out the export documentation. The next topic was a rather lengthy diatribe on why U.S.

7

firms cannot entrust the distribution of their product to anyone in a foreign market without the services of an accomplished international attorney. The result would be stolen patents and lost market share. The hapless victim would be driven from the company, lose his or her spouse and eventually wind up wearing fingerless gloves and begging for money. And it got worse. There were dire predictions of what would happen if one did not hire a professional to handle all of the laws surrounding the export licensing regime imposed by the U.S. government.

Certainly bad things do happen. The problem is that we tend to fear those things, especially in the international arena, and then we build an entire mythology around them rather than viewing these incidents in context. Bad things happen everywhere. But much like newscasts, dog bites man (problems that occur with your business at home) is not news, whereas man bites dog (problems that occur with your international operations) gets a bit more attention due to the novelty of it all, if nothing else.

Having completed the required seminar, I left for the first assignment in my international career: teaching technical seminars on heavy equipment maintenance. I did not dread the subject matter, having a good technical basis for the discussion, but the thought of conducting the classes in Spanish was alarming. "No," my boss assured me, "all our mechanics are required to speak English. How else could they read the manual?" he finished triumphantly. That seemed reasonable. After all, my predecessor had taught these classes in English.

My students did not seem overly intrigued. Several of them slumbered through class and not one asked even a single question. At each pause I found myself greeted by vacant stares and general malaise. I could conclude only that they either already knew everything or were uninterested in general. By the third stop, in Costa Rica, I tired of the blank vacant stares and, somewhat dubious, began to question if any of these mechanics spoke English. Consequently, I set out to develop and then launch a Spanish version of my program.

The response was staggering. As it turned out, not one of those mechanics knew a transmission from a spaceship—at least not in English. Oddly, my teaching in Spanish was regarded as a discomforting problem for the distributors, because they had always assured everyone in my company that all the mechanics did, in fact, speak English. So, for the first time (but certainly not the last) I found myself acting as "translator" between a disgruntled group of distributors and an immovable front office. I was to later learn this situation is the position in which many international executives find themselves.

Certainly, it defied common sense that these mechanics, most of whom had not completed grade school, would speak English. It seemed equally improbable the distributors would attempt to teach them English; it would have been expensive, and the turnover rate of these workers was so high that the majority would be working elsewhere before any advantage could possibly be derived from their language skills. At the same time, the distributors could not plead their case to headquarters; they feared that if it were known that they employed non-English speaking mechanics, my company would cancel their distribution contracts. After careful consideration, I decided to forget the whole thing and was duly sworn to secrecy by the distributors.

This was my initiation to international trade: working for one of the nation's largest companies, in an international division that had existed for decades, but in which nobody knew that for years we had compelled our overseas distributors to conceal their mechanics' inadequacy with the English language. As a result we were unable to provide adequate service to our clients because we refused to acknowledge that training in their language was a necessity! The lesson burned indelibly into my mind: Top management, even in large companies that derive high percentages of their total revenue from international operations, often lacks knowledge about the conduct of their international operations.

Most of those executives would greatly benefit from reading this book, which is, admittedly, only a starting point for the larger process. I would hope they would then embark on a formal program to begin to deal more effectively with both the problems and opportunities that face U.S. business in the international arena.

The whole effort commences with what I call "learning what you need to know." It also involves "learning why you have to be international and effectively communicating the need to others." In some cases, these "others" are within the company, but just as often they are outside of the company, involved in some support function, such as an attorney or accountant. They may have no knowledge of the international marketplace and may even discount it to management, or they may make it appear perplexing, to increase billings. Either of these situations presents a real problem to the potential exporter, who is trying to enlist support from others in the company for seeking new business abroad. I know of many cases in which top management of a company is so ignorant of export operations that they refuse to act. They shy away from international operations because of illusory legal complications and a host of other fancied pitfalls.

Some years ago, I was speaking to a CEO of a medium-sized corporation who contended he didn't want to get into export sales because it involved foreign currency. Apparently ignorant of my background, he lectured me at length concerning the unwanted tax exposure his firm would generate from export sales (completely false in his case); he imagined legal entanglements that would cripple the company and a variety of other disasters lurking just outside the borders of the United States.

Although many companies profess to be international in nature, very few, especially manufacturing firms, are truly global in outlook. The reason, in part, is that many companies never manage to break out of perceiving themselves as a U.S. company, a perception that eventually becomes self-limiting. The company will fail to grant overseas opportunities the same importance as domestic ones, and the resulting lack of market development abroad will create the illusion that overseas potential is not as great as that in the United States. This sort of thinking manifests itself in all sorts of ways, perhaps the most common being that an overseas assignment is seen as a poor career move, or discussion centers around the firm's need to protect itself in the international arena rather than how to exploit the opportunities international marketing presents to the company.

Certainly some trepidation about the hazards of international operations (not getting paid, getting your product ripped off, having your factory nationalized, and the like) is natural for novices. (I have even heard this sort of self-defeating talk from large, supposedly sophisticated companies.) But if you are to succeed, you need to get around this inward-looking, self-defeating, and self-perpetuating nonsense. How do you do this? Quite simple: Make the international arena a part of your daily business, and place it on an equal footing with the domestic side of the company. The steps are straightforward and begin with the most obvious: commitment from the top of the company to cultivate the notion that a foreign assignment is not only a career maker, but is required to stay on the path to the top. Increase the desirability of these assignments by granting greater autonomy to your foreign managers, promoting only after the successful completion of an overseas posting, and establishing a clear career path for those who return. Put the word out throughout the company that top management has identified international business as the future of the firm and thereby attract the best managers in the firm.

Even in companies that do not yet have overseas operations, top management can still require that executives spend time on international issues. As they become conversant with overseas operations, those at lower levels of the company will realize that experience and knowledge of these operations are required for their success. Management will gain the added benefit of exposing mid-level managers to international operations and thereby assist them in beginning to debunk the myth. In most cases, managers will quickly develop new confidence with international issues, and they will begin to seek out new opportunities.

The CEO, CFO, and chairman of the board should take trips abroad routinely to visit staff, facilities, distributors, and customers, in part so international staff understand they are not "out of sight, out of mind." One board meeting should be held at an overseas site every two years—either at the company's overseas offices or at the site of an outstanding distributor. In the latter case, you can pay this person the enormous compliment of addressing the board. Not only is this a great morale booster; your board might learn something as well.

Create the perception that no bias exists within the company for where a dollar is earned and that international sales not only offers a chance to excel above what could reasonably be expected in the United States, but also offers truly unusual opportunities (including frequent exposure to the top levels of the company).

Hire, retain, and promote foreigners in your company. You will create a pool of language talent and cultural knowledge about other countries, and your international corporate image, within and outside your firm, will be greatly enhanced. Treat foreigners with the same standards and fairness applied to any other employee, American or otherwise. Consider promoting top foreign distributors into the head office (assuming the firm can afford them) to assist with recruiting and supporting other distributors, and to assist in generating additional sales, especially in countries and regions with which they are familiar. Distributors will be impressed with the company's willingness to draw from the distributor pool, and your firm will gain someone who is knowledgeable about picking distributors and committed to supporting them.

Involve lower levels of the company in international travel. Motivate them to learn more about foreign business methods, languages, and cultures so the fears of the international arena become dissipated with time. This will be especially important for marketing, finance, and technical support staff.

If your company does all these things, it will become a truly international corporation, with the myths shattered and the ability to respond to the opportunities.

INTERNATIONAL EVOLUTION

No set profile seems to exist with regard to what makes a particular company fly internationally and what creates failure. But in looking across the spectrum of successful multinationals and U.S. exporters, it becomes clear that almost all firms heavily oriented to the international marketplace have two attributes.

The first has to do with the products involved and is an important, but not sufficient, explanation of why they became accomplished exporters. Essentially they are blessed with highly exportable products that will, if properly managed, eventually generate around 50 percent of their total revenue from international sales. These products are usually patented and benefit from those patents. Put another way, if the products were not patented, they would create a great deal of additional competition. Generally, well-managed companies undergo the expense and effort of filing patents only if the technology or product is truly novel.

Usually the product will have a price advantage over existing products that perform the same function—or they will achieve the same purpose more quickly or cheaply, and perhaps not have a price advantage but enjoy a cost efficiency edge. These products may possess some other unique characteristic, functional or aesthetic, that makes them more desirable to the end users. They may be products used in conjunction with existing products, making them quicker, better, or easier to use.

In some cases, they will be products or services that are relatively new to the U.S. market and are characterized by a broad geographical acceptance in the United States, given the short period of time they have been marketed. Usually the product enjoys a high rate of domestic sales growth. This rapid acceptance often leads to inquiries from abroad, essentially unsolicited, during the early stages of growth. These inquiries normally will be generated by spillover from the domestic marketing campaign or by favorable press reviews.

If the product does not enjoy broad application, it will occupy one of the dominant positions in a smaller niche market, and be widely perceived as possessing some unique characteristic or use, which will lead to inquiries from abroad. These niche products, often characterized by a relative absence of competition, are often the ones that receive attention from abroad almost immediately.

The second characteristic, and the one that determines the ultimate success of the international marketing effort, product characteristics aside, is the attitude of the company management. The internationalization of a U.S. firm is often an evolutionary process and at the early stages is marked by indecision, dread, and a perception that international operations are beyond the capabilities of the company. In many cases, management believes the domestic market is not yet fully developed and that international efforts cannot start until the last unit has been sold in the United States.

Over time, the company management becomes a bit less tentative in its approach to international operations. They begin to develop expectations about international sales and wonder how to pursue these opportunities. By the time the U.S. firm reaches this stage of development, it may already face foreign competitors marketing in more than one country. This is especially true for products not so highly technical in nature that they preclude rapid development by other firms.

As the company explores this new area, it begins educating itself about exporting and/or international operations. Seminar attendance becomes evident, and the company begins to seek out governmental and nongovernmental sources of information. Corporate staff may be thrashing around in a completely unfocused manner, but at least they are aware of the opportunity. Often the person heading the international efforts is from the domestic marketing group and will focus on the technical issues surrounding international operations rather than generating business. This person will greatly fear the possibility of making a costly mistake.

Finally, the company begins to investigate specific international opportunities and starts an effort to place distribution systems abroad. Missteps along the way are not unusual. The companies almost always follow a premium pricing policy in foreign markets (which will eventually create problems with their foreign representatives). They often pass up opportunities for sales because they do not feel sufficiently familiar with a market to undergo the decision process of how to enter it. The executives may feel quite intimidated by the entire process, and that attitude leads to a continued lack of aggressiveness, which will cost market share. When they do make a decision with regard to appointing a foreign representative, marketing executives often grant territories that are extremely large, at times granting exclusive distribution rights for entire continents to one distributor or export management company.

While the company is establishing distribution, the focus tends to be toward the psychologically close countries, such as the United Kingdom, Canada, and other English-speaking developed markets. Many decisions are made based on a desire to enter markets that seem familiar, and therefore less threatening, regardless of the market's actual potential for the firm. For example, among medium-sized U.S. firms, Canada is the highest export destination (26 percent), followed by the European Community (21 percent). Not surprisingly, the Middle East trails all other regions (10 percent).

Most often the U.S. company comes to rely heavily on its overseas representatives for information regarding how international business is conducted, market conditions in their countries, and even some of the technical information about international operations. This is a period when the company, which has not yet learned how to develop independent sources of information, can fall victim to an unscrupulous representative.

Eventually our firm will either develop the required international skills in-house or seek experienced international staff from outside the company. Typically the company begins to experience dramatic increases in its international sales, and this stage is somewhat chaotic because the company is simultaneously striving to maintain its growth, struggling with required product adaptations, and institutionalizing its international efforts. The firm may open its first overseas offices and begin to contemplate joint ventures and other investment postures in its primary markets. These proposals occur due to pressure, or, at the very least, strong encouragement, brought to bear by overseas representatives. Decisions are often made without a completely rational basis, but they are often correct since the markets are sufficiently well developed to support a more direct presence.

This is also the time when rapid turnover in international staff will occur, because the staff has become attractive to competing companies and management's focus begins to narrow. In many cases, management may for the first time be sufficiently interested in international operations to distinguish additional opportunities that may be realized by replacing the existing international staff. Quite often this changing of the guard will lead to a loss of product knowledge by the staff, distributorship defections as old staff move to other companies and take their distributors with them, or the cancellation of existing distributors by new staff (which may be undesirable from any number of perspectives).

Over time, with additional experience, the company completes its evolutionary cycle. For well-managed companies, the cycle will continue as new products and staff work their way through the company.

COMMON MISTAKES

Common mistakes are very much linked to the evolutionary process. In most cases, they are quite understandable—and in all cases, they are avoidable. Perhaps the best way to avoid mistakes is to recognize the nature of the evolutionary process and use this understanding to raise the sophistication of the effort from the beginning. However, this does not seem to be a common approach to the problem.

Many companies that embark upon an international effort suffer from two maladies. First, if they are not immediately successful, they give up, presuming no market exists for the product. This determination is usually the consequence of not doing enough homework. Any investigation the firm undertakes is normally unfocused and tends toward understanding the technical detail surrounding export operations rather than the marketing issues and the sales opportunities. Staff members are shortly engulfed with the technical issues, which can be quite daunting and lead to the conclusion that international operations are beyond the scope of company resources. These companies are out of the game before the clock starts—not because they have no market but because of a failure to focus on the market research and trade contact information that is available. They never determine whether their product is marketable in a particular foreign country because the knowledgeable representatives or end users in that market never get the opportunity to examine the product or engage in any test marketing of it. The result is that the formal marketing effort is shelved; by now the company has already "determined" it has no international potential and views these orders as anomalies, thus putting the company even farther behind in its efforts.

Companies that move beyond this first mistake and find that they have truly exceptional products sought by overseas customers, may promptly perpetrate the second error: shipping product with little or no idea of the identity of the ultimate end users. Often these orders come through trading companies, or they are direct, unsolicited orders from overseas users. If the product does get out in the market, other pitfalls await. The product may be used improperly or lack adequate service, and eventually the quality image of the product may be tarnished. Finally, the manufacturer, having no idea who the end users are or why the product is valuable to them, is unable to repeat a success achieved by accident.

Any degree of sustained success with these unsolicited sales lends credence to the fiction that being international does not really require any effort. This misperception leads to the belief that the international portion of the business is really gravy, and not the core business of the firm. This misunderstanding can be the most dangerous of all outcomes because it will lead the company to shelve the entire effort, perhaps for decades.

If the company has generated enough interest to begin to receive requests for distribution rights from overseas markets, the tendency is to issue a flat no to these requests or to authorize anyone who wants to market the product to do so. Saying no is walking away from the revenue that will allow the company to begin the more enterprising approach to expanding international operations (with greater degrees of comfort). Saying yes to *any* request often results in getting a group of distributors that may create a great deal of uncertainty by poorly representing the product line. Aside from the damage that might accrue to the company's reputation, many firms end up with a number of distributors who, through ineptness or neglect, do nothing with the product. The company may conclude it has no potential in those markets serviced by that distributor group. The end result, once again, is to ignore potentially lucrative markets because of a faulty conclusion.

The evolving company will find that many of these distributors will have to be canceled as it begins to formalize the international process. These terminations can be costly and time-consuming, and they will engender a great deal of confusion with the end user group, which has come to associate the product with a particular distributor (assuming that the distributor has sold the product widely in the market). Additionally, the canceled distributor will seek out another supplier, or even produce the product in-house, in order to safeguard the market developed for that product. Because this distributor may be identified as the leading supplier in that country, he or she can delay or dilute other efforts to establish a beachhead in the market.

At the same time that overseas customers are pursuing the U.S. firm, export management companies (EMCs) also notice their products. Most companies will fail to recognize the usefulness of these export managers in pioneering product introduction in difficult or costly markets and refuse the request for distribution rights. Or, they may offer to sell the EMC the product but not on an exclusive basis, so the EMC will cast about elsewhere for a supplier, again creating unwanted and costly competition. Very few EMCs will work on a nonexclusive basis, and very few of the good ones will even discuss the possibility of expending their funds in the marketing effort with no guarantee their investment will be protected.

Assume, by now, that the company has begun its international effort and is moving up the evolutionary scale. The next misstep is when it begins to disregard the international business. Perhaps the firm's growth is such that management is having difficulty rationalizing the sales increases, and the international side is sacrificed to secure development of the domestic market. Or maybe the company has established differing pricing strategies that clearly favor the domestic distribution system, to the displeasure of distributors, who may defect.

By now, the international side has begun to demand additional resources: more frequent travel to other markets, product modification, foreign language brochures and technical manuals, and increasing warranty payments and service requirements. The next lapse is the one that eventually costs the company more in lost revenue than any other: Management declines to acknowledge the need for additional investment to continue international sales growth. Companies that have not made the investment to maximize their international operations may begin to balk at expending funds on the effort. Management contends they have not done so to date, and the firm is doing quite well! They are unable to see that a change of approach is needed because executives have nothing against which to measure "quite well," and their experience is that they can sell product in these markets without the additional investment. This decision, usually made by the most senior of company management, will go unchallenged in all but the rarest of circumstances.

It is often at this point that luck appears—a trusted colleague of some senior management member who happens to have already lived (or suffered, depending on perspective) through the evolutionary process. This person might be able to force a rethinking of the decision, pointing to his or her own experience and how a more aggressive approach paid dividends. If this agent of change does not surface, the effort may be set back years, or at least until new management appears on the scene.

Let us assume now that the company has overcome its reticence and begun doing everything it can to market the product worldwide. With success, management will sense they are knowledgeable with their conduct of international operations, and sales staff may begin to pull out the stops with regard to the effort, sometimes recklessly.

Then the next bombshell drops. A distributor is convinced that the product needs to be produced or assembled in a foreign market. The first reaction from the U.S. company is usually negative. Management feels that an overseas operation is fraught with peril, that the company may lose profitability, that intellectual property will be threatened, that the company might undergo an unacceptable foreign exchange risk, and the like. The recent cockiness will quickly disappear as the firm's executives realize this is a whole different level of effort, where capital will be at risk and the company will no longer be able to retreat to the domestic business should anything go awry with the overseas operation. If the company delays so long that it loses market share to a more audacious competitor that establishes the foreign facilities, it will eventually grasp the need for that sort of presence. If this happens, our firm will again begin the effort, but without the advantage of being first to the marketplace. It will take longer to recoup the initial investment as the competitor, in an attempt to conserve a hard-won market, uses price and any other tool to discourage the entry of the newcomer.

Then our company will begin the next step toward international excellence, building a truly global company, and confronting a fresh series of potential mistakes. We look at them later in the book.

We, as businesspeople, must begin to think of a firm's international growth as a process of maturation. Companies beginning the effort should seek out more accomplished firms and study their international expansion, in an effort to better understand their own decision-making process, and their fears in a larger context. That context is one of understanding the problems that accompany the evolutionary process and tackling them before they divert the company from the quickest route to failure avoidance. The wrong decisions will be costly at every stage of the evolution. Often the blame for these decisions can be laid at the door of docile and fearful managers who allow their own lack of knowledge to hold the firm back from its rightful position in the market.

Chapter 2

Cultural Factors: Are They Really Important?

U.S. executives must come to a better understanding of the role that cultural differences play in the conduct of international business. These differences, however, are entirely overestimated as a factor with regard to individual fortunes in international operations. I have never seen a case in which a deal that was advantageous to both parties was not struck because of a cultural difficulty. But I have seen deals become more costly or delayed because individuals, most often Americans, were unprepared for the negotiation or failed to understand what the other party wanted from the meeting.

CULTURAL TRAINING OR GOOD MANNERS?

An entire industry has sprung up around the perceived need for cross-cultural training, but most examples used to demonstrate how dissimilar other cultures seem to be are, in fact, not unique to that culture. More often, it is a matter of degree that constitutes the uniqueness a particular society places on a manner of behavior. Let's begin with some examples and compare them to typical American behavior.

One of my favorites is the old saw that one should never touch the head of a Thai, because the head is considered sacred in Thailand. But it is *never* proper, in any society, to go around patting relative strangers on the head. And it most certainly is not behavior that is considered businesslike in the United States (or any other country, for that matter). Yet this old saw has become part of the lore employed to demonstrate how radically different other societies are from our own. There is no arguing that societies differ; the argument is with how the differences affect the conduct of business.

In the Arab world, it is extremely discourteous to point the bottom of the feet in the direction of another person. To effectively accomplish this maneuver, you must slouch down in a chair with your legs crossed. This is not a position anyone would normally assume in a business meeting (at least not for long). Again, the fact that presenting your feet to someone in a business setting is rude is relatively universal. That this gesture has special significance in the Arab world is not arguable. But assuming one exhibits simple good manners, it is not a problem.

Customs vary widely from one country to another. But it is also true that people with whom U.S. executives do business are often quite a bit more cosmopolitan than their American counterparts. The vast majority of the individuals with whom we do business abroad are, with some exceptions, better traveled, better educated, and more worldly than most Americans, and they often fathom American culture better than we can know. In almost all cases, they are far more familiar with our culture than we are with theirs. This is, in part, due to American television and movies, which have, by virtue of their wide distribution overseas, exposed even the most unsophisticated to American culture. It also has a great deal to do with the fact that so many foreigners seek an education in the United States or are frequent travelers to America. Your contact typically will have a set of expectations about how you, as an American, will behave. In terms of the business relationship, the greater jeopardy may well lie in adapting your behavior to his or her culture to the degree you shatter expectations about how you will comport yourself.

On to another case—belching, which is not, in most countries, acceptable behavior in public. Imagine that you have a meeting with someone from an Arab country in which belching is quite commonplace. After lunch you emit a deafening, moist burp. However, your business partner (who probably speaks excellent English and was educated in the United Kingdom or the United States) knows this behavior is loathsome in American culture and is quite rightly aghast; it is something he does among Arab friends in private but not with a foreign business partner. He might well view the belch as being condescending or implicitly critical of his culture. At the very least, you have certainly managed to confuse him about what you might have meant by the belch. You have meddled with his perception of what behavior he should expect and perhaps made his dealings with you somewhat more unpredictable from his standpoint.

Remember that the business meeting is taking place for a reason—one that has nothing to do with any cultural considerations. Rather, each party has something the other party wants. There are many times when the effort to impress one another with our cultural awareness begins to impede the process that motivated the meeting in the first place: to do business.

The Japanese bow is a well-known form of salutation and symbolizes respect. The handshake discharges a similar function in many Western countries. Both are universally acknowledged forms of greeting, yet they can lead to a great deal of discomfiture. In the early 1980s, I accompanied a group of American businessmen to Japan with the objective of negotiating a joint venture agreement between the two firms. This negotiation was of extreme importance to the U.S. company, and the executives who were to attend the initial meetings, anticipating difficulties, had contracted with a U.S. university for a course in American-Japanese cross-cultural communications. On the flight over, these executives discussed the various aspects of what they had learned concerning Japanese business protocol. (I would have spent the time going over what we hoped to achieve from the negotiation.)

We were met at the airport by some of the lesser executives of the Japanese firm and taken to the Tokyo office. When the two negotiating groups finally met, outside the boardroom of the Japanese firm, our hosts strode forward with hands extended (yes, they too wanted to be culturally sensitive) while the Americans, after quickly dropping their briefcases, all peered at the floor in a deep bow. This scramble seemed to carry through the next two days as both sides undertook the establishment of cultural ground rules for the meetings—while making no headway toward the business objective. The Japanese contingent was unusually forthright, probably in response to their own training about the "American way" of doing business, while the Americans were untypically circumspect. At one point I heard one of the Americans state that he was somewhat displeased by the directness of the Japanese side because he understood directness was discourteous. But eventually, both sides decided to be themselves, and we finally began to make progress, with each side fulfilling the role the other initially assigned to it. With the disorganization out of the situation, a bargain was eventually reached.

This example helps show that when two sides meet with the intent of doing business, they should not be entangled by making the business at hand secondary to the manner in which the business is conducted. In many cases, the individuals with whom you are dealing are much more conversant with your culture than you are with theirs. If it makes sense to be "American" in how you go about the business, then do so. If, on the other hand, you are engaged with someone who is clearly uneasy with your method of conducting business, you may well have to shift gears and conduct meetings as he or she prefers.

In Indonesia, it is considered churlish to hold the level of your head higher than that of a superior. At the same time, it is practically impossible for the average American to maintain a head level lower than the average Javanese. Any attempt to do so normally results in gales of laughter from all sides—a result just as negative as no attempt at all. Hence, using the "culturally acceptable" method of showing obeisance is quite impossible, a fact that is obvious to the average Javanese and one he or she clearly understands. At the same time, using simple common sense, you can quickly conquer whatever possible affront may be tendered your Indonesian counterpart by something so simple as arranging for lunch to be Indonesian cuisine and expressing a genuine interest in the country. This is just simply good manners, not the result of any sort of cultural training.

CUSTOMS OF IMPORTANCE
IN BUSINESS RELATIONSHIPS

There is a portion of the cultural area that is directly consequential to the conduct of international operations, and it generally tends to be differences in business styles, attitudes toward business relationships, punctuality, negotiating styles, gift-giving customs, and customs regarding titles. That these areas do have a true importance does not mean that they are truly different from the general manner in which Americans go about their business. Rather, they are differences in degree.

It is generally accepted that personal relationships are more important in international business than in domestic transactions, perhaps because of a greater uncertainty in international transactions. It may be that a deeper personal relationship makes sense to all involved. After all, your counterpart has the same fears as you with regard to the potential for something going awry in the transaction or with the longer-term relationship.

Attitudes toward punctuality vary greatly from one culture to another and can be the cause of serious misunderstanding. Attitudes are somewhat more relaxed in South America and Southern Europe than in many other areas. But even this statement has to be viewed in context. Arriving late to a business meeting is rare, even in Latin America, if it is the first meeting, if the businessperson is serious, and if the relationship between the two parties has yet to be established. Once the parties have promulgated a relationship, or if the event is social in nature, then tardiness is more common.

Individuals in the United States seem to differ in this regard as well. There is a distressing tendency, especially in large urban areas on both coasts, toward a more relaxed attitude with regard to punctuality. Parisians seem to have a greater degree of problem arriving on time than their more rural counterparts in France. Hence, these differences may have more to do with population density, and the resultant difficulty in getting anywhere on time, than culture. What is important is not to let someone else's arriving late to a meeting interfere with the business at hand.

Correct use of titles is often a source of confusion in international business relations, but simple good manners will suffice in most situations. As a general rule, formal addresses are a good idea, although this sort of formality does seem to be rapidly going out of style almost everywhere. In most cases, the best idea is to let the other person take the lead and suggest when it is time to become less formal. This is not to suggest communications should be stiff or unnatural. Rather, it is simply allowing the other party to become less formal with regard to names when he or she is comfortable with doing so.

Customs concerning gift giving are of some importance to avoid potentially embarrassing situations. In some countries, gifts are expected, and receiving a present is not uncommon; in other nations, offering a gift is considered offensive. I normally carry several small gifts in my briefcase—pocket knives, pen sets, and the like—so I am prepared in the event a gift is offered. This has been most useful in Japan, where gift giving is an important part of doing business.

UNDERSTANDING DIFFERENCES

Negotiating across cultures can become complicated, as several examples show, dramatizing how convoluted things can get when U.S. executives attempt to develop deeper relationships with overseas trading partners. Most often, I tend to think of a negotiation that took place in the late 1970s, with the People's Republic of China, as a good example.

We had gone over to begin talks on locating a production facility on the mainland, and at our first meeting with our Chinese counterparts, we were introduced to the Chinese method of doing business. It began with our side sitting across a long table staring at the Chinese delegation for the better part of five minutes. This was a tremendously uncomfortable situation, especially since we had no idea who was leading their delegation, or if they even had a leader.

Eventually the president of our company got impatient and launched into an exhaustive list of what we wished to discuss. During his monologue, I saw the Chinese side furiously scribbling notes, and I recall thinking they had no clue as to how to go about this negotiation, since private enterprise was somewhat new to them. In fact, they gave all the attention to our president that an attentive student would pay a tremendously well-respected professor. At one juncture, while we were discussing the difficulty of locating a plant site, I noted a gleam come to the eye of one of our Chinese counterparts and realized he had just come to understand they could actually charge for the land. To this day I am quite certain that moment was the first time it occurred to them. The following day we began our session by establishing the price of the site for the building.

The long and the short of this discussion is we did not think about the Chinese negotiators and what level of knowledge they brought to the table. As a result, we spent the remainder of the time we were there assisting them with establishing what they could charge us for and how much it was going to cost! So although cultural considerations did not directly affect our misfortune in this negotiation, our lack of attention to the method by which we negotiated, due to our desire to use an approach with which we were comfortable, led us to an unfavorable conclusion. A great deal of patience, especially in the preliminary stages of the negotiations, can be the best policy.

It is not a bad idea to become familiar with the customs and cultures of the people with whom you do business, but do not let these cultural differences be the primary focus of dealings, and do not let attempts to be culturally sensitive interfere with a trading partner's expectations. As a general rule, display good manners, indicate a desire to learn more about his business and his country, do not become too familiar too early on, learn when it is best to follow, and learn when one can (and should) dictate the pace of the relationship.

Bear in mind that despite what the "experts" would maintain, cultural differences are not absolute. Rather, they are the reflections of an individual's experience, education, and outlook. The only successful approach is one that recognizes each individual as unique and responds appropriately. There is no question that an individual's culture will have quite a bit to do with how this person views the world, business, and foreigners (including you), but do not assume this cultural bias will lead to any forgone conclusion with regard to what will be comfortable in dealing with someone of another culture.

When overseas business requires U.S. expatriate staff abroad, that staff should exhibit higher levels of sensitivity because of the time they spend there and the contact they maintain with locals. Formal education of this sort prior to departure from the United States is not the best way to learn what is needed. It should be done on site. There is actually only one means of demonstrating true sensitivity with regard to another's culture: learn that person's language so that you can conduct business in that language. This is impractical for most international staff, but it should be a requirement for expatriates.

Discussions of culture always seem to focus on the mistakes Americans make due to ignorance of the cultural issues in other countries. They never center on the advantages Americans have in doing business overseas. There is no question in my mind that Americans are regarded by most foreigners as honest in business dealings, open and forthright in manner, and predictable in behavior (at least in a business setting). Additionally, Americans are seen as highly innovative, good marketers, and technologically adept. All these perceptions can clearly work in our favor—so long as we do not lead the other party to conclude we are something different from their perceptions.

The key to understanding cultural differences and their impact on international operations is to focus on what is truly important to the process of getting business done and recognize that stereotypes cannot apply when dealing with individuals who have a high degree of exposure to the rest of the world. Be sure to start every negotiation by understanding that the individual nature of the person with whom you are dealing—not his or her culture—is the primary issue.

Chapter 3

Conducting Market Research and Targeting High Potential Markets

There is probably no greater misstep one can make than believing that everything about international operations must be studied and mastered before starting efforts to develop, or further refine, international marketing efforts. In most cases, this sort of rigorous investigation is required only when considering a capital investment abroad. Nor should executives necessarily go outside their companies and hire consultants to perform the investigation on their behalf. Many market research firms use government-developed research or other existing information to produce the report they ultimately submit. Often U.S. firms end up paying the consultant not for research but for the knowledge they possess about where to find information. Further, executives are often doing themselves a great disservice by not requiring their own staff to learn how to find this information.

Even where information is not readily available, there are other steps to take before paying for professional services. One example is to ask the relevant industry association in the target country to survey the existing research.

GOVERNMENT DATA

All developed countries (and many developing nations as well) conduct government-sponsored research about foreign markets. For example, most useful research conducted by the U.S. government in the field of international business is performed by the United States and Foreign Commercial Service (US&FCS), a small group within the International Trade Administration (ITA) of the U.S. Department of Commerce (DOC). (Throughout this book, you will see references to the US&FCS, ITA, and DOC. In all cases, unless otherwise specified, I refer to the United States and Foreign Commercial Service.) Normally they supply this research only to companies in their own countries. Thus, another enormous benefit accrues from being an international firm: access to all of the information developed by any number of governments about overseas markets. Some of the best research I have uncovered was ferreted out by my overseas distributors from their governments, and we made good use of their research for our operations in third countries.

In addition to foreign market research, other governments also conduct research about their own markets. Most developed countries have a counterpart of the U.S. Small Business Administration, numerous statistics-gathering agencies, and any number of trade associations that discharge domestic research in that country. This information can greatly assist U.S. firms in exporting to that market. To be a global business, companies need to think like one and gather data and information about international operations from multiple sources. Let me outline one example of how foreign governments assisted me with my conduct of international business.

In the late 1970s, we could not pinpoint any research concerning the market in India for a computer product. After conquering my initial frustration with being unable to locate the required information, I finally called our British distributor, who, in turn, called the British Foreign Office and uncovered the research. It stood to reason that a former British colony would likely be thoroughly researched by the United Kingdom, and, in fact, that turned out to be the case. Although the research was over a year old, the project at hand involved exporting to the country, not investment in it. Hence, the information was sufficient for our purposes.

The significance here is that international operations necessitate that you think creatively about problems rather than accepting no for an answer. The longer you are at it, the faster you will move to the unorthodox solution for a particular obstacle. The intellectual gear shift required is breaking free of the assumption that since your company is an American firm, it has only

American resources at its disposal. Once this self-limiting approach is put firmly behind a U.S. company, informed decision making becomes greatly facilitated.

When I use the term *market research* in international operations, I most often refer to secondary research, not primary data collection. This research may be as simple as getting a list of overseas importers of your product and faxing them to inquire if it is, in their opinion, marketable in that country. These lists are generally available through the U.S. Department of Commerce (or other countries' counterpart agencies), U.S. or other country trade associations (I have found the German associations to have the best information and assistance), or commercial sources (discussed in detail in Chapter 10).

It may mean simply getting the U.S. or U.N. export-import data for a product. These data provide the historic level of imports by country and product category and are indicative of the future potential demand for those products in those particular countries. You may see sporadic blips in these data, especially in the developing world, where governmental policies concerning imports, together with the general economic uncertainty of the country, tend to be somewhat capricious. This situation will create spikes and valleys in the data that at first seem somewhat perplexing but are usually easily explained.

Generally, large swings in import data result from one of two occurrences. First, when governments face deteriorating economic conditions or hard currency shortages, they may impose exchange restrictions, which lead to dramatic drops in the level of imports across the board. If this is the case, you should note declines in the overall level of imports for all products. The second occurs when a government, most often due to a local firm beginning its own manufacturing operations for the product, imposes high import duties for imported competing products. If this is the case, the overall decline does not occur to the same degree as the decline in the now-protected industry in that foreign market.

U.S. export data are available from any local Department of Commerce office. The U.N. data are generally found in university libraries or can be purchased directly from the United Nations. I tend to prefer the U.N. data, which track imports, by country and product, from all supplying countries. In contrast, U.S. export data track only imports by country and product from the United States. Hence, the U.N. data not only provide a better vision of total market demand for imports but also identify the foreign competition by virtue of identifying the country where the exports originated.

Several countries seem to have import and export levels out of line with the domestic market potential. These outward anomalies are readily explained by what is known as "pass-through" shipments—shipments that transit through the country, either because they have been sold by companies in that country to customers in third countries or because the shipments are broken down, in one location, into smaller shipments and then dispatched to the ultimate destinations. These countries tend to be well located geographically (Netherlands and Singapore, for example) or have a history of being important trading bases (Cyprus, Singapore, Hong Kong). It is easy to discount these countries as potential markets because of this pass-through phenomena, but do not be hasty. Traders in these nations might well be the best candidates to handle nearby markets. Hence, although the import data will not reflect the local real demand for that product, they may well be good indicators of where to place a regional office, retain a trading company, or otherwise take advantage of that location in the larger trading pattern of the region.

A good example of how much more suitable the complete U.N. data can be is found in the computer industry, where higher-priced computers tend to originate in Japan and the United States and lower-end models from Taiwan and the Republic of Korea. Information on import levels in a target market from all countries helps to determine how price will affect sales in the importing country. For example, high levels of Japanese and U.S. exports to the target country, combined with low levels of export from Taiwan and Korea, may imply a no-discount-pricing policy, together with higher levels of support for the product since quality is obviously imperative to the end user group. These same data might be used to arrive at some informed conclusions about the sort of computer the market demands. For example, if we were to note high total imports from all sources, we might conclude that the market demands the more powerful computers from the United States for business application and the lesser developed models for home use.

The U.N. data also provide a good sense of how market demand has changed over time and identify the traditional source countries. In our example, let's assume we noted in a particular country that shipments of U.S. computers had declined rapidly over the past five years and Taiwanese and Korean imports were burgeoning. We would use that information to rethink pricing policy because price was obviously becoming the dominant consideration in that market.

Research, however, may be considerably more complex than looking at U.S. and U.N. data and in some cases may involve hiring a professional market research firm to conduct primary data collection and investigation in a foreign market, although this avenue is most often undertaken by large companies with consumer products. Note, however, that the expense of having a consultant engage in primary research is rarely justifiable unless the research is conducted with the objective of facilitating an investment decision.

There are exceptions to this rule—for example, when the cost of introducing the product to a particular market is so high that more information is needed to gain company approval for the product's introduction. Another arises when entering that market requires a protracted and expensive registration process for intellectual property purposes, together with a standards approval requirement from the local government that is also expensive, and at the end of the process product adaptation is required for market entry. In this case, there might well be a need to ensure the company will be able to recoup this investment. The situation in the second example, however, is rare. Usually the market can be overlooked until such time as other markets are providing a sufficient revenue base to undertake the market entry.

For more developed or larger U.S. companies, often with manufacturing or sales facilities abroad, the conduct of primary market research is more common, either directly or through a contractor, because the costs of uninformed decisions become more expensive than the cost of the research. U.S. firms that remain somewhat parochial in outlook will attempt to direct this research from a U.S. base. These firms usually come up with findings that are consistent with the home office preconception rather than ones accurately portraying the reality of the marketplace. In large part, this occurs because of the reluctance by corporate staff to decentralize the research function or to allow a foreign subsidiary to contract directly with more knowledgeable local firms.

THE INITIAL RESEARCH

Research at its initial stage should focus on the following issues: the product's marketability overseas, identification of the markets already acknowledged to be good prospects, and identification of other high-potential markets. Most of the information related to these issues is available through market research reports from the U.S. Department of Commerce, which are designed to help U.S. firms make a preliminary cut with regard to the best markets. While there are complaints that these reports do not provide enough specific information for particular products, the purpose of these documents is to indicate which market might be good for particular industry sectors, not specific products.

Is the Product Marketable?

Assuming no existing export operations, the first piece of research is to determine if the product is marketable in foreign countries. An adequate method for a firm that decides not to engage in the limited research we have discussed above is to attend trade fairs and talk to foreign participants about the marketability of the product. Another good method is the "fax polling" formula: the potential exporter faxes prospective buyers or distributors in foreign markets with information about the product and asks if the foreign firm finds the product interesting. (Both subjects—which trade fairs to target and how to develop a "fax polling" list—are covered in Chapter 9.)

Which Are the Best Prospects?

Uncovering the best markets for the product in terms of total market demand and import demand can begin with the U.S. Department of Commerce "best prospects" list: a listing, by country, of which U.S. products enjoy the best market in which countries. Look for countries designated as good prospects for the product, and begin to build lists of potential distributors, representatives, or end users. Contact these prospects as the information accumulates. Do not be overly concerned with dealing with one potential distributor at a time or retard the effort to get representation because your staff thinks they have insufficient information about that particular market.

A next step might be to identify U.S. manufacturers that produce and market products related to yours. This information can serve to indicate your product's market potential. Look at corporate reports to identify good markets, or contact a counterpart in that firm, explaining carefully your noncompetitive situation, and ask where they have been successful. Meanwhile, continue to build your list and contact your prospects.

What Are the Best Potential Markets?

To identify the markets that are likely to enjoy increased demand for your product, look at the *Foreign Economic Trends* and *Overseas Business Reports,* available from any ITA office. Additionally, a glance at the export statistics or the U.N. import-export data will quickly indicate if demand for imported items has generally grown or declined. These sources of information together can provide a good snapshot of the potential of a particular market over the next several years.

If you have difficulty pinpointing a category in these data that is directly applicable to your product, look to leading or indicative product categories. For example, a leading category would be the use of hardware sales data for a conception of what future sales of software are likely to be. Or, it might be the total petrochemical production numbers, if you are selling replacement parts for equipment typically found in petrochemical plants.

An indicative product is one that indicates that demand is likely to be good for another product. For example, if a country has high import levels for consumer goods such as clothing, it is reasonable to postulate that imported personal care products are desirable. You can check your hunch by determining the import duty for the product (from the U.S. Department of Commerce country desk officer). If the duty rate for the commodity is much higher than that of the indicator (i.e., the clothing), then it is likely that entry for personal care products will be more difficult, regardless of the indicative indicator's seemingly positive result.

USING THE INITIAL RESEARCH

By reviewing the "best prospects" and other import data, you will have established countries that are promising prospects: countries that have high levels of import of the product *and* are identified as "best prospects," and those where import levels are high *or* the country has been identified as a "best prospect." By now you have probably identified several or more markets that are good candidates for your company. As your marketing staff proceeds to interview potential distributors in those markets that occupy the first two tiers (getting the necessary background and credit information on them and becoming more familiar with the legal issues that surround distribution contract law in their countries), management should, at the same time, be forming some judgment about the third-tier countries: those for which the potential is low or staff doesn't have time to pursue. This determination should result in one of three decisions:

1. Engage an export management company (EMC) to pursue these third-tier markets on your firm's behalf. By retaining the primary and secondary markets, this offer may be less alluring to the EMC, but you will probably be able to find EMCs to handle these markets. If you cannot, then marketing staff should proceed to look to the regional trading centers. Trading companies or EMCs in regional centers cover that region and are not interested in the rest of the world. Hence, they tend to be flexible with regard to the size of the territory they seek.

2. Be essentially passive. Your staff will respond to inquiries from third-tier markets but will not pursue them. Over time, a number of markets will fall into this category, typically as the result of meeting customers from those markets at trade fairs or through advertisements placed in the trade press. Since it makes no sense to turn away business, proceed with these sales as long as your marketing staff remains circumspect about granting exclusive arrangements to this group of distributors—at least until staff are prepared to address those markets in a more organized fashion.

3. Do not grant anyone rights to sell the product in that market until your firm is prepared to take an active support role and/or handle the support directly. This option is most often chosen when the product requires a great deal of support. If this is the case, the correct course is to be prepared to extend that support on a selective basis, as the firm's resources allow. While this may drive your export ship a bit off course, at least with regard to the execution of the remainder of your plan, upper-level management may well have to accept that unique targets of opportunity will arise.

As a practical matter, at least at the outset, marketing staff may find they must pursue these opportunities to foster continued support from upper management, who are often dubious of the whole effort and demand that rapid and ongoing progress be demonstrated. Hence, they are not in a position to turn down business from any source.

If you endeavor to master everything about international operations prior to beginning the marketing effort, you will never begin because there is too much diverse information to embrace. So, get started, and work efficiently with regard to how your staff amasses and uses data. During the first stage of your effort, do not gather more information than needed to place overseas markets in one of the three categories just listed. Once a prospective distributor is qualified, do the additional homework to avoid any potential pitfalls. Understand that marketing plans are not cast in concrete and that deviations from the plan are not only acceptable but desirable if they generate revenue.

INFORMATION SOURCES

Some good sources for compiling your research follow. Almost all are free or inexpensive.

You will inevitably face some problems in compiling information, so do not wait until it is all on the desk to begin the effort. The most efficient way to proceed is to make a list of the publications and other needed information, order it, and begin to work, as the information flow allows, toward getting distributors or sales up and running.

Reports

The following information sources have proven to be useful in the real world of international business operations, and should be carefully examined and used to support and supplement information received from distributors and industry associations.

Export Statistics Profiles. Indicates U.S. exports for a single industry, by product and country of destination, for the previous five years. The profiles normally include industry growth projections, competitive information, best prospects, and an overview of the industry. Contact any ITA office.

If your product is not covered in the Export Statistics Profiles, a custom report from ITA can be generated for a fee. It will allow you to choose the measurement to be used (dollar value versus weight, for example). Contact any ITA office.

International Market Research. This in-depth research service, conducted by embassies overseas, allows exporters to draw up the specifications for the research, to some degree, and typically will include general market information, end user analysis, business practices, and competitive information including pricing, trade barriers, and lists of potential distributors. This service is generally more expensive than most of the others listed, but it is still a bargain when compared to the cost of commercially produced research. Contact any local ITA office.

Market Share Reports. This report provides data to evaluate trends in the size of export markets and compares the competitive position of U.S. exporters with other foreign exporters of the same products. They are particularly useful to help establish the three tiers. Contact the National Technical Information Service, (202) 487-4630.

Export Information System Data Reports. Available for approximately 1,700 product categories, they contain a list of the 25 largest import markets for the product, the 10 best markets for U.S. exporters of that product, general information about the markets, and competitive information on non-U.S. exporters to those markets. They too are useful for establishing tiers. Contact any Small Business Administration.

Directory of Market Research Reports, Studies and Surveys. This publication, developed by a private firm, contains over 10,000 listings of market research reports, studies, and surveys from all over the world. Contact FIND/SVP, Information Clearinghouse, (212) 645-4500.

Foreign Economic Trends. These reports cover current business and economic developments by country and provide macroeconomic data for those countries. Contact any ITA office.

Overseas Business Reports. These reports provide statistics and information on specific countries and include economic and commercial environment information, and statistical profiles on U.S. trade with the country. It is the most complete country-specific, business-oriented report available from public sources. Contact Superintendent of Documents, U.S. Government Printing Office, (202) 783-3238.

Background Notes. This series surveys the people, geography, economy, government, and foreign policy of approximately 60 countries. Although not directly useful from a market research standpoint, they contain good general information, useful for a preliminary understanding of a country. Contact Superintendent of Documents, U.S. Government Printing Office, (202) 783-3238.

Exporters Encyclopedia. The bible of exporting, it contains market information in reasonable detail, including shipping information, on over 220 markets. This is my favorite reference book. Contact Dun's Marketing Services, (800) 526-0651.

Doing Business in Foreign Countries. A series of doing business guides, organized by country, these are published by a number of the Big Eight accounting firms. They provide information on specific countries and generally include demographic data, economic climate, restrictions and incentives to trade, duties, documentary requirements, tax structures, legal information, and a host of other topics. Although these reports are geared toward providing information of use to potential investors rather than those seeking export market, they remain an excellent source for both. My favorite is the Price Waterhouse series. Contact the nearest Price Waterhouse office.

Statistical Yearbook. This is the most complete source of export-import data by country. It is the compilation of individual country trade data done by the United Nations, with information on importing countries and exports by country. Order by calling (800) 521-8110.

The Encyclopedia of Associations. Many U.S. trade associations can provide information for research through publications or contacts with their foreign counterparts, who often have extensive industry-based research for that market (and others). In addition, the membership lists of the overseas associations can be good leads for a distributor search.

Databases

When using databases to conduct research, remember that they often charge for both connect time and the information downloaded. Make sure you understand both the fee structure and where to find what you are looking for before going on line. The following are good sources of information:

Predicasts. A collection of machine-readable databases from Predicasts Inc. of Cleveland, Ohio. It is available on Dialog, and other dial-up vendors. Predicasts includes information on domestic and international market trends, new product introductions, competitors' acquisitions and mergers, and a host of other information.

Harfax. A compendium of international market research done by private firms worldwide with information on available reports. Offered by Dialog.

Findit. An on-line database that is a compendium of available research. Offered by Dialog.

Business International. An on-line database that is the best source of information on country political and economic risk. It also contains demographic data.

The National Trade Data Bank (NTDB) is a U.S. Department of Commerce database with a wealth of information about international trade and economics. It is available on CD-ROM and is updated monthly. The material, gathered by 15 government agencies, is a valuable resource for firms involved in exporting or international operations. Users can gain a great deal of confidence about a new market from this source because it provides enough information to allow for intelligent discussion of the industry with foreign businesspeople and sufficient insight to handle negotiations well. Several sections of the database are of particular use to international executives.

The Foreign Traders Index contains over 50,000 foreign importers identified by products carried. This is not only the most accessible database in the world but also the cheapest and the easiest to use. Often you can find several (or more) distributors per target market from this list. This database is developed by U.S. embassies abroad and submitted to the Department of Commerce headquarters in Washington, D.C., where it is loaded onto the disk and sold to users in the United States. The records contain information about each distributor's operations: which products they carry, how long they have been in business, the size of the company, and contact information, often including fax numbers. The database is not completely current and some countries have much better distributor lists than others, but the convenience of this tool means that it is the most valuable resource.

The NTDB's "A Basic Guide to Exporting" is useful for learning the nuts and bolts of exporting. And even those more developed in their international efforts will find that it contains a wealth of information concerning investment-related issues. It can be a valuable reference tool that allows answers to specific questions by keyword searches.

The NTDB contains more than 8,000 market research reports, developed by country and industry sector. They are usually based on industry subsectors (such as microcomputers, food processing equipment, and the like) and provide good information to exporters about particular markets. Even if specific product research isn't available, researchers can often find information that provides good indicators of market potential (for example, much of the research about computers is valuable to a whole range of allied industries, such as software, printers, and data communications). In addition, it contains a wealth of country-specific information about doing business. The following reports are the best:

Country Marketing Plans: Provide information about the best potential products for import into that market and the general market environment.

Foreign Economic Trends: Gives an excellent overview of the general economic climate and the government's policies toward trade and investment.

Overseas Business Reports: Provides detailed information about the commercial environment in that country.

Foreign Trade Barrier: Notes problems U.S. firms may encounter in operating in a particular country.

Trade Finance Highlights: Describes any unusual financial requirements the country has with regard to payment by letters of credit and the like.

In general, the data contained on these disks are sufficient to support country-specific needs for export operations.

The export statistics data portion of the database can be used to determine where good markets exist for a product by virtue of determining the level of export from the United States to individual countries by product grouping. The data are not as good as those from the United Nations, which tracks imports from all countries to individual countries, but they are adequate to allow work to begin for countries that have obvious high levels of U.S.-sourced imports.

For potential investors or companies that wish to investigate overseas production, the NTDB has useful data on foreign labor costs and rates, foreign direct investment by country, and a host of country-specific demographic information.

The NTDB is very user-friendly, featuring pull-down menus that are highly intuitive and allow novices to get up and running with very little need to refer to a manual. I often download information from the NTDB onto a diskette before a trip overseas, so I can carry all the information I need on a single diskette rather than reams of paper. I review the country-specific information on the plane and arrive with most of the information I need to know the lay of the land.

An annual subscription to National Trade Data Bank costs $360; single-month CD-ROMs are available for $35 each. I recommend buying every third disk. Although the full year's subscription is worth the price, it is overkill from an informational standpoint. In addition, the NTDB is a cumulative document, so anything missed in earlier releases will be included in later ones. To order, call (202) 377-1986.

Other Sources

Piers. A port import-export reporting service that scans all ocean-borne bills of lading to identify exporter and importer and where the product is being shipped. Offered by the *Journal of Commerce of New York*.

Duns. A service that provides customized international mailing lists, market statistical information, and credit reporting. Offered by Dun and Bradstreet.

IN SUMMARY

A good friend, and a highly respected colleague, once told me that conducting market research for international operations is a bit like peeling away the layers of skin on an onion. He was right. At each layer of the research, we understand that while we can experience the joy of discovery, there are many additional layers to get to the core of the matter. Obviously, at some point in the process, should we wish to enjoy the onion, it's time to take a bite. The real trick is knowing when to stop peeling and start eating.

I have concentrated here on the essentially free or inexpensive research available, in the main, from U.S. government resources and associations. The reason is that money will be an issue at the start of this effort, and these are the best sources available for the dollar. As time goes on, your firm will become more sophisticated and need greater detail in the research than it can get from these sources. When that happens, there are any number of companies that can conduct or provide existing research. Should you choose this course, select a company from the market you intend to study. It will know the method by which the study should be conducted, understand the existing work in that area, and have better sources of information in that marketplace.

SUMMARY

C h a p t e r **4**

Managing Foreign Distribution Networks: What You Want from Foreign Partners

WHAT YOU NEED TO KNOW
ABOUT DISTRIBUTORS

Most U.S. companies rely more on commercial or governmental sources for information about a potential distributor than on testimonials from other U.S.-based suppliers. There is nothing wrong with these written reports, but often they cannot provide the kind of information that another supplier company has available. In most cases, another supplier is in a much better position to understand the internal dynamics that could affect distributors, the marketplace in which they operate, the position they occupy within the universe of competing distributors in that country, and what individual potential distributors are like in terms of dealing with suppliers.

I was once told by a U.S. factory representative who serviced a distributor I was considering appointing in Venezuela that the principal of the distributorship was terminally ill, and his son, who would inherit the business, was unlikely to carry the same weight with large government buyers the father enjoyed. The owner had been a political appointee in a previous government and held the rank of minister. As a result, he maintained excellent relationships throughout the government. This was a very good match for us, because my company was highly dependent on government purchases to maintain sales growth, so I entered an agreement with him. And, based on my knowledge of his fading health, the agreement included a termination-upon-transfer-of-ownership clause. Two years later, the father died, and, consistent with prediction, the son was unable to continue the same level of sales. We quickly terminated the agreement and moved to another distributor, with no loss in sales growth.

The lesson here is that databases and reports are very good at indicating where companies have been but often less useful about where they are going. Information about the future is best obtained from those close to a company, both in the market it serves and from other suppliers. In short, spend some time talking to customers, the sales force and technical people within the prospective distributorship, other suppliers, and anyone else with direct knowledge of the company's operations and personnel. The judgment of others is important, but remember that your marketing staff cannot rely upon it to the exclusion of your own evaluation. The one constant is change, and ultimately your staff is responsible for these decisions. If you are uncomfortable with a distributor candidate, proceed with caution, and try to pinpoint what is troublesome about the distributor. These marriages are extremely easy to make and can be difficult to dissolve.

Product Support

Many products cannot be sold without adequate service and parts support. IBM and Caterpillar Tractor Company are two U.S. firms that made their business one of solving customers' problems with good service and support rather than simply selling a product. The tricky part of this approach is that these requirements are rapidly changing, as the recent evolution of the computer industry shows. Not long ago, it was unthinkable to buy a computer by mail order. Yet today many are sold in just such a manner, probably because many Americans have become comfortable with managing their own computer problems. Hence, cost, rather than service, has become the primary consideration when purchasing a computer.

The response of IBM to this competitive challenge was quite poor, in part because it seemed to view the issue of customer support as the overriding consideration and assumed it would carry the day against price pressures that the clone manufacturers generated. But when the support requirements for a large segment of computers users rapidly changed, with price becoming more important than service, IBM's inability or unwillingness to adapt to this market segment essentially spawned (and allowed to flourish) a competitive industry. As the number of computer-literate Americans continues to grow and as software becomes more user friendly, service requirements will continue to diminish in importance, at least when compared to price.

This same scenario is unfolding, albeit somewhat more slowly, in many foreign countries with any number of products. Most foreign markets, even in Europe, still require much higher support levels than the United States, with its technologically sophisticated population and large infrastructure of third-party service firms. Support tends to be more important in markets with low levels of economic development or when product sophistication increases. There are, however, some notable exceptions. For example, India (which seems to generate an unusual number of excellent mathematicians and engineers) seems to have a greater degree of comfort with new technology than many other developing countries. The same is true of "Tiger" countries such as Korea, Singapore, and Hong Kong.

For some firms, these differing requirements translate to the need to have two or more levels of service available for different markets. In many cases, suppliers will offer higher levels of support for developing countries than offered in the developed world. In other cases, it will be just the reverse; the newer and more advanced product lines are not appropriate for Third World application, and hence the need for product support in these countries declines as the life cycles of the older products are extended.

Service and support are not static as a component of marketing strategy. Rather, they change with time and require U.S. firms to adapt with them. U.S. executives may well find that the future of their international business will require that their firms provide either better service or lower prices to end users through the establishment of directly owned sales and support offices in primary markets. The decision to open these kinds of offices in primary markets is becoming much more common as U.S. companies become more familiar with the conduct of international business.

An added consideration for a direct presence is that it is often a competitive response to increasing price pressures from competitors already selling directly into those markets, thereby avoiding the distributor markups. There is something of a transformation already underway, especially in Europe, where many U.S. firms are moving away from the distributor approach and going direct. In part, this is due to the competitive situation. However, there are two additional considerations. The first is that most view E.C. 92 (the economic integration envisioned by the implementation of the European Community) as removing many of the logistical and marketing barriers that made a presence in each country necessary. The second is that recent export expansion has increased revenue streams for many U.S. firms on the Continent, to the point they need to take the next step in the evolutionary process: a direct presence in Europe.

Regardless of how firms have traditionally approached service and support issues in the United States, the decision must become less automatic with regard to supporting the product overseas. This is part of the 10 percent of domestic operations, which I discussed in the introduction to this book, that is not directly transferable and is one area that can cause failure. As a result, it is worthy of careful evaluation, in each market, prior to committing your firm to a particular course of action with regard to service and support.

The best way to determine the specific level of support required, by market, is to use some common sense and maintain, at the outset, close ties with end users in the overseas markets so your company can make any adjustment to the market. As it matures and develops a facility with the technology, the marketing and service approach may have to adjust yet again.

It is also important to listen to distributors and rely on them to help develop adequate support policies for each country. However, the last leg of this effort is frequent and direct contact with the end user group, throughout the life of the effort, by your technical and marketing staff. This contact will also help smooth the transition from distribution sales to direct sales, if for no other reason than that your firm will know who the end users are and what they want.

The Perfect Distributor

The perfect distributor is one that already sells to your end user group, has good service and support in place, and is financially strong. You can rule out all but the most established distributors by applying these criteria.

A good distributor, in all likelihood already distributes similar but noncompeting products, and this is both good and bad news. The good news is that it becomes easier to target a prospective distributor by identifying those that carry compatible lines and approaching them with a proposal to assume the distribution of your line. Additionally, the candidate is very likely to already sell to your end user group, be familiar with the technology, and understand marketing techniques unique to the industry. Yet another bonus is that this person is often familiar with issues such as service and support, the need for adequate training for staff, import and payment procedures, the need to stock product, and how industry changes in the market are likely to affect your efforts to sell in the country. All of this background makes your life as a supplier much easier, because your staff will not have to spend the first year educating the new distributor about the industry and marketing approach.

The bad news is the distributor's energies will not be focused entirely on your product. The solution to this seeming dilemma, is not at all complicated: Narrow the search to foreign companies that meet the criteria, with the understanding if you cannot recruit one of them, you will move on to the less desirable alternatives. In each case, exhaust the list of potential distributors (most often based on the other products they sell) beginning with the most desirable group and moving toward the less desirable. Eventually the right one will appear.

If no one seems right, bypass that market for now, seek to establish some direct presence, or attempt to recruit the right person from an existing distributorship (to start a new company with the rights for your product line). The last is often the best approach since a direct presence, prior to generating substantial revenues from that market is, for the most part, unlikely. Bypassing a market identified as a good prospect is painful. So the problem is often solved by offering some incentive to an employee of an existing distributor to strike out on his or her own. In some cases, the distribution rights for your product will be sufficient incentive. However, you may need to sweeten the pot by offering credit or some other concession to allow this person to get started. Once you have located your distributor, your firm must understand the need to do everything possible to divert this person's attention from other product lines and give the maximum attention to yours. Frequent visits and allowing the distributor the best possible margin on sales of your product (so that it is the most profitable of those he or she carries) are two simple methods of getting the distributor to devote more time to your line.

A good example of how to target distributors comes from the office supply business. Let's assume your company manufactures machines that recharge laser printer cartridges. The best potential distributors are currently selling printer ribbons. That would be my guess for a number of reasons. First, the potential distributor (the ribbon distributor) does not have to make a substantial investment in training a new sales force to distribute the new product; he or she is already in the office supply business and selling to large users of printer supplies. What you are proposing is simply to put another item in the distributor's sales brochure, one that will generate extra revenue for this person, provide customers with greater ease in purchasing their office supplies, and perhaps even allow the distributor to secure some new accounts because of the new product. Your product requires little additional effort and returns a great deal to the distributor. As an astute businessperson, he or she will be attracted by the highest return on investment.

An additional factor that serves to make your product more attractive in this case is the fact that this theoretical distributor is in a dying industry: Print ribbon sales are declining rapidly as other technologies move into the forefront. There are a lot of good distributors out there in dying industries. Target them. They are much more likely to take on additional lines than someone who sees no threat from new technologies or is already marketing cutting-edge products.

Now assume for a moment that no ribbon distributors are interested in your product. The next step is to build a list of potential candidates based on another product line carried—perhaps distributors of computer paper or personal computers. They are not the ideal candidates but can still do a nice job in a market with which they are familiar. Initially they will require additional levels of support. They may have to invest a great deal of money and time in a promotional campaign and may even need to hire additional salespeople to market the product. The impact on the supplier is often the need to lower price or otherwise increase support for this sort of distributor to ensure that the initial effort is successful.

Many companies fail to achieve good international sales because they do not understand how to target distributor groups. Often they begin with too much of a shotgun approach, which results in little expression of interest from the potential overseas representatives. The lack of response is often interpreted as signifying a lack of market for the product, and, usually, additional efforts to seek overseas business will not occur, often for years.

If all of your initial efforts fail, conduct an evaluation of how your staff targeted the distributor group. Make sure to ask every distributor candidate who declines your product why it is not attractive. Talk to other U.S. suppliers, active in your target markets and industries, about their approach and what has worked and not worked for them.

Legal and Regulatory Limitations

The fact that U.S. business is subject to an entire set of business rules with which many other third-country suppliers do not contend (including such regulations as the Foreign Corrupt Practices Act and transfer pricing rules) has long been a subject of bitter complaint from the international business community in the United States. An overseas distributor with experience in dealing with U.S. companies is more likely to understand the legal and regulatory limitations American firms face in the conduct of international business.

I can think of any number of instances in which one of my distributors abroad began a conversation with, "In order to get this business we have to pay the minister . . ." At this point, I always responded, "I don't want to hear this discussion," and explained that under the terms of the Foreign Corrupt Practices Act, I could be guilty of a criminal offense if I had knowledge of any illegal transaction that involved bribery of a foreign government official. This was normally the first and last time that discussion took place, because my colleague would now understand that any action violating the act could not be undertaken with my knowledge. The Foreign Corrupt Practices Act does place an unfair burden on U.S. firms abroad and is not a very good law, all things considered. The fact is that American law is not going to change the way business is conducted in foreign countries, and restricting our companies from operating in a manner consistent with the business practice of another country serves only to place us at a competitive disadvantage. However, it is a fact of life, and the way to handle it is to explain the rules of the road the first time this sort of discussion comes up. Having said that, I hasten to add that familiarity with U.S. regulations should not be the primary factor in selecting distributors. Factors such as market coverage and other products handled should take precedence over any prior dealings with American firms.

There is a flip side to the issue of the Foreign Corrupt Practices Act that most U.S. companies largely ignore. Many U.S. firms have ethics codes in place that would prohibit this sort of conduct, independent of any legal constraint. In a sense, this law provides protection to U.S. firms in that they may use it as an excuse to refrain from behavior that they would not otherwise condone anyway.

Sales Force and Other Staff

There are many schools of thought with regard to the ideal structure for a foreign distributor's sales force. Some maintain that the best method is to establish a separate force for each product line. This structure is often desirable with highly technical products, but it is a very costly approach and not often employed.

Experience has taught me that the real issue is not the structure of the sales force at all but how long the distributor's salespeople have been with the firm. One axiom of business does not change across international borders: Good salespeople stay in companies where they make money. If sales staff do not make a good living, they move on. Hence, a favorite tactic of mine is chatting with the distributor's sales force before making a decision as to distribution rights. I often ask indirect questions to assist me in determining if the sales force is content, stable, and earning up to expectations. It should come as no surprise that the only requirement for coaxing a salesperson to speak at length is a mildly attentive audience.

Such questions as, "How many sales reps have been with the company for more than three years?" can be revealing. Questions concerning specialization in the sales force (do certain salespeople handle major accounts or specific product lines) will also indicate quite a bit about the professionalism of the company. Questions about technical qualifications and educational level will reveal if the distributor is able to recruit and maintain the caliber of salespeople likely to ensure the successful introduction of your product into that market.

Although sales staff are the best indicator of the distributor's effectiveness, service and support people, and any other individuals who may represent your product line in that country, should be assessed. With these individuals, ask about their training, education, contact with the customers, and the like. I have found that the best distributors are often those who encourage their technical people to get into the field and maintain contact with the customer base.

What They Don't Know

A number of foreign distribution firms have very little idea what to do with the product once they gain the distribution rights for it, so it is essential to determine if other products in the line will have educated the distributor about the need for vigorous promotional campaigns to support the sales efforts. Something as simple as requesting a schedule for major account calls can set the agenda in such a way as to make clear that your company expects an active campaign to sell the product aggressively and will not tolerate "order taking" as acceptable business practice.

Different products, even within the same industry, are marketed in radically different ways. That the prospective distributor has enjoyed some success with a similar product does not always mean he or she understands how to market your product. Depending on the degree to which the product requires a more in-depth and formalized promotional campaign, you may also consider sitting down with the potential distributor to establish budgets and map out the first year's marketing plan. It is crucial that the plan be a shared one in which your firm actively participates.

Give the new distributor all available information concerning how your company markets the product in the United States—and anywhere else for that matter. This will allow him or her not to have to reinvent the wheel and also assist in determining which, if any, of your promotional techniques will be effective in this marketplace. It will also assist in uncovering, before a formal agreement is reached, any areas of major disagreement with regard to how the product should be promoted, marketing budgets, and the like. Resolving these disagreements prior to launching the product will result in less confusion for both the distributor and the customers.

Some distributor candidates immediately understand your product, how it's marketed, and what requirements for technical support exist. They may become so enthused by the product that they begin selling the American executive on their distributorship and what it can do for the supplier. I refer to these distributors as individuals who share my vision. They often do a wonderful job because they share a commitment to the product. I don't claim to understand what leads to this shared vision, aside from the fact that these people seem to be excellent businesspeople and do not see products so much as they see the product's utility. They are an enormous assets. For the most part, your staff won't spend a great deal of time convincing them the product is marketable, and they don't waste time agonizing over making the necessary investment to get it launched in their markets. This aggressive approach can cut years off the time it normally takes to penetrate the market fully. These distributors will also require much less support from your firm, because their own curiosity will lead them to fully investigate the product, its uses, and how to maintain it. In short, they will do as good a job with your product, almost unassisted, as they would if your staff devoted a great deal of time and effort to supporting them. This will allow your firm to free up time and move on to other opportunities.

Language

English-language skills are not the most important factors with regard to selecting a good distributor. In fact, many poor selections are made by U.S. firms because they consider language skills the paramount concern when appointing overseas distributors. This mistake will usually be made when the individual selecting the foreign sales organization has little or no experience in international marketing and mistakes the comfort he or she feels with being able to speak directly to the candidate for the comfort he or she should feel with the overall business ability of the potential distributor.

The situation can be worsened by the American habit of scheduling meetings every two hours. Business meetings that are conducted through interpreters require additional time (to wait for the English version of what was said, to respond, and then to listen to the translation of your counterpart's statement). These meetings can become unacceptably abbreviated by the press of the next appointment, leaving both sides with a sense of frustration. The result, most often, is that the candidate who does not speak English is not considered for further discussion, regardless of other abilities.

English-language skills, however, can be a very attractive characteristic. If the distributor lacks good English skills, consider the following issues:

- How will others in your company communicate with the distributor, should that become necessary?
- What additional costs may be incurred to ensure that staff at all levels of your company become involved with the support of that distributor's staff (shipping, service, parts, etc.)?
- How will your staff handle meetings that involve overseas distributor and domestic personnel?

It is important as well that key staff in the distributorship have good English skills. Much like your company, the owner of that distributorship will not, in all likelihood, be overseeing the day-to-day operations of the business. Additionally, there will be times when that person is unavailable, and accurate communications must take place between your two firms. How can this occur if there is no English-speaking staff in the distributor's offices, or if you do not have foreign language capability in the home office? Ask yourself how many employees you would hire to cover all the languages needed to operate worldwide.

Remember, too, that English is the language of international business. Most distributors of any size and reputation will have some English-speaking staff. While these language skills are not a requirement, they certainly do make the conduct of business abroad much less trying and allow you to get a leg up on building your international company by providing for quick and accurate communications (and the ability to integrate the international and domestic sides of your business).

Distributor Size

The optimal company size is a true double-edged sword. There are good arguments to be made for both large and small companies.

You may find greater difficulty in getting a rapidly growing or large distributor candidate to take on a new line, and your product may not get the attention it needs by virtue of the fact it does not, in percentage terms, represent a great deal of the distributor's total volume. At the same time, a history of well-managed increases in sales volume and a track record of successfully introducing new lines to the market indicate you may have the right distributor, even if your product does not enjoy the dominant position within the distributor's lines. If this distributor is your choice, it's best to ensure your product very quickly becomes the dominant one, or it may wither on the vine.

Don't walk away from the small or beginning distributor; often newly emerging companies are the most aggressive representatives in that group, and they tend to do more by virtue of the fact that their attention is not divided. With this breed of distributor, however, you must seek out an individual who already possesses a great deal of product knowledge and good industry contacts. Most often this person will have worked for one of his or her now-competing distributors. The chances of getting the attention your product warrants are greater with these firms, but newcomers typically have liquidity problems and may require an extension of credit much earlier than you would like.

Market Share

Market share is one of the primary considerations with regard to your ultimate choice of representation in a particular country. This measure is not so straightforward, because your firm begins its efforts with no share at all. By necessity, the performance measure becomes the market share held for a product in the distributor's line—one that acts as an indicator of likely sales levels with yours.

It is improbable that you will pick a distributor currently selling a competing product line (although this does happen more often than most firms would like to admit). Hence, there are no primary data with which anyone can divine the likelihood of obtaining a given market share for the product on a projected basis. More often, marketing executives look at a similar product sold to your end user group and, based on your estimate of the distributor's ability to service this group, decide if he or she enjoys a dominant position in the market or has the ability to get to the dominant position. This approach requires a leap of faith, but my experience is that distributors that already enjoy a dominant position with your end user group (with other noncompeting products) are most likely to use their existing relationships effectively to get the new customer to try your product. If the product is good, this approach greatly reduces the time needed to get it introduced into the market.

This approach may seem unscientific, but you are unlikely to find independent data covering market share by overseas distributors. Hence, a look at the distributor's sales history, together with discussions with customers and other individuals in the industry, will provide the best data you can get. Remember that perfect is the enemy of good enough in these situations, and you will have to make judgments that may not be entirely verifiable with independent data. (Later we will discuss the means by which U.S. firms can prevent a bad decision or inaccurate judgment from coming back to haunt them.)

Territory

I wish someone would give me a nickel for every time I heard my distributor say he or she could sell in China, via a shirt-tail relative, from a home base in Peru. Most distributors greatly exaggerate their ability to service the markets surrounding them and in some cases test the credulity of the most naive. This is part of the game.

Like most other human beings (and other businesspeople), a distributor's sight will almost always exceed his or her grasp. Part of the reason is that overseas distributors are accustomed to dealing with American companies that possess a startling tendency to lop off grand chunks of the earth and give them to one distributor. I have often puzzled at this phenomenon and recently concluded that a possible explanation for it is laziness. We want to stick one pin in all of Southeast Asia rather than the seven or eight that would protrude from that part of the world with a minimum of responsible behavior. Additionally, many of these U.S. firms are more concerned with filling in the blanks on the distribution map at the home office than with ensuring that the distribution network will effectively exploit the potential the various markets offer.

It is very easy to grant large territories, and very difficult to divide them later. In some cases, the only legal means of division is to "buy" it back from the distributor to whom you so foolishly granted the too-large territory in the first place. In other cases, the attempt to divide territory has been so filled with conflict that the entire distribution system defected to competitors. Surrounding distributors will often watch your attempt to reduce territory in other markets and fear they will be next. They may even take preemptive action and seek out other suppliers. In one case, 32 distributors defected en masse to a competitor, setting a U.S. company back ten years in its efforts on the European mainland. This is, admittedly, an extreme example, but never underestimate their reaction to any change in the perceived rules of the game. The only way to avoid this problem is not to succumb to the temptation of doing things the easy way.

Conventional wisdom claims that the best method to establish overseas distribution is to grant an exclusive by country. This is a good example of what is wrong with conventional wisdom. What does geography have to do with market coverage? Would you grant an exclusive for the United States to one individual in South Dakota? Of course not. The issue is what territory the potential distributor has demonstrated he or she can cover. The questions are: Where are the offices? How are they staffed? Who manages them? Do staff in remote areas fully understand the supplier's needs with regard to product introduction and support?

I know distributors who successfully covered entire continents, and some who literally covered only one city. There is only one rule of thumb here: Do not grant more territory to one distributor than historical performance indicates as proper.

There are other issues involved as well. In Germany, for example, three outlets are needed, at minimum, to cover that marketplace. In Spain, at least two are required for reasons related to the cultural and political environment of the country (Madrid and Barcelona). In Japan, I've had very good luck with a single distributor—but have never been completely happy with any French distributor, despite my best efforts.

Never assume anything when it comes to granting a territory overseas. Each distributor and country will require your firm to apply the same rules of thumb that it applies to its domestic operations. Grant territory consistent with the candidate's abilities to market your product in that area. When in doubt, err on the side of caution; it is much easier to grant additional territory, should the distributor work out, than to cut existing rights.

Stock

There is one constant of distribution sales if you are going to appoint a stocking distributor: she or he will need to carry inventory. I normally require that new distributors hold a fixed level of stock, for two reasons. The first, commonly discussed in textbooks, is to ensure that customers have ready access to the product when they want to buy it. The second is equally important: Distributors have a lot more incentive to move stock if it is sitting in their inventory, not mine. In addition, a fixed level allows for much better production planning and delivery execution for the supplying company.

In some countries, however, the cost of capital is so high, most often because of high inflationary pressures, that nobody can afford to hold much of an inventory. This has been the case for a number of years in Latin America and will probably continue to be a problem for the foreseeable future. Often, Latin American distributors will not hold a sufficient inventory and besiege suppliers with ongoing requests for "emergency shipments." In these instances, U.S. firms must find ways to speed delivery to distributors, even if the per unit price rises. Buy-backs from your existing domestic distribution network, when your product lines allow you to take items off the shelf, can be an attractive way to fill these "emergency" orders.

Financial Strength

One of the classic reasons for selecting distributors is the financial strength of the candidate. This trait is among the most sought after, primarily for reasons of alleviating concerns over payment. Payment certainly is a legitimate concern, but it is only part of the reason. The other part has to do with the fact that a distribution system is an asset. Your company will invest considerable time and effort to get a new distributor up and running properly. You spend money on training, and your firm generates travel expense to support this person. Hopefully, the local market strongly identifies your product with that distributor. If he or she goes out of business after all of this effort on your part, a great deal of your time and money are lost.

When examining a distributor from the financial side, pay less attention to this person's bank account balance and more to his or her general credit-worthiness, as well as outstanding debt. Do not be fooled by extravagant entertainment and premises. Be sure the company has a strong asset base.

Premises

As a young man I made the classic mistake of not actually visiting a distributor's facilities. It so happened he was the last on a long list of interviews I had done that day, and I, at the end of a lengthy trip, was more interested in getting home than getting the right distributor in the United Arab Emirates (UAE). As a result, I interviewed him at my hotel, just prior to leaving for the airport.

I was impressed when a very well-dressed gentleman appeared in the lobby. More impressive still, he brought with him his financials and a beautiful company profile, including brochures. To this day, I regard that gentleman as having made the best first impression of anyone I ever met. He appeared to be the perfect distributor.

I returned to the United States, and some days later as I reviewed my notes on all the companies I had become acquainted with during my swing through the Middle East, I continued to return to the company in question for the UAE. It seemed perfect. I was a little reluctant to appoint them, given the briefness of the meeting and the fact I had not visited their offices, but they were, by far, the best candidate, and I appointed them. Six months later, on my next trip to the region, I discovered he was the perfect distributor for one very good reason: He already represented my leading competitor. He had neglected to put that particular brochure in the profile and never mentioned it during the meeting. His reasoning was as sound to him as it was distressing to me: He felt his firm could delay our market entry for some time by getting us to sign a contract with him and then simply make no effort whatever to market our product. He recounted all this, to my mounting horror, as though it were the perfectly logical thing to do and completely understandable under the circumstances. The subject came up because, as I was getting out of the taxi in front of his office, I couldn't help but notice my competitor's logo on the building's windows and their machines on display in front of the office. I was to learn that while this did not, in my mind, constitute acceptable business practice, it was highly effective.

It took two years to dissolve that contract and get another distributor in place. The process involved waiting him out and did not cost my company a great deal of money for legal fees and other expenses, but it was acutely embarrassing for me personally. Had the UAE been one of our primary markets, this miscue would have cost dearly indeed from the standpoint of lost revenue. If I had been the boss, I would have fired me.

Lest I begin to engage in "export terrorism" and begin to sound like some of the consultants I criticized in the introduction of this book, note that this disaster occurred not because of any inherent danger in the conduct of international business but because I acted rashly and with some youthful abandon. Learn this lesson: Always visit the potential representative's office. In some countries, your competitor's distributors can tie you up for years if you sign a contract with them.

Because many distributors overseas own a number of interlocking companies, often through family ties, the need exists to exercise diligence in investigating a potential distributor's business interests. When in doubt, ask the U.S. embassy to perform a world trader data report or, at the very least, check with his or her bank and the U.S. Chamber of Commerce in that country. These steps may slow the process of getting the distributor up and running in that market, but your firm has already survived a number of years without being there, and a few more months will not matter.

My experience in the UAE is an interesting anecdote, but this sort of thing is not common, and there are other important considerations with regard to what the potential distributor has to offer:

- Does the distributor have the sort of test equipment and shop on premises to service and support your product?
- How does the office feel? Are the people working there generally content and productive?
- Is the office well organized for the efficient conduct of business?

Assets

Perhaps the greatest comfort in the world to an American company is appointing a distributor with substantial assets in the United States. Should you ever get into an unworkable situation with a distributor with regard to payment or intellectual property issues, there is no quicker and easier way to force a rapid and favorable resolution than having readily attachable assets in the United States or other "friendly" jurisdiction. In general terms, an individual's taste for this sort of legal conflict lessens to the degree he or she is forced to engage in judicial combat in a foreign jurisdiction. Aside from the natural discomfort of being in a foreign court system, the costs also increase. And if the distributor has U.S. assets, the cost/benefit ratio radically alters in favor of the U.S. company.

In a recent case, a U.S. company was able to attach the assets (a commercial building in New York) of a Turkish distributor that had not only refused to pay the company for goods shipped but solicited a competing supplier as the new source, apparently with the intention of evading payment to the first exporter. When the U.S. firm discovered what had happened, they recalled seeing a U.S. asset on the credit application form, submitted by the Turkish distributor months earlier. Sure enough, the building was listed on the application. After attaching the building, the U.S. company was paid in full, severed its relationship with the Turkish distributor without indemnification, and as part of the settlement received his agreement to sell no competitive lines for a three-year period. Absent the ability to threaten the U.S. asset, this settlement would have been absolutely impossible as a practical matter. The amount of money involved would not have warranted the cost of the legal proceedings in U.S. courts and the subsequent attempt to get the judgment honored in the Turkish court system.

It is unlikely that many foreign distributors will have U.S. assets, but it is a question you should ask every potential distributor against the day you need some additional leverage.

GO WITH YOUR GUT

There have been several instances where I have gone out on a limb and granted distribution rights to individuals who met none of the criteria. They were just starting out, poorly capitalized, did not have adequate staff (if they had one at all), and were not able to support the product from a service standpoint because they could not afford to stock parts. Yet I took them on. Why? Sometimes you have to throw the book out the window and go with your gut.

In each of these cases, there were mitigating circumstances. All of these people were young businesspersons who would be entirely dependent on my product line for financial survival. Every one was aggressive and had good product knowledge (they came out of similar industries), good industry contacts, and excellent recommendations from major end users. These recommendations were most often the factor that swayed the decision in their favor. And I liked them. For whatever reason, my instinct told me to place my trust and my company's fortunes in their hands.

They all became good representatives. I often wonder, in retrospect, if part of the reason for this success wasn't my willingness to do almost anything to make them successful—if for no other reason than to ensure I didn't get taken to task for appointing such unqualified distributors. I recently reviewed my travel records for the time I worked with this group of new distributors and discovered I traveled to see them with greater than twice the frequency of my other, more traditional, distributors. My conclusion is that it wasn't necessarily that I chose them well. Rather, by choosing them, I created a situation of mutual dependence between us that had only one logical outcome: success. Neither of us had any choice, and we were both willing to do whatever it took to ensure we were successful.

DISTRIBUTOR SUPPORT

Once a new distributor is in place, your company is faced with the challenge of getting the best sales performance possible. Contrary to popular belief, distribution sales is not a passive activity for manufacturers. It requires a great deal of work, especially during the initial effort, to get the new representative to the point at which he or she can operate somewhat independently, at close to optimal levels. Further, at no point will marketing staff be able to rely entirely on the distributor for the best possible coverage of the market. No set guidelines exist with regard to how to milk the maximum performance from a distributor. However, this should be viewed as a competitive advantage, assuming that you are willing to be flexible in the manner by which you approach your overseas distribution system. By letting other suppliers operate under the assumption that the distributor's "job" is to market the product, your company can (assuming sales staff choose an active approach) very rapidly gain market share from suppliers that take a passive approach to their distribution sales. An added bonus is that your firm will become less dependent on your distributor as your knowledge of that market, competitive distributors, and the client base steadily increases.

General Guidelines

There are some general guidelines (although your firm will have to adapt the way it approaches the various markets to maximize penetration). Begin by attempting to become the distributor's partner in the effort to expand his or her company. Work with this person in the development of new approaches or to adapt existing techniques in this marketing effort. Help by providing competitive information from other foreign markets, the United States, and the distributor's own country as well. If your company can't, or won't, travel frequently to his or her location, then maintain regular contact by telephone and mail. Try to persuade all distributors to visit the head office at least once a year (in addition to the regional conference your company should hold annually). In short, do everything possible so that communications are frequent, friendly, and responsive to the distributor's needs. Understand your role: that of a business partner who will put his or her shoulder to the wheel in the quest to make your mutual efforts rewarding for both parties.

You can sell your product without traveling frequently to your distributor's country, but the lack of travel will make the effort that much more difficult. I could predict, within a 10 percent margin, my distributors' monthly sales based on my travel schedule. Usually they made enormous efforts to generate sales prior to my arriving on a regularly scheduled visit, so they had something to demonstrate that they were making an effort with my line. They also wanted to be able to close several deals while I was at the location. If nothing else, my arrival forced each distributor to spend time with my line and created additional attention for my customers because I always used these trips to do cooperative client calls with my distributors.

Remember that your products are competing with a number of other products in the line for the distributor's attention. To get maximum focus and to force efforts to close pending deals, a regular visit is critical. Additionally, your firm may want to offer terms, additional discounts, better technical support, or incentive programs to ensure that time spent with your product is more profitable than that lavished on the remainder of the line. Distributors always allocate their best efforts to those products and companies that are the most profitable for them.

In responding to these needs, understand that a joint effort also means that costs should be split. Encourage the use of free samples, if it is appropriate, and share the cost of promotional campaigns and unusual service requirements. If your firm agrees to this cooperative spirit up front, the distributor will be encouraged to invest funds in promoting your product and you can avoid later disputes about who should bear what expense.

Distributors, like the rest of us, have egos. Reward outstanding performance of recognition with plaques, achievement prizes, making sure corporate staff are present during important trade fairs, calling on his or her best customers, and bonuses (my favorite is a free trip that includes spouse and children). You can also reward distributors by granting additional support, such as allowing them to grant warranties directly, additional training for their staff, granting an exclusive or otherwise deepening the business relationship between your companies, or putting them on open terms (or better terms).

In many countries, duty rates are substantially lower if the product is shipped disassembled, and the local distributor (under license, joint venture, or simply by agreement) assembles the product in country. This can be a tremendous reward for good performance; it will give the distributor the increased status of being a "manufacturer" and make the business much more profitable. Many countries have minimal requirements to qualify a product as "locally manufactured," so gaining the duty reduction can be as simple as allowing minor assembly work. Your distributor may also be able to qualify for local investment incentives by doing some assembly to the product on-site, yet another way to enrich your distributor—and perhaps share in the additional profit. Bear in mind that a successful program is one that will both reward financially and stroke the distributor's ego. One without the other can be as bad as neither.

Performance Evaluation

Perhaps the most difficult of all jobs is to develop standards for objectively evaluating a distributor's performance. Performance evaluation can be a vital means of cementing the relationship between your company and its distributors, and getting better performance from both. Hence, the approach should be, "What can *we* do to improve performance?" Not only are you able to remove the element of conflict from this discussion, it also impresses upon the distributor that your firm is dead serious about accomplishing targets and goals and your staff are willing to include themselves as a possible impediment to achieving them.

The best quantitative method is to compare your sales levels to those of competitors and other distributors. These data may not be difficult to find since public companies throughout the world often have similar disclosure obligations. Your marketing staff can also identify and interview the highest-consumption end users of the product and extrapolate total sales from these data. A simpler method is to use customs service data (import data of the foreign country, usually collected by its customs service or equivalent) to determine total levels of imports and then describe your sales targets in percentage terms. When historic foreign customs data are combined with the historic sales levels of your distributor, a clear picture begins to emerge with regard to total import market share for the product. Then your staff can begin to develop meaningful achievement goals and projections for future sales. Give some thought to the wisdom of defining goals in terms of market share gained, if that is your highest priority.

As a practical matter, both your staff and the distributor will know when performance is not up to standard without looking at data. At the same time, it is critical for your executives to have a basis to discuss the matter other than stating, "I think you are not getting the job done." Some measure is needed, if for no other reason than to avoid an argument, that could lead only to a further deepening of the problems in your relationship with the distributor.

Before holding a performance review, chat with customers to determine if they have any complaints about or recommendations to improve service or support. Check out their general satisfaction or dissatisfaction levels with the distributor. When the criticism comes from customers, the personal element is removed from the discussion, and it can proceed based upon what is good for the customer, not what the distributor has failed to do. Not only does it make for a more dispassionate and focused discussion, it places the emphasis where it rightly belongs: on the customer.

Termination

If you are dissatisfied with performance, be very slow to terminate. Rather, try to locate and correct the problems. Remember that both parties have a great deal of money invested in the distributor's success, and your firm cannot terminate this person without reinvesting a similar amount, usually with no guarantee that a new distributor will be better.

If termination seems possible, start by setting close deadlines for achieving results. Begin with three months and continue with three-month cycles as long as it takes to get the distributor back on target. If he or she does not respond quickly, consider taking this person off open account or reducing the term of credit (if any). If that does not work, inform him or her of your doubt that it is a solvable problem and that your company may have to search for another distributor in order to protect market share. The intent here is not to penalize the distributor but to establish that the situation is serious and that personal relationships are not going to be sufficient to get around the problem. It also demonstrates that past incentives granted are not sacred cows, and your company is going to make every effort to remedy the situation.

The next step is normally to switch (if applicable) from an exclusive to a nonexclusive agreement to allow both parties time to line up new partners and, if possible, to make a last-ditch effort to save the existing distributor. If you must cancel, advise the distributor in person, and be honest. Share the responsibility for failure, and do everything possible to reduce any animosity created by the termination.

Finally, make sure that the termination is consistent with local law and is recognized by the appropriate authorities (if any). This information is generally available from your ITA office or the U.S. embassy in that country.

Chapter **5**

What Foreign Partners Want from You: The Hidden Agenda

Let us take a step back from your desires with regard to foreign distributors, and put the shoe on the other foot for a moment: What do foreign partners want from you? The result will be a little startling.

WHAT ABOUT YOU?

For your company, payment is the primary question. For the purchaser, however, the biggest fear is that your firm will not ship the goods on time, will not ship what was agreed upon, or will ship a product of inferior quality. From the perspective of the trading partner, the risk in this transaction is almost entirely his or hers, and your hazard is minimal. Yet you certainly do not see it in the same light as the distributor.

You intend to check out new potential distributors carefully before agreeing to grant distribution rights. Distributors have the same concerns. It is quite possible that other firms have taken advantage of this person on prior transactions—perhaps by not shipping on time or shipping inferior products. The distributor feels, and rightly so, that his interests need to be protected as well. He may also want to know if your company has a history of management turnovers that may lead to capricious changes in the distributor network and threatens his ability to hold on to the distributorship during these changes. He will wonder if your company will deliver on the support that is so vital to push the product into the marketplace. He may have very real concerns about your firm's desire to honor warranty and to send technical staff to his location should he require assistance.

He will want to know if your company has firm underpinnings financially. Perhaps in the past, he ordered from a company that underwent bankruptcy, and, as a result, he was left on the hook and never received goods for which he paid.

If the potential distributor is relatively sophisticated, he may inquire if you are a division of another company that might, at some point, consider merging international operations and put his distribution rights at risk by virtue of changing company management or consolidation of overseas distribution. If he has been around long enough, this has very likely befallen him at least once, and thus is a very real fear.

He may investigate your company history with regard to allowing domestic distributors to sell into foreign markets, thus violating the exclusivity provisions of the overseas contracts. He may be particularly inclined to do so if there is a substantial margin between your domestic and international pricing structures—yet another argument for parity in pricing levels between the international and domestic list prices. In fact, many U.S. companies do allow this sort of leakage to occur and eventually suffer the consequences of viewing the international distribution network as a second-class citizen.

THE PRODUCT

Distributors will want to know if your product line is the best one available, or whether other lines could better serve their needs. After all, for the most part, they are taking your word on the quality and marketability of the product; it is understandable they might harbor doubts about your credibility. If they assume the line and tie their fate to your firm's, they will fear that their company may miss another product that would be more marketable. The greatest concern is that this superior product, should it appear in their country, will place them at a competitive disadvantage—after they invested capital in your product line.

I have never ceased to be amazed at how U.S. companies go to great lengths to describe their product in glowing terms but never tell a potential distributor why he should undertake the distribution of the product. Let's face it. There are a lot of good products and any number of products that are of lesser quality but are cheaper or easier to use. All distributors understand there are a number of alternatives and that it's possible to make money on any of them.

THE DEAL

The potential distributor wants to understand, as a businessperson, what's in it for him or her. Yet fully 90 percent of the faxes, letters, and distributor packages I see make no mention of anything but the product itself. Nowhere is there information about margins, freedom to price, factory training for staff, cooperative advertising, or anything else that gives the company an advantage over any of the other products competing for attention. Do not ignore the quality of the product, but realize that it is only one of the considerations. Having said all that, I would acknowledge it is important, and does need to be addressed in your communications with distributors, along with the other issues.

Overseas distributors want quality products at good prices, preferably with good market recognition worldwide. If yours is a newer product, high degrees of acceptance in the U.S. market and surrounding overseas markets are desirable from the standpoint of the potential distributor because this sort of product will require the least exertion to market and make the best return on investment. However, if the product fits this category, the supplier should get something back because the distributor's job is greatly facilitated by virtue of what has already been accomplished in other markets. It is a grave mistake to price product too cheaply or settle for an inferior distributor when the product is already successful in other markets. What the supplier wants in return can vary greatly. One possibility is to trade the prestige of the product for greater commitments from distributors in terms of the number of salespeople devoted to the product, the amount and kind of factory training required for service and support staff, and a highly leveraged commission (or discount) plan that recognizes that a great deal of the sales will be essentially order taking. The commission (or discount) structure should create very real incentives for going beyond that passive activity and into a more active marketing effort.

If the product does not have a great deal of recognition, the focus should turn to price and quality. You must be more competitive in areas such as financing the sale of the product to the distributor or offering payment terms. Your company will also need to consider offering a cooperative budget for the product's promotion in that market and giving the distributor greater latitude in pricing.

THE CONTRACT

I have never not been asked for an exclusive territory in all the years I selected and supported overseas distributors. It is a given. Your policy should be to establish initially that exclusives are not perfunctory and are tied to achievement of sales goals. (Bear in mind, though, that some countries require an exclusive distribution agreement. This subject is discussed in Chapter 6.) The distributor must have a reasonable prospect of achieving the desired goal, and thus gaining exclusivity for the period of time specified in the distribution agreement.

Many U.S. firms should begin to think of exclusives more in terms of end user groups than geography, especially in the less-developed countries, where most distributors sell to a fairly narrow group in a particular industry. If the product enjoys a number of applications across a multiplicity of industries, then your firm will want to carefully consider offering exclusives based on industry sectors rather than geography. Some would maintain that the best situation is to have no exclusivity with any one distributor in a particular market. However, this is quite difficult to accomplish, without a product that does not really require any investment from the distributor. In fact, should your firm choose not to offer exclusive distribution contracts, efforts to recruit and maintain good distributors can become considerably more difficult.

Most potential distributors will demand that the supplier assume some responsibility for protecting their territory from other distributors in the region or country who will undertake (should you grant geographic or sector exclusivity) to poach in the market. No assurance from a supplier can or should be iron-clad (after all, what can one really do but press the other distributors not to poach or cancel them?), but a good-faith effort should be made.

THE SUPPORT

One of the more important calculations for many products is training and support. My preference is to mix factory training with on-site updates, as needed. This not only gets the distributor staff into the factory for the bulk of the initial training, where it does not affect marketing budgets, it also forces technical staff out into the field to meet with customers and update distributor training, as needed, for new products or applications.

Good distributors usually press for more assistance in staff training and support. If the products lend themselves to the approach, they also press for their technical staff to spend time in the field with your domestic sales force or technical support staff, or both. Technical support staff can be excellent salespeople for products that require some degree of sophistication, and they should be required to spend time with the sales staff in the field. An added advantage of pushing technical staff into the field is that a great deal of applications knowledge (which will lead to additional sales) can be spread around in this fashion. Finally, it gives the distributor's sales force the self-confidence they need to promote the new product to their best customers. Good sales representatives never lead valued clients down a risk-filled path with regard to a new and untested product. They want to know the technical support is there for customers before they sell the product.

Technical newsletters, distributed to both support and sales staff, keep the level of product support high and ensure that new applications reach the field as quickly as possible. If your company cannot provide ongoing communications to distributors, they will often request some sort of informal arrangement to ensure that any new product or applications developments reach the distribution staff quickly.

If your company has an aftermarket for the product, consider making available (for a price) an emergency parts service to speed needed parts to the customer. This is especially needed in Third World countries, where stocking levels tend to be quite low because of financial necessity.

An emergency parts service my company created in the late 1970s for Latin American distributors led to enormous growth in parts sales. It got to the point that we shipped other manufacturers' parts to our distributors, who sold them to their customers because we could deliver the part within 24 hours of the request. We filled a void not only for our equipment but for other noncompeting manufacturers as well.

Your distributor candidate will often want some flexibility from your firm for help in maintaining high levels of service to customers in the face of sometimes unusual or difficult circumstances. Do not view these requests as onerous or asking more of your firm than it should be willing to deliver to an overseas distribution network. Rather, view it as an indication of the distributor's desire to deliver good service to customers, despite the difficulties of doing so.

WARRANTIES

I have sold more product through distributors by promptly paying warranties than I ever would have by calling on customers. Manufacturers offer warranties so they can sell more product, not because they like losing money on honoring them. Think of warranties more in terms of using them to generate additional sales than an issue of right and wrong. I have paid many over the years that were not the fault of our manufacturing but resulted from misuse in the field. I paid them anyway, because I knew we would get the money back a hundred times over by not quibbling and paying up.

Most of your competitors do not pay warranties in foreign markets as readily as they would at home—yet another reason that smart companies pay them gladly (it gives them an edge over the competition). In fact, I have picked up several very good distributors who defected from their suppliers over unpaid warranties. Never underestimate the importance of prompt, honest, and, sometimes, slightly excessive payment of warranties. Warranties are of critical importance to distributors, not only because warranty payment involves their credibility with customers but also because it is a leading indicator of the supplier's commitment to the international marketing effort. Ultimately, warranties are important to both parties, for the same reasons.

Consider empowering the distributor to authorize warranty payment up to a certain level. This strengthens your relationship with the distributor and better services clients, who do not have to suffer long delays to get the replacement (it also saves money because you do not have to ship the part back and forth for factory inspection). Your warranty should cover the distributor's labor cost as well. Why should they pay for labor to fix a defective device? Distributors will press to extend the warranty to any labor or other expenses they assume to honor the warranty.

PROMOTIONAL ASSISTANCE

Distributors are proud of their businesses and want to participate in local trade events and the like, but trade shows are costly. A good cooperative advertising budget—for trade shows, media, or developing foreign-language brochures—is often key to getting the product before the end user group in the most forceful way.

It is only fair that this should be a shared expense; both your company and the distributor are making money on the increase in sales that results from the promotional effort. Gear the cooperative budget to a percentage of gross sales achieved over a period of time; discount cooperative advertising expense from invoices, if need be; and offer discounts and other special offers if a distributor agrees to hold higher levels of inventory or needs to stock up before a busy season. Make it easy for distributors to stretch to get those additional sales. If your company is unwilling to spend money to expand sales in that market, distributors may wonder why they would undertake an expense that accrues benefit to both parties.

TERMS

Give careful thought to establishing the same credit policy with your international distributors as you maintain with the domestic organization. Many American companies have allowances for bad domestic debt on their books and none for international. But if you accept that bad debt results from open accounts, which you have established to sell more product in the United States, why would you not apply the same criteria abroad? The answer is ignorance.

The response I usually get to this assertion is that it is more difficult to collect abroad. This may be true, but there is very little instance of bad debt occurring with distributors that does not result from one of two circumstances: a distributor has gone bankrupt and your company is probably well down the line of creditors anyway, much as you might be in the United States under the same circumstances, or a conflict arises from your business operation (failure to pay warranty, invoice dispute, etc.). Most often these latter should be worked out between the parties: if no solution can be reached, the contract should call for arbitration, with the dispute settled by a third party.

Several collection agencies operate internationally, and they can offer assistance. However, as a general rule, a relationship with a distributor should never sink to this sad state. A negotiated settlement of some sort should be possible.

The distributor's risk factor in this arrangement is at least equal to yours, and in some cases it is even greater. As a result, during negotiations, the distributor will press your firm to assume a portion of the risk in the payment transaction. It is not in your best interest to begin the relationship with an open account, but it does make sense to go to net terms within a reasonable period of time, assuming good credit reports and a relationship of trust between you.

PRICE MAINTENANCE

Your distributor may want freedom to price the product. Price maintenance is in your company's interest, but costs in each country are unique, and price maintenance clauses in contracts can become a real obstacle to getting product sold. In general, freedom to price, within maximum limits and expressed as a percentage of the entered cost of the product (the cost of getting the product into the warehouse), will keep painful discussions and conflict to a minimum and allow the distributor to move price, within the limits defined by the contract, as costs change.

Many suppliers succumb to the temptation of comparing distributors' margins to their own. Let's assume, as an example, that a supplying company works on a 20 percent gross margin. Its position may well be that the overseas distributor should not operate on a mark-up any higher than the manufacturer's. However, this position misses the boat because the distributor's costs may be radically different from the supplier's. In many countries, employment benefits, taxes, and business fees, among other expenses, are much higher than in the United States; in other countries, these costs are lower. So in almost all cases, manufacturers are not using a fair or accurate basis for comparison. Additionally, the cost of freight, duties, import fees, warehousing, and inland transportation may serve to make overseas distributors' expenses much higher than those of a domestic distributor.

The bottom line is not to compare margins of foreign distributors to either the manufacturer's or domestic distributors'. Understand the unique costs in each market and how they affect the final price of the product to the end user.

TERMINATION

Termination is a two-way street. Distributors will want the right to drop your product line, with short notice, should your firm become difficult to work with or if other, higher-potential, products appear. They will likely want some sort of indemnification for your termination of the distributorship, as well as restocking provisions that are generous and some provision to allow a continuation of extending warranty to customers until the new distributor is up and running. A general rule of thumb is to follow the legal guidelines of each country in which a distributor operates.

A NEW VIEW

We must change the way we view foreign distributors and begin to think of them not as customers but as business partners. All partnerships inherently contain elements of conflict and cooperation. How exporters define this relationship and attempt to minimize the element of conflict will ultimately determine their success or failure with overseas distributors.

International marketing is not a matter of selecting a distributor and resting content in the assumption that the distributor is now responsible for our fortunes in that market. There are many products and companies pulling at the attention of distributors. Good suppliers must be competitive not only with regard to the products that directly compete with theirs but also those that vie for the distributor's time and money, from both within and outside of the current product offering. In short, U.S. marketing executives must become familiar with a distributor's whole operation and try to ensure that their company is the best supplier, offering the highest levels of support, the best margins, and the like.

Go beyond your own fears with regard to selecting distributors, and begin to understand that they are counterbalanced by the concerns of the overseas representative, who is equally anxious about protecting his or her interests. Understanding the need to balance the two will lead you to greater success with regard to attracting and maintaining the best possible representation for your product line.

Finally, things change. The relationship with a distributor is a dynamic one. Distribution operations are sold to new owners, current owners retire or die, new products come in and out of the distributor's product line, companies go out of business, and so on. Your likelihood of maintaining a profitable relationship with a distribution network will depend on your ability to recognize the changes before they occur and your willingness to adapt products and approaches as needed.

C h a p t e r **6**

Legal Considerations

I doubt there has ever been so much smoke generated by so little fire as has been the case with international distribution agreements and the need to have enforceable contracts with overseas distributors. For the vast majority of companies that export, these agreements are not worth the paper they are written on from an enforceability standpoint. The bottom line, from a practical perspective, is that these agreements will be respected so long as the suppler-distributor relationship is mutually beneficial.

Many companies take great comfort from the words, "This contract shall be interpreted under the laws of the Sovereign State of X." What most don't understand is that although the clause will allow you to sue an overseas party in the courts of the State of X, it will not automatically force an overseas party to pay you the damages you have won. Unless the foreign party has some readily attachable assets in the United States, you may be required to convince a foreign court to uphold your U.S. court judgment in order to force the other party to honor the contract.

The long and the short of it is that, most often, the cost of enforcing these contracts, for either party, far exceeds the amount of money to be gained by pursuing a lawsuit in a foreign jurisdiction. In most cases, problems with distributors will arise prior to that distributor's generating a sufficient revenue base to warrant the legal action, should a dispute arise. The flip side of the coin is that once that level of revenue has been achieved, both parties have too much to lose to allow the situation to deteriorate into an adversarial one.

Hence, the practicality of the situation lends itself to a business solution rather than a legal one.

The relative unenforceability of international distribution contracts, when compared to domestic agreements, does not mean you should not have a distributor agreement. They contain many useful and important features that will provide you with a moral high ground, if nothing else. Additionally, the agreements will, if properly written, be enforceable should you reach a level of sales where it is worth the time and effort (and expense) to enforce it if something should go amiss with the distributor. Finally, the entire exercise of drafting the contract will assist you in identifying any potential disagreements that may occur down the line and get them solved before they become issues.

Early in my career, when I had the luxury of working for a large Fortune 500 firm, I would simply call our corporate attorneys and request they draft a distribution agreement for country X. After I had been through a number of these agreements, I realized the attorneys were not customizing the agreements to conform with the applicable foreign laws unique to each of the markets in which we had contracts drawn. Consequently, in many cases, our contract would not be enforceable in the market in question should a dispute arise. I began to search for cheap, readily available sources of information that would be of assistance to us in drafting these contracts. I found that the U.S. Department of Commerce published a good guide, *Foreign Business Practices*. Unfortunately, the guide has never been updated. However, updates for most countries are readily available through another U.S. Department of Commerce publication, *Overseas Business Reports*, which are published by country.

I do advocate the use of attorneys to draw updated distribution contracts when a particular market reaches sales levels where enforcement might, in fact, become worthwhile. And you should use them when the contract governs such ventures as a foreign investment or licensing agreements. In general, however, I grew to rely less on attorneys and more on readily available sources because I found that by including a few customized provisions, I could perform this function myself using a template contract, which was kept on computer. Over the years, I saved clauses and provisions that cover most contingencies in most countries. I even discovered a great deal of similarity within regions, at least with regard to laws governing distribution contracts. These laws tend to be quite similar throughout Latin America and, in different ways, the Arab Middle East. You too will find that you can churn out these contracts with some ease.

SOURCES OF MATERIAL AND ASSISTANCE

Become familiar with the source materials for drafting these agreements, and ensure that your attorney not only has them but studies them. It is also a good idea for your marketing department to review the documents.

The U.S. and Foreign Commercial Service of the U.S. Department of Commerce has commercial officers in 67 countries. These officers are located in the commercial sections of U.S. embassies and consulates and can be reached by telephone, telex, or fax. They offer advice on foreign law in their country of assignment and often have, on file, reports and other information developed by local consulting firms. This information can be useful for indicating the practicalities of a distribution agreement and how it can be structured to ensure that you can quickly and cleanly break your relationship with a distributor, if need be. These officers can advise as well on whether the contract is, in fact, beneficial for your company.

Attorneys in the target countries often are less expensive to use than American attorneys, especially if they specialize in contract law. The foreign attorney has all of the basics down and needs to do only minor customization to draft the contract. Embassies often keep lists of local attorneys by area of specialization.

A bonus to using foreign attorneys is they understand the practicalities of the country in which they operate. I once used an attorney in a Southeast Asian country to develop a contract for a distributor. That country's indemnification laws were quite draconian, and I was uneasy with the individual with whom I had been negotiating. I expressed this doubt to the attorney, who informed me we could draw the contract and delay registration with the local Ministry of Industry until I was comfortable with the new distributor. In that country, the law provided for no recognition of the contract until it went through the registration process and was filed in a particular office. As it turned out, after a year's time, we did file the contract; the distributor, despite my misgivings, had turned out to be quite adept. But until the filing occurred, we could have thrown the contract away and found another distributor, should that have become necessary.

Other good sources with regard to the legal requirements surrounding distribution practices in foreign countries are the *Doing Business In* series, published by the Big Eight firms like Price Waterhouse. They contain quite complete information on the regulations and laws of doing business in a particular country, including a section on any legal considerations that may govern commercial relationships.

Probably the best single source, in terms of completeness, is Business International's *Investing, Licensing and Trading Conditions Abroad.* This publication, updated annually, contains information for most foreign markets on laws involving taxes, corporations, joint ventures, licensing, patents, trademarks, copyrights, investment, foreign exchange controls, antitrust, labor, distributorships and sales representatives, and a host of other topics.

A template distribution agreement can be requested from foreign chambers of commerce and the U.N. Industrial Development Organization. These models, however, will not, in and of themselves, solve your legal needs. They are only a starting point and will still require some customization. In addition, the level of service these organizations can offer varies widely. I found that roughly half of the chambers do not have template contracts available and that finding the right person at the United Nations requires some digging. Regardless of the difficulty you may face in getting these documents into your hands and their admitted shortcomings, they still are a good means to help you understand the issues before you.

Among the better introductions to drafting international business agreements are the following:

> *International Commercial Agreements* (by Fox; Norwell, Mass.: Kluwer) "A Foreign Sales Representative Checklist and Agreement," by Douglas in *Practical Lawyer* (December 1985)
>
> *Digest of Commercial Laws of the World: Forms of Commercial Agreements* (edited by Nelson; Dobbs Ferry, N.Y.: Oceana Publications)
>
> *International Business Planning: Law and Taxation* (by Streng and Salacuse; New York: Matthew Bender & Co.)
>
> *International Exporting Agreements* (by Ezer)

There are also useful monthly or quarterly publications, which have the advantage of being somewhat more up-to-date than yearly publications. Two are the *International Contract Adviser* (published monthly by Abacus Press, Ltd., Washington, D.C.), and the *Exporter* (published monthly by Trade Data Reports, Inc., New York).

CONTRACT PROVISIONS

From a practical standpoint there is only one basic difference between an international and a domestic contract: The international agreement must consider the laws that regulate commercial relationships in the foreign market. It is just that simple—and that complex. Several rules of thumb can be used to avoid most of the problematic situations and expense that may arise from the need to have somewhat different contracts for your international operations.

Several provisions in your contracts are the most important and need to be given careful attention.

Exclusivity

Spell out clearly if the contract is exclusive and, if it is, what kind of exclusive you are granting: geographical (the right to sell in a particular area) or sectorial (the right to sell).

Pricing

We all want distributors held to some sort of price maintenance in terms of the final price they will charge the customer and normally want to work it into our agreement. However, in most cases, if you need a price maintenance clause in your contract, you may have the wrong distributor. You are, in part, allowing this person a margin with the idea that she brings value-added to the product through her knowledge of local markets. To interfere with her determination of the proper markup is to negate this concept.

A good distributor will make every effort to keep the price competitive in the marketplace. Moreover, many developed countries (notably in Europe and

Japan) prohibit or restrict price maintenance from distribution contracts. As a result, you may want to consider a standard clause in your contract that allows you to impose price maintenance but does not do so initially. This clause should be removed when the contract is used in countries that prohibit price maintenance. For the remaining countries—the vast majority of the world—you can then impose it as needed rather than applying it across the board, which would serve to impede your recruitment of good distributors.

Price maintenance has several drawbacks. It makes you a less attractive supplier to overseas distributors, and if you cannot attract good representatives, in part due to their objections to this sort of clause, then there is nothing to argue about because you are not selling anything and, hence, have no price to maintain. In a sense these clauses put the cart before the horse. An additional drawback is that if you impose this sort of clause, you have to police it and be willing to terminate distributors that violate the agreement—another basis for conflict. Finally, price maintenance will require customization of contracts and does run afoul of the laws in some countries.

Returns and Warranties

Returns and warranty handling is often an area that leads to substantial disputes between distributors and suppliers, typically because the need to lay this out contractually seems to be overlooked or the matter is not seen as one that is sufficiently important to warrant the attention of the attorney. Issues such as who is authorized to pay warranties and to what dollar level should be expressly stated. Additionally, some attention to which party pays for shipping, handling, and customs clearance, should the product need to be shipped back to the factory, should be considered. The need to reimburse the distributor for any expenses incurred in honoring your warranty should be included in the contract.

Promotion

Cooperative advertising, the nature of the marketing program, development and modification of sales material, and translations of materials and presentations can be addressed in your contract. Should you anticipate these policies changing and not want them in the distribution agreement, at least take the time to develop a clear and explicit verbal understanding with your distributor, and be prepared to offer additional discounts to distributors willing to undertake these endeavors on their own.

Service, Training, and Inventory Levels

The agreement should strive to offer greater levels of training and support to distributors willing to engage in factory training for their staff, commit to greater levels of inventory, and develop adequate service facilities. The translation of service and technical manuals is every bit as important as sales brochures. All of these factors are more important internationally because of the distances involved and because their absence from the contract often lead to accusations from the distributor with regard to the supplier's not offering adequate levels of support for sales and service efforts. Although it may be difficult to quantify, for purposes of the contract, the specific levels of support and inventory you will require of the distributor, some standard language that commits the distributor to engage in best efforts to maintain stock and provide service is generally a good idea, because some distributors do not see their role as being anything but a sales organization.

Compliance with Foreign Law

Compliance with foreign law provisions, especially those that require the distributor to advise the U.S. supplier of any local technical product requirements, is a good idea. This responsibility should be placed directly on distributors to ensure that they familiarize themselves with the local requirements, especially if the product is in a high-liability sector (such as health care) or the industry sector is new to them. Try to work a clause into the contract that requires that the representative be responsible for any government approvals (standards or safety approvals). This clause can save you an enormous amount of money and shorten the time required to get the necessary approvals in place so that you can begin to market the product.

There is a practical side as well to having your distributor undertake these sorts of approvals on your behalf. The authorities that issue these approvals tend to be much more responsive to a local businessperson than a foreign one. Additionally, the distributor is on the spot, so it is easier and cheaper for him or her to monitor the progress of the approval procedure.

Patents, Trademarks, and Copyrights

Patents, trademarks, and copyrights should be registered in that market, and the return of these rights, including "know how," should be provided for by the contract or a separate agreement. The registration process is your responsibility. However, having this clause will help ensure that you regain your rights to your intellectual property if you abandon the market or choose another representative.

Performance Evaluation

It is critical to include performance evaluation requirements in the agreement so that a commercial relationship can be cleanly broken. If the distributor needs to be canceled based upon nonperformance (the most commonly invoked provision, as well as the one with broadest acceptability around the world), it will be important to indicate clearly that the requirements were, in fact, contractual. It is a simple matter to update the performance requirements with a yearly review of the contract.

If the performance goals are unrealistic or clearly designed to allow you to terminate the agreement regardless of the efforts of the distributor, you will find it more difficult to enforce the termination. Having unattainable goals may be comforting to you to the extent it provides a basis for you to get out of the relationship, for whatever motive, but such a clause is unenforceable in many countries and bad business practice. It will be damaging to your reputation in that market, should you terminate unjustly, and you will have great difficulty attracting a suitable replacement for the terminated distributor.

Performance requirements are important to ensure that the distributor and the supplier understand, at the beginning of the relationship, what is expected from each. Should you establish high levels of sales as a requirement, be prepared for pressure to provide greater levels of support for both the sales and the service sides of the business. Your representative will expect you to take an active role in assisting him or her to get to the targets you have established, perhaps also demanding higher discount structures in exchange for higher sales goals.

The contract should state clearly that termination for cause is without indemnification. As a practical matter, this may be unenforceable in countries that have laws that require indemnification for terminated distributors (notably many of the Middle Eastern nations, although there are others). In some cases, they will require payment in an amount expressed as a percentage of total sales achieved, and in others, base the compensation on the number of years the distributor represented the supplier.

One case, in the Middle East, comes to mind. We had a distributor in a relatively small country whom we had to cancel. He went to his Ministry of Industry and got a judgment that would prevent us from naming another distributor in that country until we indemnified our terminated representative for his service. Although we enjoyed some sales in that market, the revenue did not justify the legal expense we would have undergone in attempting to enforce the nonindemnification clause in our contract and cleanly terminate our representative. The ex-distributor (through some creative math) had come up with an indemnification number that was not at all realistic.

I was unwilling to pay the amount requested or to undertake the legal battle and spent some time trying to think through a viable alternative. Eventually I decided to give the distribution rights to our representative in Saudi Arabia, who was able to market the product in our ex-distributor's country. The law did not and could not keep us from selling through a third party because the distribution contract was with our original distributor, not our Saudi representative.

Eventually our terminated distributor realized, much as we had, that the cost of enforcing the judgment and attempting to stop the Saudi distributor from marketing the product in his country was too high, at least when compared to the potential revenue he could generate from the legal action. Soon the uselessness of opposing us became apparent, and he allowed the judgment to expire rather than paying the additional expense of having the attorneys renew it.

Applicable Law Clause

Getting an applicable law clause—one that requires that the contract be interpreted under U.S. law and that any action takes place in a U.S. court—may be difficult or impossible. The distributor may be unwilling to sign an agreement that creates jurisdiction away from his or her country. In some cases, foreign law makes it a practical impossibility or outright illegal. Again, an arbitration clause may well avoid losing a good potential distributor or being forced to accept foreign jurisdiction to recruit the distributor. In many cases, you might consider a neutral third-party jurisdiction that is acceptable to both parties.

Termination

Nobody enters into a relationship with the idea of later getting a divorce. However, it does happen, and you need to be prepared to deal with it by constructing a good agreement and by paying careful attention to the laws of the country in which the distributor is located.

Be careful not to imply an extension of the agreement in the absence of meeting performance goals; at the same time, realize that the offer of extension of contract is also a great incentive for the distributor to make every effort to meet those goals. State expressly in the contract that nonperformance is a basis for unilateral termination, with no recourse to the representative.

Be sure that the period of time between notification of cancellation of the contract and the actual cancellation is reasonable, so as to allow both parties time to find a new counterpart should termination occur. Failure to do so may be interpreted as unreasonable in many countries. As a practical matter, this approach is also good for you; it allows for continued sales and service to existing clients while you are searching for new representatives.

The agreement should clearly specify that it is a contractual relationship between the parties and avoid the use of the term *agent*. In some countries, the absence of this specific language could lead local authorities to conclude that your distributor is, in fact, an employee and that you are liable for employment benefits. In some countries the use of the term *agent* is interpreted to mean that the individual can make legally binding financial commitments on your behalf.

Specifically include a clause that prohibits a distributor from asking for any amount over the initial purchase price for restocking after termination. There are many examples of distributors' attempting to add on "lost interest" or other inventory costs to make the termination much more expensive and more difficult for you to accomplish. Include language that provides for who pays shipping and import duties to accomplish the restocking.

In some countries, noncompete provisions are either highly diluted or unenforceable. Make allowances to get that sort of protection through other contractual agreements, should you need it. In any event, ensure that the provisions are reasonable in scope and do not constitute an onerous provision. In many countries, "unreasonable" provisions will not be recognized.

Always require customer lists during the life of the contract because you will be unlikely to get them in the event of termination. The distributor will claim to have lost the list or be otherwise obstructive. Getting the distributor accustomed to sending you these lists periodically is the best means to avoid an extended dispute later. If you cannot get lists, then demand that the distributor engage in cooperative calls to major accounts with you when you travel to his or her country. At the very least, this will ensure that you have some knowledge of the identity of your major end users.

Product Registration

If you have a product that lends itself to copyright or patent infringement, additional study will be required in drafting contracts. In these cases I recommend that you retain professional assistance to ensure that all foreign registration and maintenance requirements are met. However, U.S. companies' fears of infringement are not consistent with the actual danger. The coverage given to the relatively few cases of piracy does prey on our minds, and as a result, we tend to focus on the few cases where things went wrong, not the thousands where everything went right. Of course, this is little solace to anyone who has suffered from piracy. Hence, if you are vulnerable, take steps.

Before you undergo the expense of registration for your product, explore two issues: Is this business sufficiently profitable to attract the "rip-offs," and is the product really protectable in the sense that it is a truly original technology?

While I certainly am not recommending that you seek no protection for your products, I do know of any number of companies that never bother to register products. Their reasoning is that the product is so difficult to copy that they don't have to be concerned with piracy or that the technology is moving so fast that by the time someone could copy the product, they will be producing the next-generation technology. I even heard one executive state that the market for his product was so small that nobody would want to get into competition with them. The first two lines of reasoning make some sense, although I would be uncomfortable with leaving truly unique technology unprotected.

YOUR ATTORNEY

Your contractual agreements with foreign representatives have to be drawn with an eye toward the business and practical aspects of your relationship. The fundamental points should be those that define the business relationship. Only after the two parties have drafted an agreement, based upon the business considerations, should attorneys, if you feel the need, be called in to supply the necessary language for the remainder of the document.

Make sure that you outline such key issues as exclusivity and territory, products, the legal relationship between the parties (always disclaim any form of legal relationship aside from that laid out by the contract), the terms of sale, and the specific obligations of both parties with regard to performance. In all cases where possible, include binding arbitration as the means of dispute resolution.

Hire a specialized attorney who keeps current of the trends with regard to international contract law. If you are unwilling to do this, refer to the U.S. Department of Commerce's *Foreign Business Practices*, and update it with the latest information from the *Overseas Business Reports*. Better yet, get the attorney (whom you are paying for this) to do it for you.

FROM THE DISTRIBUTOR'S PERSPECTIVE

To the extent that you can, keep the contract in plain English. Many foreign governments require bonded translations, and the smart thing to do is make that translation straightforward. Bear in mind that your distributor probably is not a native English speaker or a lawyer and needs to understand the nature of the contract to avoid later misunderstandings.

The relationship with a distributor can usually be characterized as satisfactory (profitable for both parties) or unsatisfactory (unprofitable). With a few notable exceptions, in the latter case, there is nothing to fight about if the relationship goes bad. It is not worth anyone's time and money to have a legal battle when nobody has yet made any money or is likely to generate a profit in the near future. Most often the distributor will understand this and act accordingly. (I do know of a few cases in which foreign distribution contract law conspired with a particularly vindictive ex-distributor to create an uncomfortable situation with regard to terminating a nonperforming distributor. However, this is not a common situation.)

The vast majority of the relationships that turn bad when the situation is mutually profitable occur for one of three reasons.

The first is bad planning. This most often happens as the result of a dispute over commission, sales territory, payment terms, changing personnel within the distributorship, failure to pay warranty or inadequately support the distributor, or unforeseen acts of a foreign government that cause (or provide an excuse for) the distributor to violate the agreement. All of these causes spring from the failure to anticipate changes and deal with them before they occur, and all can be remedied—assuming that the relationship with the distributor is one of mutual trust and there is a desire to solve the problems before legal actions become necessary.

A rule of thumb for handling this sort of situation is to begin negotiations by outlining the benefit that you have both enjoyed from the relationship and by stating your firm intention to find a solution that is fair and equitable to both parties. Outline what you can agree upon, and then tackle the issues dividing you. Next, work through the issues with the idea that this process will involve some give and take. At the same time, look to your contractual agreement as the basis to resolve areas of disagreement and understand that if the topic is not covered in the agreement, you must work through the problem. Always keep an eye toward how your new agreement will affect the general ability of the distributor to meet the expectations of your company with regard to performance.

The second, and most common, cause of a good relationship's going bad is changes in the U.S. firm's personnel. It seems that every new international salesperson, or regional manager, or vice president of international marketing starts his or her tenure by attempting to get rid of "bad" distributors and re-placing them with a group of "better" choices. In 90 percent of the cases I have witnessed, the "bad" distributors were not, in fact, bad, and the replace-ments were worse.

Be very slow to change income-generating distributors based on the new staff's perception of their performance. In most cases these changes reflect not inadequate performance by the distributor but a poor understanding of the local market on the part of the U.S. executive. Moreover, it is important to understand that the act of terminating a distributor, especially when it is done by personnel new to the firm, creates great tension throughout your corps of representatives. This uneasiness can lead to distributors' beginning to court competing suppliers against the day that they too are terminated. Termina-tions are a fact of life, but they should be used only after all other methods of getting the distributor on track have failed and a reasonable period of time has elapsed. My favorite speech to new regional manager started with, "Any idiot can get rid of a liability. Only a true manager can take a liability and turn it into an asset."

The third, and most uncommon, cause of souring a profitable relation-ship is when the distributor is stolen by a competitor. A defection within your distributor corps usually reflects a weakness in your products, margins, or sup-port for a distributor. Breaking an ongoing relationship is just as costly for the distributor as it is for you. When this happens, go out to the remainder of your distribution network and find out if anyone else has been contacted. Then beat back whatever competition is targeting your group. Use the defec-tion as an opportunity to improve relationships with the representatives and the means by which you service them. Find out why your distributor defect-ed, and make some attempt to court this person back. Your distribution net-work is an asset, and you need to take steps to protect it.

THE ROLE OF ARBITRATION

With very few exceptions, and wherever possible, use arbitration as the vehicle for dispute resolution. When the international arbitration process functions well, it can provide substantial savings in time and expense. Another important benefit is the comfort both parties to the contact derive from avoiding the national courts of the other contracting party. Without arbitration, both parties are concerned, in many cases with some justification, that the local party will be better able to manipulate the legal system should a dispute arise from the contract.

An agreement to arbitrate is an arrangement between the parties involved in a contract. The effectiveness of the arbitration clause depends on the degree to which the foreign legal system will accept arbitration as binding. However, courts in both countries, should one of the parties choose to negate the arbitration clause, must agree to enforce the clause. This will ensure that a party cannot avoid the agreement by refusing to arbitrate. Additionally, courts must enforce the results of the arbitration.

The New York Convention is the most widely accepted international agreement in place and was responsible, in many ways, for the explosion in the use of arbitration. It is likely that the convention will continue to offer the broadest coverage for your arbitration efforts.

Arbitration provides great benefit to U.S. exporters and their foreign customers and representatives. It is, however, a bit tricky, and I have used attorneys for drawing standard arbitration language and to help me determine where we could use it effectively. It is binding to both parties, and you could find that it could be used to force you to honor agreements that you wish to slip out from under. However, on balance, at least for firms that conduct their business in an ethical and above-board manner, arbitration is a wonderful innovation.

Arbitration does not help you avoid problems and should not be seen as the cure-all to all potential conflicts. Rather, it provides a faster and cheaper means of resolving international contractual problems than anything else currently available.

For more information on arbitration, contact your local ITA office.

TRANSFER PRICING

For years transfer pricing represented one of the best tax dodges in corporate America. To avoid U.S. taxes, foreign subsidiaries of U.S. firms in low-tax countries sold product at inflated prices to the U.S. parent company. At the same time, the U.S. firm was selling technology at low prices to the foreign subsidiary. The result, until recently, was an enormous tax break for U.S. companies, especially large firms. The principle that governs these transactions is known as arms-length pricing. This is the concept that the prices used in these transfers should reflect the prices that would be used if the transfers were going to a third-company customer, and not a company affiliated with the producer.

Recently the U.S. Internal Revenue Service (IRS) has cracked down on U.S. firms that have improperly managed transfers, and this action could affect many U.S. companies. Although the exact magnitude of corporate trade between U.S. companies and foreign affiliates is not known, it is estimated that this trade amounts to well over $200 billion annually. The IRS looks for several telltale signs that companies are engaging in illegal pricing: the opening of a new subsidiary in a low-tax country (such as Singapore or Ireland), excessive foreign company profits, or products priced well above or below industry standards by the subsidiary or parent companies.

The best way not to run afoul the IRS is to follow one of two price calculations consistently. The first, known as comparable uncontrolled price, involves comparing your price to that of a competitor and making sure that the two are close, if not the same. The second, known as the cost-plus method, is calculating the cost of manufacture and adding a markup reflective of industry standards. File the proper documents with the IRS (Form 5471), and make sure that you carefully document not only the transfers themselves but the means by which the pricing was determined.

FOREIGN CORRUPT PRACTICES ACT

There has been extensive discussion about this provision of U.S. law, with the business community being vocal critics of it, and often using it as an excuse for failure in their international markets (particularity in the developing countries). Others claim it is a barrier to entering foreign markets as aggressively as they otherwise would.

The basic provision of the law is that it is illegal for a U.S. citizen or resident of the United States (or U.S. company and related company) to bribe foreign officials or political figures (especially foreign government officials) to get or keep business with them or a related entity. Not only does the law prohibit the payment; the offer to pay is illegal as well. However, the law does allow for "facilitative payments for routine governmental action," defined as a number of actions that a foreign official might take to issue permits and the like.

In all the years that I have done business internationally, including in a number of countries where bribery is quite common to gain contracts, I have never been asked for anything by a foreign government official because I have never led them to believe that I would be willing to violate this law to get a contract. I have, however, made attempts to ensure that deeper discounts were available to my distributors for large government purchases.

PRODUCT LIABILITY

Product liability issues in foreign markets are generally less onerous than in the United States; however, the large exception to this rule may well shortly be Europe. Until recently, most European jurisdictions required that plaintiffs in product liability suits establish fault with the manufacturer of a product. However, the EC Council has adopted a directive that appears to be based on U.S. principles. Under the new rules, the plaintiff must prove that injury occurred, the product was defective, and the defect caused the injury.

The specific nature of these directives and how they would be modified in practice by the domestic courts of the individual member nations is yet unclear. What does seem to be clear is that the primary responsibility (and liability) for imported products will fall on the importer or distributor of the product. This does not mean that you as supplier could not be sued, only that the suit would likely be brought by your distributor, rather than the injured party, because the distributor would seek to establish your primary liability in the lawsuit. For those producing the product in EC member nations, the liability is much clearer: the producer would be on the hook.

Even with these changes, most industries will not suffer from dramatic increases in insurance premiums (with some exceptions in high-liability sectors) because it is generally more difficult to recover punitive damages in most EC countries than in the United States. National health insurance will serve, in most countries, to lower your liability, and contingency fee arrangements are illegal for the most part. The latter tends to decrease the number of actual suits filed.

INTELLECTUAL PROPERTY

U.S. businesses need to protect their intellectual property as vigorously abroad as they do at home. The mistake that many companies make is assuming the product is protectable, when in fact it is not. Another mistake is allowing fears of piracy to keep them out of overseas markets, which most often serves as a catalyst to the pirates since they can produce and market the product unchallenged from a competitive or a legal standpoint. Yet another mistake is that U.S. firms often do not investigate the issue with sufficient depth to know that the cost of this activity is not as great as myth would have us believe. When you go about registration, it is important that you use such cost-saving measures as filing with regional entities, where possible, which will effectively gain the same protection for a reduced cost.

You need to ask questions of the attorney, and be prepared to suggest some shortcuts to the process. There are few general cost-saving principles that are widely applicable. Understanding them will ensure that you gain the maximum protection for the least cost.

The Basics

Intellectual property refers to a broad collection of rights relating to works of authorship, inventions, trademarks, designs, and trade secrets. Although substantial progress is being made toward easing requirements to register rights in every country, the fact is that U.S. registration does not extend to other countries. There is no truly international patent, trademark, or copyright. To secure rights in any country, you must apply. Nevertheless, several agreements do work to your benefit. The Paris Convention for the Protection of Industrial Property, for example, provides for no discrimination in the granting of patent and trademark protection to foreigners or foreign firms. Additionally, the convention provides for allowing the applicant one year from the date of the first application filed in another convention country (six months for a design or trademark) in which to file in other countries. Not all countries adhere to the Paris Convention, and those that do not are usually covered by other treaties or agreements. In some rare cases, however, they are not covered by any entity.

The Patent Cooperation Treaty (PCT) provides procedures for filing patent applications in its member countries. It allows an applicant to file one "international application" designating member countries in which a patent is sought, with the same effect as filing national applications in each of those countries. This treaty does not cover all the countries in which you will probably need to file a patent, but it can greatly reduce the time and expense for a great number of countries. Currently you can gain coverage in 49 countries, including the vast majority of the industrialized nations, through the PCT process.

During the procedure, the application will be reviewed by an examining authority to ensure that the invention meets the standards established for novelty, invention, and industrial applicability (these are the basis for patentability determinations in most countries). If this report is positive (they determine that you are likely to be granted a patent in member countries), you then proceed with the "national" phase of the applications process. In this phase, where you begin submission to the individual member state patent authorities, you begin to undergo increased expense by virtue of having to provide translations of the application, and undergo the cost of the individual application fees and associated legal expense. Bear in mind that you are facing time limits once the international phase has begun with regard to deadlines for filing in the individual countries.

There are also several other foreign regional patent or trademark offices. The European Patent Office examines patent applications and issues national patents in those of the member countries (currently 14) chosen by the applicant. These procedures are undergoing some change and simplification (in part due to the more general integration with the EC), and the new procedures are not yet completely defined. Updates will be available through local ITA offices.

Other regional offices are the English-speaking African Industrial Property Office (AIPO), the French-speaking African Intellectual Property Organization (AIPO), and the Benelux Trademark and Designs Office (Belgium, Luxembourg, and the Netherlands).

The Berne Convention provides copyright protection for nationals of any Berne Union country, for works first or simultaneously published in a Berne country, without registration or compliance with any other formality of law in any member nation. This is true for works first published in the United States on or after March 1, 1989. Older works may also be protected by virtue of other agreements. In any event, the requirements and protection available vary from country to country and should be investigated before first publication anywhere.

As with most other issues surrounding international operations, the issue of protecting intellectual property has both a practical and a legal side. The legal side should be left to the attorneys. Once registration is taken care of, the question of enforcement remains.

Enforcement

In the United States, you can protect yourself against importation of infringing goods by recording a trademark or copyright with the U.S. Customs Service or by soliciting the intervention of the International Trade Commission to prevent the goods from entering the country. Hence, the old saw about having your patent stolen and subsequently having to compete domestically against foreigners who steal them is just not so—at least not for those who have adequate protection for their products in the United States by virtue of holding current patents. The legal fees for this sort of relief can often run into the hundreds of thousands of dollars. U.S. firms that qualify as small businesses can obtain free legal assistance from the government.

Some foreign countries also provide criminal penalties for infringement, either as the exclusive remedy or in addition to private legal actions. The ability to bring criminal proceedings assists you with enforcement, assuming a cooperative and efficient foreign government is in place. In countries with criminal provisions, the offender will usually cease and desist with the initiation of some civil action (and the implied threat of criminal proceeding).

In reality, the expense of enforcing a right is often greater than the damage done by the violator. In addition, many countries have lax enforcement standards that further complicate efforts to bring violators to justice. Most often, efforts to exert pressure through the U.S. government should precede legal action. In most countries, the initiation of legal action will preclude the embassy from intervening on your behalf, as that sort of action is seen as interfering with local justice systems.

For additional information, contact either the U.S. Patent Office or:

World Intellectual Property Organization
1211 Geneva 20
Switzerland
Telephone: 41-22-730-9111; fax: 41-22-740-1435

The following U.S. government sources can provide information on intellectual property:

Copyright Office
Library of Congress
Washington, D.C. 20559

Copyright Public Information Office, (202) 479-0700. Publications: *International Copyright; Copyright Basics; International Copyright Relations of the United States.*

Patent and Trademark Office
Department of Commerce
Washington, D.C. 20231

PTO Public Affairs Office, (703) 557-3341.
Patent Information, (703) 557-7155.
Trademark Information, (703) 308-9000. Publications: *Basic Facts about Patents; Basic Facts about Trademarks; Q&A about Trademarks.*
PTO Office of Legislation and International Affairs (OLIA), (703) 557-3065. Publication: *Protecting Intellectual Property Abroad.*
PTO Patent Cooperation Treaty (PCT), International Division, (703) 603-0465. Publications: *PCT Helpful Hints* and sample applications and forms.

U.S. Customs Service
Intellectual Property Rights Branch
1301 Constitution Avenue, N.W.
Washington, D.C. 20229

Intellectual Property Rights Branch, (202) 566-6956. Publication:
U.S. Customs and Protection of Intellectual Property Rights.

LEGAL ISSUES IN CONTEXT

The bottom line with regard to international legal issues is that they are neither more complex nor inherently more dangerous than the legal issues you face in the United States. In fact, the international arena is significantly less risky in many ways.

The area of product liability is instructive. For the most part, other nations are far more reasonable about what they will award for damages resulting from use (or misuse) of a product. Could you image what would have happened if Bhopal had occurred in the United States? There are U.S. laws that can provide judgments that would be viewed with horror in most foreign countries.

What you do face are legal issues that are slightly different and danger areas that are somewhat novel. Getting the right information to effectively skirt the issues that could be potentially damaging is simply a matter of doing some homework.

THE GOOD NEWS

Up to now, we have explored how to protect yourself when operating in the international environment and have left to the end, intentionally, the legal and regulatory structure that has been put into place to motivate you to export. The human propensity to accentuate the negative has the international community so focused on defensive measures to protect themselves from imagined and real pitfalls that they have effectively ignored laws designed to try to get us out of our chairs and into the international fray.

Duty Drawbacks

A duty drawback is a refund of custom duty paid to import materials or components needed for processing or assembly of the final product. You can obtain the drawback for all duties paid on the imported merchandise that is re-exported as a part of your finished product. Customs does keep 1 percent of the total duty paid, and the refund is only for inputs that are subsequently exported as part of the finished product. The drawback makes you better able to compete by not having to pay duty twice (once to get the component into the United States and once when the finished product is imported into the foreign country).

You may also qualify for a drawback if you buy products from someone else who has imported the goods, use them to manufacture a product, and then export that end product. In such a circumstance, the importer must supply you with the documentation in order for you to claim the drawback. Further, you can claim the drawback if you purchase goods from someone else, store them, and later export them without making any transformation to the goods.

To claim the drawback, you are required to provide documentation about the import, plant receiving information, an inventory of the raw materials and finished goods (input and output), bill of material information, and the export documentation. When you file the required documents with the regional customs office, payment processing begins, and you may receive payment, under an accelerated procedure, within eight weeks. In the event that you have not yet applied for a payment, the drawback is retroactive for exports made over the last three years. As a result, you may find quite a bit of money waiting for you at the customs office.

The drawback will continue to be an important tool for U.S. business, especially as the need to import foreign components increases. This may be particularly true for the electronics industry, where the tendency is clearly to import components (mostly from Asia) and export finished product. It also is a stimulant to the U.S. firms with existing facilities overseas to begin to think more globally in terms of how and where they produce the component parts for their finished products.

Model drawback proposals to assist you in developing your own submission to U.S. Customs are available from the Drawback and Bonds Branch, Customs Headquarters, (202) 566–5856.

Foreign Sales Corporations

It is possible, through the formation of a foreign sales corporation (FSC) to obtain a corporate tax exemption from 15 percent to 32 percent of the earnings generated by export operations. FSCs can, with some limitations, be used by an individual company, or a group of companies can form and "share" an FSC, which can lower the burden of administering the FSC.

The requirements for setting up and administering an FSC seem daunting. However, there are several methods of easing the practical impact of the requirements and, at the same time, taking advantage of the FSC benefits. Several private companies have sprung up that will, for minimal fees, create and manage your FSC. Some of these companies are U.S. based. (I have had good luck with using U.S. Virgin Island companies, which also are quite reasonable in their fees.) The FSC requirements can be met with little effort on your part, assuming that you retain the services of another company to manage the paperwork required. A general rule of thumb is that any company exporting over $1 million a year should carefully examine the FSC. A friend who owns a company that exports around $7 million of product annually found that the tax savings for the company, after administrative costs, would be $78,000 a year.

Despite the fact that the FSC offers many benefits to exporters, it is underused because a number of business owners regard it as "dangerous" or "likely to stimulate an IRS investigation" or any one of a hundred other excuses not to engage in the work necessary to get that additional revenue. They need to understand that the IRS is concerned only with the FSC's meeting legal requirements and that the reporting be accurate.

Chapter **7**

Logistics: How to Get the Product to the Overseas Customer

FREIGHT FORWARDING

One of the requisite maintenance functions that surrounds export operations is that of the freight forwarder. The forwarder is responsible for developing the documentation required for the export shipment and ensuring that the goods arrive at the overseas destination with the suitable packaging and crating, markings, and documents to ease delivery to the overseas customer.

Freight forwarders can assist with an order from the beginning of the process by helping you determine your costs, including their fees, the cost of special documentation, and insurance costs. Good forwarders will be able to recommend the sort of packaging that should be used to safeguard your merchandise and will arrange to have it packed and/or containerized. If these services are well executed, they are worth every dime. Unfortunately, there are a number of forwarders who have not administered the service that the fee demands. Forwarding is not a capital-intensive business and, hence, attracts a number of companies that are not sufficiently funded to survive over the long term.

Think of the forwarder as you think of the freight company with your domestic shipments. However, there are some dissimilarities in terms of skill levels in that the forwarder should review the letter of credit, commercial invoices, packing list, and other documents to ensure that there are no surprises in the execution of the export shipment. They should reserve the freight space, by whatever means are chosen and make the necessary arrangements with custom brokers to ensure the goods comply with customs export documentation regulations. In addition, they should prepare the bill of lading and any special documentation that may be required. After shipment, they forward all documents directly to the customer and/or to the paying bank if desired.

Insurance

Export shipments are usually insured against loss or damage while in transit. Damaging weather conditions, rough handling by carriers, and other common hazards to cargo make marine insurance important protection for U.S. exporters. If the terms of sale make the U.S. firm responsible for insurance, it can consider insuring under a freight forwarder's policy, for a fee. If the terms of sale make the foreign buyer responsible, the exporter should not assume (or even take the buyer's word) that adequate insurance is, in fact, in place. You may need to change the terms of sale to ensure that the buyer cannot back out of payment if, after not insuring the goods, he chooses to decline them based upon real or imaged damage.

Packing and Shipping

In packing an item for export, shippers should be cognizant of the demands that exporting puts on packages. Consult the forwarder to get the information you need to guarantee that the product arrives unblemished. If at all possible, you should pack in moisture-resistant material, on pallets, and with adequate internal bracing for the crate. It is also prudent to shrink-wrap and strap what you can to avoid pilferage. The buyers may dictate the packing. Follow their advice; they are probably more mindful than you of the kinds of problems that can occur in their locales: arduous handling, inclement weather conditions, temperature extremes, high humidity, and a host of other conditions that can severely damage your product. Certainly any additional or special packing is at the buyer's expense, although this expense can be negotiated between the parties.

Normally, air shipments do not require the heavy packaging used with ocean shipments, but they must still be adequately protected, especially for highly pilferable items. Standard domestic packing is usually satisfactory, especially if the product is durable. If you are not willing to package for export, use a professional firm to perform this task—either your freight forwarder, who may have the necessary facilities, or a professional packing firm.

Often specific marking and labeling is used on export shipping cartons to meet shipping regulations and to assist the receivers in identification of shipments. The buyer will normally specify the markings. Any questions you may have about them should be referred to the forwarder, although you may want to ask for advice about the need to include the marking in English and the language of the country of destination.

Be especially diligent about inquiring as to whether or not foreign customs require certain markings; it is frustrating to both the supplier and the customer to find that a shipment is stuck in a customs area because of inadequate homework by the shipper or the freight forwarder. This sort of situation will quickly earn you the reputation of an untrustworthy supplier.

Documents

The key to doing export documentation is to get someone else to do it, in most cases. In the following, we look at documents that are commonly used in exporting to assist you in dealing with the forwarder. Some of these documents are almost always required; others will be unique to the sort of product being shipped or the requirements of the foreign customs service. The required documents will depend on both U.S. government requirements and those of the importing country.

Slight inaccuracies in documentation can prevent your product from being shipped, which can result in payment problems or worse. You can be beaten out of payment for improper documentation, but only if you are acting irresponsibly with regard to how you conduct your business. Hence, careful attention to detail is required with documentation, and often this will require that you retain an experienced freight forwarder to take this responsibility partially off your back.

Commercial Invoice

As in a domestic transaction, the commercial invoice is a bill for the goods from buyer to seller. The buyer needs the invoice to prove ownership and to arrange payment. Some governments use the commercial invoice to assess customs duties, so be sure that the invoice accurately reflects the cost of the goods. At some time, you probably will receive a request from a foreign customer to fill in the invoice with an amount somewhat under the actual value of the shipment. Do *not* succumb to this temptation, no matter how badly you want the sale. The buyer is attempting to avoid payment of duties, and when you underinvoice, the potential legal liability is shifted to you. This is not a desirable situation.

Bills of Lading

Bills of lading are contracts between the owner of the goods and the carrier. The customer usually needs the original or a copy as proof of ownership in order to take possession of the goods. Always make sure that at least two copies are forwarded to the customer, because not meeting the requirement can substantially increase the delays and costs of clearing the goods. Some countries require that the original bill of lading, not a copy, be forwarded with the shipment.

Consular Invoice

Certain nations require a consular invoice, which is used to control and identify goods. The invoice must be purchased from the consulate of the country to which the goods are shipped and usually must be prepared in the language of that country. Normally there is a fee for the consular invoice, and this expense should be calculated into the cost of the shipment.

Certificate of Origin

Many nations require a signed statement as to the origin of the export item. This form is usually obtained through a local chamber of commerce, and it may be required even though the commercial invoice generally contains this information. These statements are known as certificate of origin and most often are used to ensure that the goods did not originate from a third country. The same product may be duted at a different rate, depending on where it is actually produced; hence, the need for this sort of document. In other cases, the intent is to ensure that goods from prohibited countries are not illegally imported into the country of final destination.

Some purchasers or countries may require a certificate attesting to the specifications of the goods shipped, usually performed by a third party. This is often obtained from an independent testing organization or companies that perform these inspections, such as SGS of Switzerland. The reason for this inspection can be quite varied. In some cases, the government in the country of destination so mistrusts its own customs service that it contracts with private entities for the assessment and collection of duties. In other cases, the intent is to use the inspection to ensure that the goods comply with standards or health regulations in the importing country. In still other cases, the contracting party is not a government but a foreign buyer who wants to be assured, by an independent third party, of the quality and quantity of the good prior to concluding the payment transaction. There are other reasons as well. What is important here is simply that you understand what these services do.

Receipts

Dock and warehouse receipts are used to transfer accountability when the export item is moved by the domestic carrier to the port of embarkation and left with the international carrier for export. The reason for these receipts most often has to do with liability if the shipment is damaged or lost, to establish when and where responsibility for the goods transferred.

Destination Control Statement

This statement often appears on the commercial invoice, bill of lading, or air waybill, and shipper's export declaration (SED). It serves to notify the carrier and all foreign parties that the item may be exported to only certain destinations. Normally this statement is important only if your product or shipment is subject to export controls.

Insurance Certificate

If the seller provides insurance, the insurance certificate states the type and amount of coverage. Refer to your freight forwarder to ensure that the insurance, if your responsibility, is consistent with the risk you are assuming under the terms of the sale. See that your coverage extends to the time that legal ownership passes to the buyer.

Shipper's Export Declaration

Used to control exports and compile trade statistics, the shipper's export declaration is prepared for shipments valued in excess of $2,500 or for shipments of items subject to export controls, regardless of values, or both. For the most part, this document is required by the U.S. Customs Service and will accompany the vast majority of export shipments.

Export Packing List

This list is considerably more detailed than a standard domestic packing list. It itemizes the material in each individual package, indicates the type of package, and shows the individual weights and measurements for each package. The list should be included in or attached to the outside of a package in a waterproof envelope marked "packing list enclosed."

Inland Transport

The inland transportation of an export order is handled in much the same way as a domestic shipment. The export markings should be added to the standard information shown on a domestic bill of lading and should show the name of the exporting carrier and the latest allowed arrival date at the port of export. The exporter should also include instructions for the inland carrier to notify the international freight forwarder by telephone on arrival.

Going It Alone

If you should choose, for whatever misguided reason, to go it alone, there are some means of getting required information on foreign import restrictions and documentary requirements.

Country desk officers in the Department of Commerce are usually good sources of information regarding documentary requirements and the unique shipping requirements in the countries to which you are shipping. They will also be able to assist with getting duty rates for your product in that country and advise you of any additional fees that you will likely incur (such as consular invoices or port fees).

Foreign government embassies often provide shipping information and import regulations for the country of destination.

Two books provide guidance as well. The Bureau of National Affairs' *Export Shipping Manual* contains complete country-by-country shipping information, as well as tariff systems, import and exchange controls, mail regulations, and other special information. Contact the Bureau of National Affairs, 1231 25th Street, N.W., Washington, D.C. 20037. The *Air Cargo Tariff Guidebook* lists various regulations affecting air shipments on a country-by-country basis. Contact the Air Cargo Tariff, P.O. Box 7627, 1117 ZJ Schipol Airport, The Netherlands.

Pros and Cons of Hiring a Freight Forwarder

Although my preference is to retain a freight forwarder, some companies want to do it themselves. In some cases, the reason is a perceived cost savings (although the work involved is often far greater than what a forwarder will charge for the service). Others use a forwarder for the first shipment but do subsequent ones themselves, using the initial documentation as guidance. This approach is better than the "go it yourself" philosophy; nevertheless, changing regulations often foil any attempts to standardize the documentation. In addition, you will lose the freight forwarder's ability to help you with your letters of credit and the like. On balance, I would advise this approach only under a particular set of circumstances:

1. The goods being shipped and the destinations are highly repetitive. This situation does allow for some automation in the documentation.
2. The destinations are, for the most part, in the developed world. Developed countries tend to have fewer changes in documentary requirements, and in the event of a problem, it is generally easier to deal with their customs services than those of less developed countries.
3. The customers are characterized by a high level of ongoing orders and a relationship of trust exists between the exporting company and the customers.
4. There is some degree of expertise in-house.

Doing your own shipping will require that you bring on specialized staff to handle the function. This cost may seem worth it from a customer service standpoint, but remember the true costs of having employees, including sick time, vacation, and benefits.

Additionally, this sort of expertise may not be available for a reasonable price. Freight forwarders are running their own companies and typically are not looking for employment. Should you try to move this function in-house, you will be building from the ground up in terms of a knowledge base unless you can hire a well-trained and experienced employee away from a forwarding firm. Many companies do not feel it is worth putting their customers through the learning experience. In fact, I know of several cases where valued customers were lost as a result of an attempt to bring the function in-house.

Moreover, forwarders are often able to offset their fees by virtue of the fact that they can group (consolidate) shipments and take advantage of lower rates than you could obtain yourself, unless you are doing a high volume of export business.

What you really pay a forwarder to do is to keep up with the regulations. You can buy the same reference materials they use and, with some work, develop the in-house expertise, but it is a lot of effort to keep up with the changes that are occurring around the world with regard to documentary requirements, letters of credit and how the documents will affect the payment, changing freight rates, consolidation, containerization, and the like.

There are situations where volume or unique customer service requirements will, despite drawbacks, lead you to conclude that the forwarding function needs to be in-house. Be sure that you calculate the real cost of the employees before you make that decision and that you fully understand the costs of ongoing training to keep the staff up to date.

A new development in export transactions is electronic data interchange (EDI), which offers a paper-free alternative to export-related communications (between shipper, freight forwarders, U.S. customs, the customer, etc.). Since paperwork accounts for 7 percent of the cost of doing international business, most companies are advised to investigate the benefits of setting us these systems, and many already have; EDI expenditures are growing at a rate of 56 percent in the United States. These automated systems make the choice to do without freight forwarders more attractive, but they will not completely replace the services a good forwarder offers with regard to staying current on changing documentry requirements. For additional information, contact:

EDI Association
225 Reinekers Lane, Suite 550
Alexandria, Virginia 22314
(703) 838–8042

How to Select and Use a Freight Forwarder

Pick a freight forwarder with demonstrable expertise in the areas to which you ship and, if possible, one that has existing clients with products similar to yours. You may need to use a combination of different forwarders to ensure that area and product expertise exist across the layer of your operation. It is also a very effective way to ensure that a good sense of competition is built into the quotations you receive from the forwarders. Compare quotes every so often to ensure that nobody is getting out of line with costs.

Request information about a freight forwarder's network of customs brokers in other countries. These brokers are key to solving any problems that may emerge when you attempt to clear the goods from the foreign customs areas. Make sure that the forwarder has at least an agent in the countries to which you are shipping. An office is even better still, although this is somewhat rare with most of the forwarders with whom you will be dealing.

111

Check to ensure that the forwarder is financially sound. Some U.S. firms have suffered the results of a freight forwarder going bankrupt while their merchandise was on the water, with considerable ensuing complications. An established, sound firm is worth some premium, with regard to fees, to guard against this sort of occurrence and to ensure that it will be around long enough for you to benefit from the learning process it goes through with your product and destinations.

The issue of solvency is quite different from that of responsiveness. Demand that the forwarder give you references, and check them out. Do not assume that the fact that you have been provided references means that the clients are happy with this service.

Always require a quotation and an itemized list of fees from the forwarder, and periodically compare the charges to other quotations you get or the cost of doing it yourself, if you are so inclined. Because this is a highly technical field and one that most companies do not want to undertake themselves, there is a tendency for some forwarders to become complacent and assume that your business is, in fact, theirs. You may need to make the point, from time to time, that your business is not captive.

Look for full-service forwarders who will handle such diverse services as booking space, documentation, letters of credit, and insurance. Every service offered relieves you of the burden of additional logistics without, in many cases, increasing your cost of doing business. If you use a number of the freight forwarder's services in addition to the actual freight function, you may be increasing cost, although it might well be worth the fees generated not to have to concern yourself with additional detail.

Most good forwarders are automated and can track shipments and the progress of your transaction via computer. In some cases, you can tie into the forwarder's computer system to enable a more direct link to the information you need to respond to customer inquiries. If you do highly repetitive transactions, you may be able to negotiate a discount from the forwarder based on your ability to access quotation data directly from the database of past transactions. Some exporting companies and freight forwarders have operations that are so intertwined that the information flow concerning orders, shipping dates, terms, documentation, insurance, and carriers occurs entirely by computer, almost without human interaction.

If you are a large account, require that the freight forwarder assign a specific account executive to handle all your business so that he or she develops expertise with regard to your product and markets. A great deal of time and work can be saved if the forwarder is agreeable to this arrangement.

In the ideal world, your forwarder would be located next door to your shipping dock. In actuality, of course, this is rarely the case, and it is becoming less important in a world of fax machines, computer systems, and the like, which have created a situation where you can comfortably shop farther afield than previously. Many companies located in the interior of the United States handle the inland freight portion of the shipment themselves and retain forwarders located in major ports for the export portion of the arrangement.

One of the best measures of a forwarder's performance is if he or she advises you of a change in regulation before a problem arises. If you see a pattern of "unawareness" emerging, dump this forwarder or discuss the problem before real trouble occurs.

Usually you will be responsible for providing the forwarder with the export license, invoice, and the packing list, although some forwarders provide this service. The forwarder will usually, at the least, assume responsibility for the bill of lading, dock receipt, consular invoices, and insurance documents.

The document that drives the export process is the pro forma invoice. Contrary to popular belief, the pro forma is not for payment purposes, nor is it binding and final. Rather, it is the basis upon which the importer receives the quote and calculates the amount of the letter of credit, if that is the payment mechanism. You are wise to include a "fudge factor" in the pro forma to cover unforeseen expenses, and so note on the document with the statement that if additional costs are not incurred, a prompt and full refund will be made to the buyer. Make sure that you place an expiration term of thirty days (or whatever makes sense to you) on all pro formas. I once received an order based on a two-year-old pro forma, and, to my surprise, the Hong Kong buyer fully expected us to honor it.

Many overseas customers prefer to arrange their own shipping because they feel that they can get a better deal on the rates or otherwise save money on the transaction. If this is the case, allow them to do so, but always follow with an ex-factory price, which relieves you of all responsibility for the shipment once it is on your shipping dock outside the factory. This may seem like a small point, but a customer who is concerned with saving these sorts of typically small amounts has a tendency to be unpredictable. Hence, get the legal responsibility for the shipment transferred as early as possible. This transfer is especially important because these cost-conscious buyers may fail to insure the shipment.

There are many different possibilities for the terms of the shipment. The bottom line is that you need to be responsive to the customer's desires but with an eye toward minimizing risk in the shipment. These terms, aside from establishing the structure of who incurs which expense and the timing of payment, also define who is on the hook should something go wrong. Pay careful attention to terms, and understand that they are a vital part of the export process.

EXPORT LICENSING

There are a variety of reasons for controlling the goods flowing from the United States to foreign countries. Most often it is an attempt to keep high-technology goods or those intended for military use from falling into the hands of "unreliable" countries. At times—for example, with the U.S. embargo on Cuba—the motives are related to foreign policy. Another reason might be that the good in question is in short supply in the United States, so its export is not desirable from an economic standpoint. The first reason is the most common. The other two are much less frequently used and far less problematic than the first.

The government controls the export of goods and technology by means of two types of export licenses: general and validated. As a technical matter, almost all goods require licenses, but, in most cases, the granting of the license is automatic and does not require that you actually gain an specific approval. It is, in essence, an automatic or implied approval.

General License

A general license is a grant of authority by the government to all exporters for most products. Individual exporters do not need to apply for general licenses. Most products fall into this category and do not provide any obstacle to your export efforts.

Validated License

A validated license is a specific approval by the government to a particular exporter to export a particular product. The validated license is granted on a case-by-case basis for a single transaction or for a specified period of time. If you require a validated license, you must apply for it.

To find out if you need this for your product, inquire at a local ITA office. The determination is based on the destination of the product and the product characteristics.

The Department of Commerce determines these two issues through the use of Country Groups, a means by which the government groups countries based on their "reliability," and the Export Commodity Control List, which assigns different numbers, based on the need to protect the technology, to the individual products. Try to imagine a matrix. Down one side is listed all the countries to which you ship. Across the top of the matrix is the export commodity control number (ECCN). The boxes these two variables create in the matrix contain either the word *general* or *validated.* The determination as to which word appears is based on two considerations: the sensitivity of the product, which is classified by the ECCN number, and the country of destination.

The key to managing validated licenses is paperwork. Some rules of thumb follow to assist you in complying with the law:

- When applying for a license, include all of the technical information, including your brochures, with the application.
- You must know what the intended end use of the item is. Find out prior to making the application. This may be as simple as calling the overseas distributor or customer, or it may be more complicated, depending upon the country and the product.
- All shipments must be accompanied by a shipper's export declaration, regardless of value, and the export license number must be inserted on the declaration. You will be required to put a destination control statement on your export documents stating to the shipper and purchaser that the item is subject to a U.S. export license and diversion from the stated destination is contrary to U.S. law. Most often this statement will, at minimum, appear on the invoices.

- On the back of the license, record all shipments made under that license.
- Return the license to the Department of Commerce after it has been used or after it has expired.
- Keep file copies of everything that relates to your application for and use of the license.
- Read the paperwork carefully, and make sure that you understand what is required of you, especially with regard to the international import certificate and the statement of ultimate consignee and purchaser. These forms are most often required from the foreign government or the foreign purchaser. They essentially are promises not to resell or otherwise divert the product from the stated end use.

You may be thinking that this is an extremely complicated subject and probably more work than it is worth. You are wrong, for a number of reasons. First, the number of items that require validated licenses has been drastically reduced, and the trend is likely to continue in this direction, given events in the former communist countries. Some estimate that this easing will eliminate controls on between $48 to 200 billion of U.S. exports.

A number of service improvements have been developed that make the procedure streamlined. Telephone assistance via the Export License Voice Information System provides general information about licensing; the Electronic Licensing Automated Information System will let you submit your application electronically; and the System for Tracking Export License Applications allows you to track the application through the system. All are available through the following number: (202) 377-4811. Or you can speak directly to a person in the Exporter Counseling Division, which I recommend if you are new to the process. There is also a Western Regional Office: (714) 660-0144.

Assistance is available through two private firms: IBEK Corporation, (512) 339-7700, and OCR International, (301) 881-0532.

Should you not want to deal with this yourself, some freight forwarders will handle the submissions and applications for you, or you can retain an attorney. However, there is no need to pay for this service if you are prepared to spend a bit of time to learn the ropes.

Chapter 8

Financing the Deal

As with domestic sales, a major factor that determines the method of payment you select is the amount of trust in the buyer's ability and willingness to pay. Theoretically, if the buyer has good credit, sales are usually made on open account. Otherwise cash in advance is required. However, as a practical matter, open-account transactions rarely happen for a number of reasons having to do with fears of being unable to collect internationally, a lack of knowledge about your distributor on the part of your finance and other support groups within the company, more difficulty and expense in gathering accurate credit information, and a host of other factors, some of legitimate concern and others based in myth and ignorance.

Remember that the overseas distributor has as much to lose, should he or she no longer have access to your product line, as you do. By the time you have a distributor on open account, this person has invested a great deal of money in training, inventory, and market promotion. A distributor who fails to keep the distribution rights for the product will lose this investment.

The myth is that "foreigners" are less reliable than "Americans." The fact is that most companies have fewer bad debts from international operations than from their domestic ones (admittedly because they sell less on open account). Open account is a marketing tool, like many others that cost money. Use it judiciously, but make it available to ongoing accounts and good distributors. (If you are uncomfortable with this, we will discuss some other methods of using open account and insuring the receivable later in this chapter.)

The next myth is that credit information is not readily available. My experience is that it is, through a host of sources, including the U.S. embassy,

Dun and Bradstreet (or similar organizations), other suppliers, and commercial banks. In fact, you will normally generate better and more credit information for your international operations than your domestic counterparts will for U.S. sales because the fear factor is higher.

Another fallacy is that you cannot collect internationally. The reality is that all of the collection methods you employ in the United States are available to you internationally, including the U.S. embassy, which can exert pressure on the foreign company to pay, international collection agencies, and the court system of the country in which the bad debt occurred. In some cases, pursuing a legal option in a overseas market will be more costly and in others less, depending on how attorney fees are structured.

The best means for reducing risks is to know what risks exist. Begin by carefully reviewing such documents as the *Foreign Economic Trends* report, produced by the Department of State, and the *Overseas Business Reports,* published by the Department of Commerce. Once you have identified countries where economic risks are high, consult an international banker for an assessment of the company with which you would do business and the potential risk.

Remember that just because a country is not creditworthy does not mean that companies within that country are not. During the late 1970s the Indonesian government imposed foreign exchange controls that prohibited my distributor from buying the dollars he needed to pay me for several shipments we had made prior to the prohibition's being imposed. He ended up paying me by smuggling currency out of Indonesia and exchanging it on a secondary market in a nearby country. I have had similar experiences in Mexico.

The lesson here is twofold. First, these distributors so valued our products that they engaged in illegal activity to ensure that prompt payment was made. Second, they were willing to go to these lengths because we had placed our trust in them by putting them on open account.

In the end, as in the beginning, it all comes down to trust, which is based upon the length of your relationship with your representative and the degree to which continued payment is beneficial to him or her.

Cash in advance may seem to be the most desirable method since the shipper is relieved of collection problems and has immediate use of the money. However, many large, well-established distributors decline to pay on this basis. They will point to their good credit and refuse to be treated differently from your domestic clients. If you want this business, typically you will have to decide to go on open account. If so, make sure that you do not accept what is said at face value and seek independent confirmation of the distributor's solvency (this assumes you are starting a new relationship). Also, remember that advance payment creates cash flow problems and decreases profitability for the distributor (or increases the price for the end user; neither is desirable).

In such a situation, you may have to ask yourself if this buyer should have to pay for the product prior to receiving it. Does this situation hurt you from a competitive standpoint, and can it lead to a dissolution of your relationship? Does it hamper your ability to recruit new distributors or to retain good existing relationships?

CONSIGNMENT SALES

In international consignment sales, the same procedure is followed as in the United States. The material is shipped to a distributor to be sold on behalf of the exporter, and you retain title to the goods until they are sold by the distributor. You receive payment when the goods are sold, although you can negotiate a routine payment. Consignment sales are best used to solve problems that lead to an insufficient stock's being held, or when product sales become so great that a prepositioned stock is required to meet market demand.

Use this method only with long-standing distributors with whom trust has been established, and exceptionally good and strong foreign companies with extremely good credit ratings.

The product is your property until sold, and, as such, you would be wise to have the proper insurance in place to protect against loss or negotiate with your distributor to ensure that he or she has such protection in place.

In essence, consignment sales are not much different from putting that distributor on open account. The goods may still be legally yours, but the distributor has physical possession of the merchandise. Consignment can be a good method of getting around any fears that the finance department may have about going to open account with a good distributor. The accountants take some comfort in the idea that the goods still technically belong to the company.

PAYMENT INSTRUMENTS

With a letter of credit or sight draft, a bank ensures that buyer and seller are keeping their end of the bargain before goods and money are exchanged. Shipping and insurance forms must be presented to the bank to ensure that conditions of the sale are met. This is true for both drafts and letters of credit. Two banks are usually involved: one in the exporter's country and one in the buyer's country. Once a relationship is established with the importer, a great deal of time and effort can be saved by using the branches of the same international bank.

With letters of credit, the exporter presents documents to a bank, usually in the United States, to prove that goods have been shipped according to the conditions of the purchase order. The bank can then either pay or guarantee payment according to the terms of the deal. Drafts that require payment before goods are received are called *sight drafts*. Drafts that obligate later payment, after goods are received, can be either *time drafts* or *date drafts*. The basic difference between sight and time/date drafts is when payment is made.

In the case of a sight draft, the exporter retains ownership of the goods until paid. A time draft is an instrument that requires the buyer to pay within a specified time of accepting the draft and receiving the goods. The date draft specifies a date on which payment is due rather than a time period after the draft is accepted. The time draft can extend the payment by virtue of a delay in the draft acceptance by the foreign buyer.

The most commonly used of the three drafts is the sight draft, which most exporters will accept in place of a letter of credit in exchange for not offering extended payment terms to the foreign buyer. Drafts are best used with old and reliable customers, in stable and open economy countries, and when the goods are easily resalable if a buyer reneges on the agreement. The obvious problems, should the buyer renege, is that you may be stuck with the shipment in a foreign port and no buyer in sight. (I have never seen this happen.) Bear in mind that in many countries, drafts are the instrument of choice because of ease of use and less expense in execution of the draft, at least when compared to a letter of credit.

A letter of credit is a document, issued by a bank, which processes payment from the buyer to the seller. It provides the issuing bank's promise to pay a specified amount of money upon receipt, by the bank, of certain documents within a specified time. The documents ensure that conditions stated in the letter of credit, such as terms of sale, shipping date, and insurance coverage, have been met. Letters of credit are properly used to ensure payment in countries with unstable economic policies, when buyers are new or have proved to be unreliable, or when the transaction is of a single nature rather than an ongoing relationship.

Letters of credit are generally more secure than drafts. With letters of credit, the bank guarantees the payment, so long as you meet the terms of the purchase order and the letter of credit is irrevocable. A revocable letter of credit may be altered or revoked without the exporter's permission, hence making it less secure.

The best of all worlds is the irrevocable confirmed letter of credit, which obligates the U.S. bank to pay even if the foreign bank defaults. This sort of default is not common, but it can happen, most often in developing countries or if the foreign government is politically or economically unstable.

Because of a host of problems with documentation and a generally increasing cost structure, letter of credit fees have risen dramatically, especially away from the money center cities, where you can shop for international banking fees. Fees are usually charged by both the foreign and U.S. banks, so a letter of credit represents a cost to both parties and needs to be negotiated in advance with regard to who pays fees or if they are split.

It is usual for buyers to assume charges for their cost of the letter of credit, but some buyers may not accept terms that require this added cost. An unwillingness to pay letter of credit fees may lead to lost sales. Aside from the implication that the U.S. company considers the foreign firm to be untrustworthy, a letter of credit is more expensive and does require some effort from the buyer generally exceeding that of open account or drafts. A willingness to pay these fees often eases the negotiations with regard to the need to have a letter of credit.

The steps to collect on a letter of credit are quite simple:

1. The deal is struck, and the importer deposits funds to cover the letter of credit in his or her bank.
2. The importer's bank forwards the terms of shipment to the seller's bank together with the letter of credit.

3. The exporter's bank advises the exporter of the arrival of the letter of credit—that is, confirms that the letter of credit is authentic and that it came from an overseas bank. (Fees for the "advice" can range as high as $200.)

4. You ship the product, your bank examines the documents and ensures that you have complied with them, and it begins to process payment to you. This process is called negotiation. The bank's fee for it can range as high as ½ of 1 percent of the value of the letter of credit. (It should be abundantly clear why bankers tend to focus on the need to protect yourself in all international transactions, regardless of how trusted the distributor or end user may be or how long you have done business with one another and not suffered.)

5. A letter of confirmation goes from the seller's bank to the seller, together with the details of the irrevocability of the letter of credit (this assumes the transaction is a confirmed irrevocable one). A confirmation of a letter of credit is essentially a guarantee from the exporter's bank that when the documents are properly presented, payment will be made by the confirming bank (normally the exporter's bank) regardless of any action that may lead to nonpayment by the buyer's bank. Fees for confirmation can run as high as 3 percent of the letter of credit value; the fee normally is based on the exporter's bank's perception of the risks involved in the transaction.

6. You present the documents to the bank where, if the documents are in order, you receive payment.

The terms are contractual in nature, much like a domestic contract. If you fail to comply with them fully the deal can be invalidated.

Late shipments are the leading cause of problems, so be diligent in ensuring that you can meet all the requirements and that the terms include all of your expenses in getting the shipment out of your factory and to the overseas customer. Let the freight forwarder and the bank earn their fees, and rely heavily on them to get the transaction done right. Far too many exporters are willing to put up with, and pay for, services that are not rendered properly. If you have to get deeply involved in all the details, you won't have time to get the business. Retain good support companies (banks and freight forwarders), and hold their feet to the fire with regard to accepting responsibility for their mistakes (including financial responsibility). If they are unwilling to do that, they are not the company you need.

HOW TO SELECT A BANK

Choosing the right bank to manage your letters of credit is as important as picking the right distributor. When you accept a certain bank to handle the transaction, you are, in effect, assuming that the bank is more creditworthy than the customer or distributor who has requested the goods.

Begin by analyzing the financial services and stability of the bank, much as you would treat any other service provider. Does the bank have the services you require? Is the international department long established and stable? Can it provide references from other exporters, and do the references check out? Does it have foreign subsidiary in the major trading partner countries?

Review the bank's operating statements. Is it adequately capitalized? Does its capital position at least meet, and hopefully exceed, regulatory requirements? Is it overburdened with nonperforming loans? What portion of those are international? Will these nonperforming loans likely lead the bank to pull back from its international business?

Check with rating companies. Are the bank's ratings good? What do peer institutions and bankers think of it.

There are ten leading export finance banks in the United States:

Bank of New York
First Interstate Bank
NationsBank
Chemical Bank
Northwest Bank Minnesota
SouthTrust Bank of Alabama
Manufactures Bank
Maryland National Bank
Bank of Boston
Society National Bank

Often foreign banks are less cautious about offering credit for shipments destined for their home countries than U.S. banks. The top local banks (in New York) from the ten biggest U.S. export markets are:

Royal Bank of Canada (Canada)
Dai-Ichi Kangyo Bank (Japan)
Banco Nacional de Mexico (Mexico)
Barclays (United Kingdom)
Deutsche Bank (Germany)
Commercial Bank of Korea (Republic of Korea)
Crédit Agricole (France)
ABN AMRO Holdings (Netherlands)
Bank of Taiwan (Taiwan)
Generale Bank Group (Belgium)

COLLECTION PROBLEMS

When I think about the few collection problems I have had, I cannot help but begin this section by drawing an analogy between collection problems and a Malaysian folk tale that involves a water buffalo and a scorpion.

The scorpion is standing by a river swollen by the monsoon season and is not passable for him, when he spies a water buffalo casually swimming by.

"Mr. Water Buffalo!" he cries.

"Yes," replies the water buffalo, maintaining a safe distance.

"Can you give me a ride across the river as I cannot cross, and I wish to visit my dying mother?"

The water buffalo, after some careful consideration, decides that this is not in his best interest and responds, "I would like to, but you will sting me."

"Why would I do that?" queries the scorpion. "If I were to sting you, we would both drown, and I would not get to see my mother."

This did, after all, seem reasonable to the water buffalo, and he reluctantly agreed to take the scorpion across the river.

The scorpion crawled up the water buffalo's leg and seated itself comfortably next to his ear, and, while making clever conversation, they proceeded across the river.

Around midstream, where the water was a frothy torrent, the scorpion arose, walked to the water buffalo's back, and stung him repeatedly.

"Why have you stung me?" cried the water buffalo. "For now we will both surely die."

The scorpion looked at the floundering water buffalo as the water began to rush about him and shrugged, replying, "Because it is my nature."

Moral: Foreign buyers who will attempt to cheat you in a transaction have, in all likelihood, engaged in the same scam prior to having met you. It is your responsibility to be diligent in checking out buyers prior to getting into a position where you have the possibility of being cheated.

In international trade, problems involving bad debts are better avoided than remedied after the fact. Credit checks and the other methods will greatly reduce risk. However, it is a fact of life that, like the domestic buyer, overseas buyers can default, and it can be difficult and expensive to obtain payment. In the event that you fall into this problem despite your best efforts, there are ways to attempt to get redress.

The best method, after you have determined that the individual cannot or will not pay the amount due, is to begin by doing what the lawyers will do later anyway, for a fee: attempt to arrive at a negotiated solution. You can often resolve conflicts to the satisfaction of both sides by accepting partial payment now and extending terms of the remainder of the debt. It is best to negotiate only when there is no party clearly at fault and the lack of payment is the result of a misunderstanding or technical problems. After all, this is what we would first do in the case of a valued U.S. customer with whom we have had a dispute.

Often, though, U.S. firms worsen the situation by assuming the worst. To some degree, this situation is complicated by infrequent face-to-face communications, language barriers, and the like. The first rule is to identify the problem and where the roots of the problem lie. After you have gained a full understanding of the problem, proceed to the solution. If negotiation prove to be unworkable or there are clear indications of bad faith, the next step is to gather documentation and submit it to the American embassy, so that the importer becomes aware of the fact that a possibility exists of souring whatever other relations he or she has with the U.S. official community and other U.S. suppliers.

In some cases, American embassies abroad can be of assistance in resolving these sorts of disputes, although usually the level of assistance seems to depend on the individual with whom you make contact and the specifics of the case. I advise direct contact with the embassies in these matters. Embassy staff are often leery of taking a strong position with the importers if they are not certain that the foreign company was, in fact, at fault. Hence, the need for very good documentation.

If neither of these approaches bears fruit and the amount is sufficient to warrant legal action, the next step is to attempt to invoke arbitration (this should be a standard clause in the distribution sales agreements), which is often faster and less costly than lawsuits. The best such agencies (in my experience) are the International Chamber of Commerce, (212) 354-4480, and the American Arbitration Association, (212) 484-4000.

FINANCING

Foreign Credit Insurance Association

An especially useful tool to reduce the risk of nonpayment in foreign operations is receivables insurance such as that offered by the Foreign Credit Insurance Association (FCIA).

Sometimes a buyer will not buy under terms that do not include some sort of financing. In these cases, or in the case of ongoing sales to an overseas distributor or customer who desires terms, you may wish to look at FCIA for support. FCIA insures export receivables so that neither the commercial bank nor the U.S. exporter suffers in the event the foreign importer does not pay.

In fiscal year 1990, FCIA insured shipments of almost $4 billion, 95 percent of which were short-term transactions. It provided insurance to over 1,100 companies, of which 72 percent were small businesses. This is not to say that FCIA is disinclined to insuring export receivables for large companies. Rather, larger companies, with more international experience, feel less need to use FCIA facilities.

These policies make bank financing more easily attainable by removing much of the risk of the transaction from the bank. At the same time, it makes your company more competitive by allowing you to offer better terms. The amount of down payment, if any, and the repayment period will depend on a number of factors, including the amount of the transaction, the buyer and his or her credit history, and the country of destination.

The range of insurance that FCIA offers is tailored to the needs of U.S. business, within certain guidelines that serve to reduce their risk of assuming unacceptable exposure. One of the programs is particularly useful for repeat sales to the same customers (such as your representatives) and is a great incentive to get distributors to hold higher levels of stock because it gives them longer terms for payment and eases cash flow concerns.

Let's review a few of the characteristics of the FCIA program, beginning with the terms offered. Short-term policies offer coverage terms up to 180 days, and often the deal can be struck with no down payment from the buyer. In some cases, admittedly rare, the short-term policy can be extended up to one year. Medium-term policies, defined as having a duration of two to five years, normally require 15 percent cash in advance by the buyer. In these cases the coverage applies only to the portion of the total that is financed (the total price less the 15 percent advance payment). Long-term policies, typically involving large projects, do not lend themselves to treatment here. Usually these projects involve many financial institutions and are sufficiently complex to warrant a case-by-case review for each application.

FCIA is concerned about assisting U.S. manufacturers, not foreign companies. As a result, it will be concerned with the percentage of U.S. content for the goods being shipped and may not insure more than an amount equivalent to the U.S. value-added. Additionally, FCIA does not stay in business by offering guarantee to noncreditworthy entities. It should not be viewed as a means of making a bad risk good, because it too has eligibility requirements. The long and the short of it is that nobody, including government agencies, likes to assume exposure to risky transactions. FCIA will demand credit reports and additional financial information from the foreign buyer to ensure that its interest is protected. If your trading partner is not capable of generating good credit ratings and reports, it is likely that FCIA will refuse the transaction.

FCIA does attempt to develop programs for the needs of individual situations and firms. Some of the most common of these follow.

The most popular FCIA policy and, to my mind, the most useful is the multibuyer policy. Most U.S. businesses build revenues on repeat sales to end users and distributors and need coverage that will apply to a number of customers in a number of countries. This program offers short- and medium-term coverage to exporters that have receivables with more than one customer or distributor in one or more foreign countries. The U.S. firm applies for the coverage once and then can renew it in one-year intervals. Hence, repetitive paperwork is kept to a minimum.

In some cases, insurance will be sought for only one buyer. With the single-buyer policy, you may seek coverage for a single transaction or an ongoing series of transactions to the same buyer. In most cases the standard coverage is three months but may be extended to one year for multiple shipments.

To assist small or new exporters, FCIA offers an umbrella policy, which allows export trading companies and other trade professionals to assist in the transaction. In this case, the policy is issued to an administrator, not to the exporter. The administrator (most often a bank, ETC, or insurance broker) then becomes responsible for credit reports, collecting premiums, reporting shipments, and completing claims forms. This umbrella policy is limited to small exporters with less than $2 million in export credit sales. FCIA also has a variant of the umbrella policy, which can be administered by a U.S. trade association.

The service policy is intended to cover the export of engineering, construction, management, and architectural services to be performed by U.S. personnel.

FCIA offers lease programs for both financing and operating leases. In both cases, they are single-transaction policies. A financing lease, where ownership of the good is transferred to the foreign buyer at the expiration of the leasing period, is similar to a medium-term sale and requires a 15 percent cash payment in advance. An operating lease policy, where the good returns to the seller at the end of the lease period, covers only lease payments due between the lessee's failure to pay and the repossession of the goods.

FCIA has developed smaller, less often used programs to assist U.S. business with uncommon situations. You can get FCIA coverage for preshipment financing, consignment sales, overseas warehouse sales, foreign currency payments, and sales of used equipment. Contact FCIA should you find yourself sailing into uncharted financial waters with overseas operations.

FCIA has long recognized that it could increase the impact of its services by offering programs for U.S. banks as well. As a result, it provides policies to cover U.S. bank losses from loans supporting the export of U.S. goods and losses due to confirmation of a foreign bank credit for a U.S. export. By lowering the risk to the U.S. bank, FCIA has also done what it can to ensure that U.S. exporters continue to enjoy support from private institutions as well.

Export-Import Bank

The Export-Import Bank (Eximbank), with which FCIA is affiliated, is another source of financing, although it is more project and single transaction driven. It can also be useful for certain kinds of operations, and both entities are helping to pioneer alternative financing methods such as cross-border leases. My experience is that Eximbank performs best for larger dollar transactions, in part because of the fee structure and the amount of paperwork required for the transaction.

In order to explore these options, contact one of the independent brokers that package these kinds of assistance on behalf of FCIA and Eximbank. They tend to offer good service and remove much of the paperwork burden from you. In addition, they often act as brokers for other sources of financing and can shop for the best deal for both you and the customer.

OTHER SOURCES OF EXPORT CREDIT

There are a number of independent brokers that package export credit support for you and several bank trading companies that will fund export transactions in exchange for a percentage of the gross margin. Several of the large multilateral development banks also have funds available for export finance, most often associated with development projects in many of the developing countries. The World Bank, the Interamerican Development Bank, the Asian Development Bank, and the Arab Development Bank are but a few. Recently, additional multilateral institutions have sprung up for Eastern Europe and Israel. And several banks have formed a new venture, the Export Insurance Company, which operates like FCIA. Yet another private company operating in this arena is PEFCO.

Forfaiting is a means to discount export receivables, generally with countries that have high risk profiles or a history of nonpayment. Essentially, forfaiting is the nonrecourse purchase of the exporters receivable by another party. The cost of forfaiting depends on the risk involved and typically involves a discount rate on the receivable. For the most part, forfaiting is done by banks that specialize in international banking and forfaiting houses.

Finally, a number of state governments, in part due to the large demand for export finance by U.S. companies, have created Eximbank-like operations. Typically they offer working capital loans and loan guarantees for export operations. They are good sources for export credits and will often be able to tap into federal sources of funding as well.

FOREIGN EXCHANGE

For payments to be made in international transactions, foreign currencies must be exchanged, normally through commercial banks. One of the difficulties of foreign trade is that if you sell in currency other than the dollar, the value between the dollar and the buyer's currency may change between the time the deal is made and payment is received. As a result, you could lose dollars in the transaction. It follows that if the foreign currency increases in value and the billing is done in that foreign currency, the exporter would make additional profit in dollar terms. However, few exporters wish to play the currency market, preferring to focus on their core business.

The easiest, and by far most common, solution is to quote prices and demand payment in U.S. dollars, placing the burden and risk on the buyer. In many cases, U.S. companies have set up accounts with brokerage houses in the countries of destination for their exports. The payment is sent in the foreign currency to the brokerage house, where it is immediately converted to dollars and forwarded to the U.S. account of the exporter. This method offers the advantage of allowing the importer to pay in local currency and increases the certainty for the exporter that foreign exchange exposure is minimized because the exposure is normally less than one day, and the markets are unlikely to make dramatic moves in that period. This method will not work when the exporter is offering terms in foreign currency because the exposure is extended far beyond 24 hours.

Sometimes the buyer cannot or will not make payment in dollars, and terms must be offered. In these cases, consult an international banker for an explanation of the risks and opportunities associated with the transaction. A banker can also give advice should you decide to accept the foreign currency in payment, as to methods by which you can hedge the foreign currency risk. A hedge occurs when the bank or other financial institution (for a fee, which has to be calculated into the quote) assumes foreign exchange risks in return for a fee or discount on the transaction. Hedges normally involve going into the currency futures market to offset fluctuation risk. They require a great deal of study, time, and effort on the part of the finance group in the company. In general terms, if a company is to get directly involved in this sort of transaction, it is best to have a professional currency manager on board.

Individual companies can also hedge directly and keep the risk, and possible reward, with the company itself. Conservative companies tend to favor forward contracts to hedge short-term exchange exposure. Forward contracts guarantee a future price at which the U.S. firm may exchange dollars for a foreign currency and eliminate the risk of exchange rate availability. However, these contracts are "done deals," and you cannot move out of them should you wish additional flexibility to take advantage of opportunities to make money via the movement of rates.

Companies with a somewhat more aggressive nature, also usually blessed with a well-grounded and sophisticated finance group, will more often hedge only a portion of the exposure and thus, have additional exposure to commit at a higher rate.

Another alternative is the currency option, which allows the purchaser to buy or sell dollars against a foreign currency at a predetermined exchange rate. The best time to use options is when the company is looking at longer-term commitments and needs additional flexibility due to the increased uncertainty associated with these longer exposures.

When using hedges or other complicated financial mechanisms, do not get too deeply involved in the details. Explain the problem to your bank or other entity involved in the transaction (such as a trading company), and let it assume the risk. Any fee involved in shuffling that risk to a third party is just another cost of doing business. Only in the rarest of circumstances should a company get directly involved in these sorts of transactions. Most often they require a much higher degree of expertise than you will have in-house, they are tremendously time-consuming, and carry (absent a third party, which assumes them for the fee) a poor risk-reward ratio.

COUNTERTRADE AND BARTER

Some countries restrict the amount of foreign exchange that can be purchased by importers to pay for goods. Most often they are state-controlled economies or countries with large foreign debt problems. In some cases, some form of countertrade may be required to make sales to these countries.

There are also cases of countertrade or barter occurring not due to government regulation but rather as the result of a purchaser who does not wish to or cannot pay cash. In either event, these sorts of transactions can considerably complicate life for the exporter.

Barter is the simple exchange of goods and probably occurred the first time a cave man looked next door and saw a tantalizing bunch of grapes that he wished to exchange for an elephant haunch steaming over his fire. Since then, not many of the fundamentals have changed, although the permutations have grown in direct proportion to the overall number of transactions. This is not something that you should be directly involved with. A number of trading companies underwrite such deals, thus relieving you of the need to sell the good that you are accepting as payment.

Countertrade is a transaction that includes the exchange of some currency as well as goods. A countertrade contract usually specifies that the seller be paid in currency on the condition that the seller agrees to find markets for products from the buyer's country. There are all sorts of variations on this theme, but the bottom line is that it involves an agreement that will take you, should you be directly involved, far afield from your core business. As such, it has not been popular with or used by U.S. firms. There are, however, alternatives to this direct involvement.

You can seek countertrade opportunities, with little cost in time or effort, through some commercial banks, large multinationals, and some of the world's larger trading companies (mostly Japanese or German, depending on where the transaction takes place). Historically, the costs for these sorts of transactions are quite high; somebody has to do the work to put them together, and by their nature, they entail more than usual risk. I have seen deals discounted as much as 25 percent, although this is a bit unusual. Remember: The deal will either fly or not with the costs that are built into the financial arrangements. The biggest mistake you can make is to spend too much time trying to develop this kind of business and miss many other straightforward opportunities while chasing an elusive one. The best thing to do is turn them over to a third party and see if they will fly. If so, great. If not, then you have not diluted your other efforts needlessly.

This treatment of financial issues is not intended to be exhaustive, nor is it written for bankers or other financial wizards. Rather, it is intended to provide international executives with no more knowledge than they need to deal effectively with the institutions involved in the financial side of international operations. Always remember that these issues are not the primary ones; getting the business is. Secure good expert assistance with regard to your needs with financial issues, and let the experts earn their fees.

Chapter **9**

Distribution Methods
and Strategies

There are many methods and strategies that can be used to distribute your product overseas. A common myth is that a product or company must follow one of these methods, to the exclusion of all others, in all markets. That is not true. The best strategy uses all the distribution channels available to the company and is based on a number of considerations.

The primary one is the level of resources a company is willing to devote to the international marketing effort. It requires little effort to retain an export management company and a huge effort to market worldwide through a variety of methods and channels. Before you select an approach, consider four questions:

1. Which channels of distribution best fit the long-term goals and the immediate financial constraints of the company? If you do not have money or time to commit to a total effort, forget the more expensive means of entering foreign markets. But this does not mean that you can't begin to adopt a long-range strategy by entering those markets where you will eventually produce or warehouse the product, and by selecting distributors who have the financial capability to enter a joint venture or licensing agreement, at some future date.

You are attempting to place your first distributors in a strategic fashion, so you can ensure that your first (and eventually longest) market presence occurs in those markets that will eventually become countries in which you will take an investment stance. This strategy gives you time to develop a good relationship of trust with the distributor (eventually to become your partner, with luck) and time to develop the market fully so that the investment decision is a more probable outcome.

2. Where should your firm produce its products in the future, and how will it then be able to use these production facilities to service nearby markets? This strategy is becoming increasingly attractive in Europe, where a growing number of U.S. companies are investing on the mainland (for the most part attempting to access all EC nations from one facility) with the idea of being properly positioned for the economic integration of the EC.

3. Since you can eliminate the need for the head office handling ongoing distribution in countries that ultimately will be serviced by overseas production or warehousing, which are the second tier of markets (which cannot be serviced from those production facilities) that you need to enter? Can the company, given its limitations, establish direct distribution in those second-tier countries?

4. Can you get the services of a good export manager, at no cost to your company, to get penetration in the third tier countries where you have so little potential that it is not worth your effort for the time being?

These four questions provide the conceptual framework for you to divide up the globe in terms of market potential and your long-term objectives. Contrary to popular belief, there is no reason to base your marketing effort on geographical considerations because geography does not always have to do with the amount of sales you can generate from a particular market. Hence, you may choose to have a distributor in Switzerland, yet go the direct sales route in Germany, and locate a production facility in Italy—or any other permutation of that scheme.

TYPES OF SALES RELATIONSHIPS

Before we go further, a brief discussion of the various types of sales relationships you can seek follows. All have advantages and disadvantages. The first two methods—passive marketing through an export management company and piggybacking (see later in this chapter)—are indirect. With a few exceptions, they are best used with third-tier countries. The other methods are more active and are intended for the second-tier countries and the first tier as well if you have no long-term goal to establish manufacturing overseas.

To some degree, if you choose a passive method (especially for good markets), you are essentially taking the risk of substantially retarding the rate at which you can fully penetrate the market in question. However, if you are not prepared to make the necessary commitment in time and money, this approach is the only method by which you can get the product to the market. If you choose the active method, the alternative you select is not important. For the most part, these terms are descriptive of the kind of legal relationship that you have with a foreign representative and not particularly important with regard to how it will affect your sales efforts.

Passive Marketing

Foreign buyers use commission or buying agents to find goods for purchase from the United States. These agents seek to obtain the desired items at the lowest possible price and are paid a commission by their foreign clients.

An export management company acts as the export department for one or several manufacturers of noncompetitive products. It solicits and transacts business in the name of the manufacturers it represents for a commission, salary, markup, or retainer plus commission. In most cases they will simply mark the product up and take profit from the margin. Some EMCs provide immediate payment for the manufacturer's products; however, they can also request terms from the manufacturer, which may or may not be passed on to the customer overseas. EMCs typically operate under exclusive marketing agreements for specific territories.

When an EMC requests a retainer, it most often means that its executives have doubts about the marketability of your product. Never make an up-front payment to an EMC, and always limit its exclusive distribution rights to three to five years, with a one-year probationary period, which, if not successfully completed, results in the automatic termination of the EMC.

If you retain an EMC, you may lose control over foreign sales and in many cases have no access to the EMCs client list. Nevertheless, it performs a valuable function in allowing you to focus on the most lucrative markets.

Most manufacturers are properly concerned that their product and company image be well maintained in foreign markets. You do have the right to request reports on efforts to market your products and may require approval from your firm for product adaptation and other similar changes.

There are differences between EMCs and export trading companies (ETCs). In most cases the ETC is an entity that basically buys and sells goods, acting as intermediary for the manufacturer and the buyer. They usually do not require an exclusive agreement with the manufacturer because they shop around each request for quote. Exceptions are entities established under the Export Trading Act, which are most often tied closely to the manufacturer. The technical difference is unimportant. What does matter is the degree of effort the ETC or EMC is willing to commit to the marketing of your product. My experience is that ETCs are less desirable than EMCs because they are, with certain exceptions, less likely to provide the ongoing marketing effort to your product that an EMC will provide.

Several countries require that imports be effected through a state-owned trading company. Many companies have been successful, over the years, in using trading companies to handle bloc trade requirements, as well as much of their China trade. Given the events unfolding in the former bloc countries, this may shortly change.

Additionally, there are some markets where the use of private-sector trading companies far exceeds the need. Japan, where trading companies import over 50 percent of Japan's total purchases from abroad, is a good example. Although the need for these trading companies has long since ceased to exist, the Japanese market is so rooted in tradition that these large trading companies continue to dominate the import market for that country. The share of imports these Japanese companies enjoy, however, has been declining slowly over the years, consistent with the worldwide pressure to flatten and make the international distribution of goods more efficient.

How to Hire an EMC

The first question you should ask is whether the EMC has sufficient funding to invest the money in actively marketing your product. I have seen some very good, well-funded, and professionally managed EMCs and some truly horrible ones. Size is not a criterion that will give you guidance on this question. Most EMCs are small operations and make their living on fairly narrow margins. As a result, professional EMC managers are slow to take on additional staff or otherwise increase the size of their operations. They also understand that their revenues need to be conserved for the marketing expenses they will incur every time they take on another product, and they tend to run lean to ensure the capital is available to take on new lines.

The second factor is knowledge of your product (preferably an experience with introducing a similar one) and experience in the territory to which marketing rights are assigned. Most EMCs tend to try to specialize in regions and products. Product specialization is especially valuable as the EMC will already know the market conditions in most countries and will have an existing base of distributors through which to test-market the product (the latter service would run you neatly into five or six figures through a research firm). This existing distribution system will allow the EMC to determine the marketability of your product very quickly. Good EMCs are rarely wrong in their assessment of the product marketability in the areas they serve.

Next in importance is the specific plan the EMC has to develop the market for your product. Ask for a proposal that outlines its efforts on your behalf. Beware of anyone who attempts to market the product without traveling to the markets he or she has been assigned. Find out how many representatives are on the road promoting the products, determine their technical capabilities with regard to product support, and ask if they have methodologies in place to deal with service and support issues. All these details, and many more, should be part of the proposal you request from the EMC.

Much like your overseas distributor, it is a good idea to get to know the EMC's business. Find out how many other product lines this EMC carries. Is it overloaded with products or can it reasonably handle an additional one without unduly straining resources.

Remember to check out the EMC with other companies it has represented. Also, ask if it tends to represent "quality" products and companies, and find out how many years it has been in business. The latter information will help you determine if the EMC's ability to select products is well developed (an EMC that does not have the ability to pick marketable products does not last long).

You will need to determine the EMC's markup policies and what you get for it. If the markup seems excessive, try to persuade the EMC to spend more money on the marketing side in exchange for the additional margin. Push for attendance at trade fairs, translating your promotional materials, and any other service to offset whatever part of the margin seems excessive.

Piggyback

Piggyback marketing is an arrangement by which one manufacturer distributes another's product through the overseas distribution network, most often worldwide. The most common piggybacking situation is one in which a U.S. company has a distribution contract with another firm in a related business. The second firm (the one that will distribute the product) may not manufacture an entire product line or wishes to take on additional lines to better service its client base overseas. The first U.S. producer piggybacks its products to the international marketplace by allowing the second firm to distribute its products overseas. Generally the distributing company, not the manufacturer, incurs the marketing and distribution costs associated with exporting. Successful arrangements usually require that the product lines be complementary and appealing to the same customers.

A good example of piggybacking is that of water well drilling equipment. Some years ago, the largest manufacturer of this equipment piggybacked its line with a manufacturer of heavy equipment. The heavy equipment manufacturer did not have a line of drilling equipment and needed one to fill the demands of its customers, who were being driven to other suppliers for their needs in drilling equipment (and increasing the danger of client defection to other suppliers). The drilling equipment company now enjoys a dominant position, worldwide, with its product line and never incurred expense in doing so.

Active Marketing

Active exporting gives you more control over the export process, potentially higher profits, and a closer relationship with the overseas buyer. You will need to devote more time, personnel, and other resources than are needed with passive exporting. Passive marketing, however, does nothing to help you build an organizational base to expand your operations. It contributes little to providing you with the necessary learning experience to improve your company's export performance, and it can, by virtue of setting your goals too low, keep you in satisfied ignorance about a market's potential much longer than if you had undertaken the effort yourself.

You will find that choices you make early on about exporting methods will often dictate your downstream decisions as you proceed in building a global company. Let's examine some of the more active methods.

Sales Representative

A sales representative is the equivalent of a manufacturer's representative in the United States. The representative uses the company's product literature and samples to present the product to potential buyers. This person usually works on a commission basis, assumes no risk or responsibility in payment, and is not likely to stock your product. You will probably have a contract with him or her, not necessarily exclusive, for a certain geographical territory or, in some cases, for sales to certain end user groups. The contract defines territory, terms of sale, method of compensation, and other issues important to your company and product line.

Foreign Distributor

The foreign distributor purchases merchandise from a U.S. exporter (often at substantial discount) and resells it at a profit. The distributor generally provides support and service for the product, maintains a product inventory and a sufficient supply of spare parts, and has adequate facilities and personnel for normal servicing operations. The distributor normally carries noncompetitive but complementary products, which can make this group very easy to target; all you have to do is follow other companies' already existing distributing systems.

The payment terms and length of association between the U.S. company and the foreign distributor is established by contract, much as the relationship is defined for sales representatives and EMCs. Most knowledgeable manufacturers begin with a relatively short trial period and then extend the contract if the relationship proves satisfactory to both parties.

Although we tend to think of distributors as "stocking" distributors (they buy and resell your product from a stock that they purchase from you), the fact is that the decision to stock will not be based upon what you call the relationship but upon the economic realities of holding that stock: Will it be more profitable for the foreign representative to have the stock readily available or to process the order from your plant.

Selling Directly

A company may sell directly to a foreign retailer or end-user. This has not been a traditional method in the past, but it is growing in importance as distribution systems worldwide flatten. The emergence of good mass market infrastructure internationally is rapidly changing the kinds of products that can be sold directly to end users and retailers. There are many examples of companies that have moved from traditional distribution to more direct methods for a variety of reasons, the most common being that competitors began to derive unacceptable price advantages via adopting more direct approaches.

Note that I have not listed agents. The reason is simple: We need to ban this vague and dangerous term from our export vocabulary. It has a legal meaning in many countries. The inclusion of the word *agent* in a contract can mean that the individual has the right to make obligations (legally binding ones) on your behalf. I am giving you the benefit of a $28,000 lesson a friend learned in Europe some years ago. Do not use the term—at least not until you fully understand its legal meaning in a given market.

There are about ten more categories that are descriptive of these sorts of relationships with representatives, but they are either permutations of the ones that I have listed or they are extremely rare.

JUMP-STARTING YOUR EFFORTS

Trade Fairs

Participate in a trade fair. The ideal method of beginning your trade fair program is to locate the largest international fair in the world for your industry, but this is not always possible from a time and expense standpoint. Often you can achieve your goal of locating foreign representatives by participating in a large U.S. fair. For example, COMDEX is one of the world's largest computer and high-technology shows, and it attracts businesspeople from all around the world. The overseas attendees at these fairs are excellent candidates for you because they are, at the very least, able to incur the expense to attend, and attendance usually means that they are seeking new products or have experience in the field.

The U.S. Department of Commerce sponsors the attendance of foreign buyers to these shows and, in some cases, has brought as many as 3,000 prospective distributors and customers to one show. Upon arrival at the fair site, go to the international business centers and make sure the staff there understand that you wish to meet with the foreign buyers' group. To ensure that you attend the shows that include these groups, ask the local ITA office for a list of the shows for which it will be recruiting a foreign buyers' group.

If you cannot afford to exhibit in the show (or don't wish to, for whatever reason), at least go as an observer. This is not as effective as exhibiting the product but can net good distributors since you will be able to track many of the foreign buyers down through the international business centers.

You can avoid the expense of going to the show by requesting, from your local ITA office, the list of the foreign buyers that attended the show. If the local ITA office cannot get the list, ask for the name of the ITA officer in Washington who is responsible for the trade fair, and contact him or her directly.

In most cases, the best way to use trade fairs to generate leads overseas is to attend overseas trade fairs. Much as a foreign distributor demonstrates a commitment to the conduct of international business by attending a U.S. fair, you demonstrate your commitment to the international marketplace by taking the time and expense to attend fairs overseas. This makes you more attractive to local representatives. It makes their life easier and does not require that they undergo the expense to find you.

The best fair to attend to get started is often one of the large international fairs in Europe. They can draw from all over the continent and tend to attract the largest number of distributors from the greatest number of countries. An added bonus is that many of the European countries have their version of the foreign buyers' groups. Hence, you may also be able to draw from their groups and will be able to generate additional leads from non-European countries. African and Middle Eastern countries tend to be well represented at these European fairs.

I have had good luck attending the major fairs in Germany. I suspect the reason is that much of the new technology introduced over the last 30 years has come out of German labs. Hence, the attendance is higher in Germany due to the fact that it tends to have more new products than many other European countries. Another consideration is that the German trade fair tradition goes back to the Middle Ages. It is the best-established program of trade fairs in the world.

Your Competitors

Get the overseas distributor lists from other companies in your field. Try to target large, well-recognized U.S. suppliers that sell to your end-user market and have similar but noncompeting products. Probably you already know who they are. It is a simple matter of picking up their international distribution lists from a trade fair or by other means—fair or foul. I have never ceased to be amazed at how many companies publish and freely distribute their international distribution lists. I have picked up many distributors over the years by taking advantage of this misplaced corporate pride. (For that reason, I have never allowed an international distribution list to be published for any company I worked for. I have recruited far too many distributors this way ever to make myself that vulnerable.) In many cases these suppliers will be companies that use the same distributors, through which you market your products.

In your communications with these potential overseas distributors, be sure to point out that your products are marketed by the same distributors in the United States. This information will allay the foreign representatives' fears about the possible negative reaction from the other U.S. company. (Why would the other supplier object to the foreign distributor carrying your line if their domestic distributors already do?) In addition, it will establish instant credibility for your company with regard to the marketability of the product because it is already marketed in the United States by similar distribution methods.

This method of identifying overseas distributor candidates is tremendously productive; it is the most targeted and least expensive, and it yields the highest-quality distributors. You already have the assurance that the potential distributor is stable (or should be if he or she is selling the products of a large U.S. firm). You can probably rest assured that the service and support capability will be in place, and you have greater assurance that he or she is already selling successfully to your end user group.

Once you have successfully recruited a distributor, advise similar distributors in surrounding markets that you will have to grant their neighboring distributors exclusives for their territory if they do not wish to assume the line. Nothing is more daunting to a distributor than the idea of nearby distributors using a new product to get the door open to his or her clients.

Follow up serious leads regardless of where they originate. There is no reason to delay because "we are not ready to move in Zambia yet." You should be ready to move wherever you can get and keep good representatives overseas. There is no reason to walk away from these sales. If you are concerned that the product should not be sold until technical training can take place, then agree to provide the support once the first sale has been made. Handle details so that any concern you may have can be alleviated by providing what support is needed either during or directly after the first sale.

You can negotiate with more than one distributor at a time. This is not considered to be a breach of faith, and, in fact, that distributor may be negotiating with more than one supplier. Do not wait to get one distributor in place before beginning to locate or negotiate with another. You will be able to handle several of these negotiations at the same time.

You will notice similarity among the potential distributors with regard to the sort of agreement they will try to negotiate with you. This somewhat simplifies the process, and it stands to reason that you will become better at these negotiations as time goes on. You will also find that you are capable of dealing with more than one issue at a time. After all, you do this every day with issues unrelated to your international marketing effort. Why would you not apply the same management skill to negotiating these agreements?

Freight Forwarders

Retain a freight forwarder. I know of no successful exporters, with the exception of very large companies, that did their own forwarding early on in their export efforts. If you allow yourself to get taken up with the logistics of export, you will not have the time to generate the business. The first rule is to get your focus narrowed to the effort to attract and retain good representatives overseas and keep it there until you have fully executed the plan.

Free Advertising

Send press releases to trade publications. The U.S. trade press is the most widely followed in the world, and you may attract foreign representatives to your products by virtue of press releases sent to industry press. Not only will you get the benefit of the additional U.S. exposure gained from the press releases, you will generate leads from abroad as well. Foreign distributors rely on this press to keep up to date on trends in their industries. A good product review in these publications will generate contacts for this reason. Keep copies of these reviews to use in later recruitment efforts. Well-informed third-party reviews are effective in establishing the quality and value of your product.

Paid Advertising

Advertise in domestic and foreign trade publications. Many overseas distributors subscribe to trade publications or secure copies in another way. This is an excellent tool for generating additional leads.

Trade Associations

Use your U.S. trade association (or the U.S. embassy if necessary) to generate contacts with counterpart organizations overseas. Advertise in their association newsletters. If translation is a problem, ask the association to provide a knowledgeable translator (often the person recommended will have both the industry knowledge and the English skills to do an excellent translation). Advertising will reach all your potential representatives in that country and is quite cheap (from $200 to $800 for a reasonable advertisement).

If you can't advertise (for whatever reason), ask the association to advise you which of its members carry products that will fit with yours, and get their addresses so that you can contact the potential representatives yourself. If it will not provide these names, get a listing of the membership. The point is that the objective is achievable if you are tenacious with your efforts to generate the leads.

Network

Associate with a company that is already active in international trade and ask for introductions to good foreign distribution candidates. As long as this other company is not competing with you directly, this will not be a problem and, in fact, may benefit the U.S. supplier by providing the overseas distributor a product that it's currently missing. If the company is reticent to make an introduction, it may be willing to share old distributor candidate lists that are no longer useful to it.

Other Resources

Quite inadvertently I discovered the most complete, up-to-date database of overseas distributors available anywhere in the world: the Yellow Pages. I had hired a college intern to assist me with some research I was conducting to gather lists of foreign prospective distributors. (I use interns quite a bit. They are cheap, ingenious, and often a great source of future employees.) I was flabbergasted when the intern came back with 2,000 potential distributors throughout Europe and Latin America from the foreign city Yellow Pages that he had dug up in the university library. My first reaction was to discount the list because it would be out of date, did not contain fax numbers, and did not address the quality of the distributors. And, quite frankly, how do you approach 2,000 distributors? What I found, upon second glance, is that all of these objections were groundless. Much like our Yellow Pages, they were current (less than one year old), they did have the fax numbers in some cases, and the size of the advertisement and the fact they had an advertisement told me quite a lot about the company, including, in many cases, logos of the other suppliers they represented.

C h a p t e r **10**

A Road Map to the U.S. Department of Commerce and Other Services

U.S. DEPARTMENT OF COMMERCE

The U.S. Department of Commerce (DOC) has a wide array of services, at little or no cost, for assisting U.S. exporters in getting established with their international operations. These services are designed to save you time, energy, and money. The DOC, despite the quality of many of its services and information, is not the only tool you can use, though it is a useful one in your toolbox for international operations. When you read this chapter, you will conclude that all of the DOC services are, in fact, services that you can and should perform yourself, especially for your primary markets. At the same time, when a market is either a knotty one or you cannot take the time to engage in a trip to a particular market, the DOC services provide an splendid alternative. Additionally, the DOC services are designed to accomplish what you want to attain with less exertion on your part and with an eye to making the process less expensive and intimidating. The DOC goal, and the thrust of its programs, is to motivate firms that would not otherwise be able to export into the game by making the whole process easier. Please note, however, that DOC does charge for most services.

Understand that the quality of the individuals who labor in this institution will vary, much as they do in any large organization, public or private.

However, for the most part, they are quite focused and knowledgeable. And with the exception of extremely costly commercially produced market research, the federal government is the only entity in the United States that is actively conducting market research abroad. Many "professional" international consultants get the vast majority of their information from these offices and charge for what they received for free. Much of what they gather is public domain information. They often repackage it, sometimes with additional outside information. In rare cases, and for a hefty fee, they may also do some original research.

The following is a brief depiction of who does what in this massive department. Make good use of what they have to offer.

International Trade Administration

The best starting point for getting information about export programs is a district office of the DOC's International Trade Administration (ITA). Its local offices have access to all assistance available in the DOC, and they can direct you to other government and private sector export services. Most of the staff in these offices have significant overseas experience and can guide you through the entire process: helping you find overseas representation, providing good information on foreign commercial laws and distribution practices, assisting you with targeting markets, checking out potential overseas representatives, and counseling you on the steps involved in exporting. You can also make use of ITA's services to assist your firm with obtaining sources for financing international deals, information on trade exhibitions, answers to documentary questions, and assistance on finding your way through the export licensing procedures.

Many seasoned exporters rely heavily on these offices, even after years of operation, as vital sources of assistance and information. You have already earned the right to these services by way of paying your taxes, so use them.

ITA provides many services. The following are the ones I consider the most useful. This list is not inclusive. Make your decision with regard to using them only after you fully understand what you need from the service.

Agent/Distributor Service. This customized search for interested foreign representatives will identify up to six prospects. It is an excellent way to pick up distributors, at reasonable cost, with almost no toil on your part. ITA will deliver your brochures to appropriate candidates in a country you target. Any interested candidates will get in touch with you.

Commercial News USA. This monthly magazine published by ITA and distributed worldwide to importers is a great way to get exposure for new product or niche products for which research and traditional targeting methods don't work well. This service is not appropriate for larger, well-recognized firms because it is a bit too broadly based for them. It works well for smaller companies, with less generous export marketing budgets.

Foreign Buyer Program. ITA promotes certain U.S. trade fairs worldwide to lure foreign buyers and importers to those fairs. Obtain a list of all of these trade fairs in your industry, and make certain that you exhibit at the fair and secure individual meetings with the foreign buyers who attend. I know of one firm that picked up seventeen distributors in fourteen countries at a single fair. As a result, the product's overseas introduction took place in a matter of weeks.

The best aspect of this service is that the foreign buyers present are normally earnest about picking up new products (hence their presence at the show), and it is a very swift process. If the foreign buyers are not interested in your products for their purposes, they can often recommend other companies in their countries that might be interested. These foreign buyers can be invaluable sources of information and referrals because they are familiar with their market and the players.

Gold Key Service. What an extravagance! If you want to do nothing but get on a plane and have the embassy do everything else for you—including setting up your appointments with potential representatives that they will identify on your behalf—this is for you. You can customize the service so that the embassy provides whatever other support you need including transportation, interpreters, and office facilities.

World Traders Data Report. These custom reports, prepared by the U.S. embassy, evaluate your potential representatives or customers and include background information, standing in the local business community, creditworthiness, and overall reliability. These reports also contain a useful "comments" section, which has dissuaded U.S. firms from making bad decisions on a number of occasions. This section is essentially the embassy's assessment of the distributor's general operations and desirability and includes information about the candidate's best customers, what other companies he or she is active with, where branch offices are maintained, which other products he or she carries, and the like. This comments section is the meat of the report; the other information is readily available from other sources.

Overseas Trade Fairs. You should participate in one overseas trade fair early on, if for no other reason than to gain the experience of meeting new customers face to face and to learn how the competition is marketing its products. ITA makes this first effort much less difficult by providing customs clearance for your materials, turnkey booth packages, and logistical support for certain overseas fairs that it schedules annually.

Commerce Officers at U.S. Embassies Abroad

Not so long ago, U.S. business could anticipate very little in the way of support from the American embassy. However, this service has improved dramatically with an increasing awareness of the importance international trade has to the overall health of the U.S. economy.

About half of the American commercial officers working in embassies have been hired directly from the private sector, and most seem to have solid international trade experience. They are backed up by a number of local employees, who are usually natives of the country and are knowledgeable about the distributors, local business law, and business practices in that country.

The commercial staff provide a range of services to help companies sell overseas: background information on foreign companies (known as a World Trader Data Report), services designed to help you pinpoint distributors, market research, business counseling, and assistance in making appointments with key buyers and government officials. In many countries a call from the embassy will effectively pave the way for your appointment.

There are still some embassies, however, where the level of service still reflects the sort of unhelpful attitudes that we saw a decade ago. Like all other large organizations, there is some unevenness to the quality of the staff. If you cannot get the sort of assistance you need from the embassy, turn to the local

U.S. chamber of commerce in that country or, as a last resort, to a business service center in a major hotel.

Country Desk Officers

These are individuals who are assigned responsibility for following all developments in a particular country that could affect U.S. business. They are an excellent source of information on trade potential in specific countries. I have found them most helpful in providing up-to-date information on the commercial situation in particular countries, especially those with unstable governments or economies. They also can confirm or deny information you pick up from other sources. They can educate you about a country's regulations, tariffs, business practices, economic and political developments, trade data and trends, market size and growth, and documentary requirements for that country.

Get a full listing of these officers from your local ITA district office.

Trade Development Industry Officers

These people specialize by industry sectors and closely follow business developments, worldwide, in that industry. Aside from the factual information they can provide, they are good sources of information about the general state of your industry abroad and can offer good counsel with regard to government-sponsored trade missions to foreign markets. These officers are most helpful with assisting in locating good international trade fairs, helping you stay abreast of developments overseas that could affect your business (such as emerging competitors), and providing good general information about where you might locate good markets for your products.

Export Licensing Assistance

Several offices within the DOC can assist you with export licensing requirements. Export licensing authorizes U.S. companies to ship sensitive products or technologies abroad and should not be mistaken for product or technology licensing for production purposes.

OTHER SOURCES OF ASSISTANCE
Commercial Banks

Almost all major banks have international banking departments employing specialists conversant with specific countries and transactions. These large banks, located in most major U.S. cities, maintain offices throughout the country. Larger banks also maintain correspondent relationships with banks in most foreign countries or operate their own overseas branches, providing a direct channel to foreign customers.

Banks frequently provide assistance free of charge to their clients. Many also have publications available that discuss business practices by country and can be a valuable tool for initial familiarization with foreign industry.

Often large foreign distributors use a U.S. bank's subsidiary in their country for conducting their business with the United States. In most cases, the bank will be delighted to set up an appointment between two customers. The added advantage is that payment details, should the deal be struck, are often more manageable if the bank is involved from the start.

In many countries, a letter of introduction from your bank can help open doors with potential distributor candidates by establishing your company as a serious international organization. Letters of introduction have fallen out of practice, but are still useful from time to time, especially in the somewhat more formal European countries.

Banks are best at assisting with financial matters and can be of great help on a variety of services, including handling international payments, advising you on currency fluctuations and the risks to your firm, and changes in the regulatory environment in specific countries. They are also invaluable in helping you conduct credit checks on foreign firms.

Industry Associations

Some U.S. industry associations can supply detailed information on market demand for their member's products in selected countries and assist members by providing information about potential distributor candidates overseas. At the very least, they can put you in touch with their counterparts in other countries, will have membership lists and newsletters to help you generate distributor leads prior to your trip. To find your association check the *National Trade Association Handbook*, available at most libraries.

American Chambers of Commerce Abroad

Another good source of information in a foreign country is the local U.S. chamber of commerce. These organizations are knowledgeable about local trade opportunities, actual and potential competition, good distributor candidates, and the like. These chambers of commerce abroad usually field inquiries from any U.S. business but ordinarily undertake detailed service only for members of affiliated organizations. Some chambers have a schedule of charges for services rendered to nonmembers.

The support they offer seems to depend on the individuals running the particular office, so services vary from office to office. However, almost all have a newsletter, a good place to advertise for your potential distributors.

Foreign Governments

Many governments conduct research on foreign market opportunities. By requesting the information through one of your foreign distributors, located in the country that has conducted the research, you can gain access to a worldwide information network. They key here is to alert all of your overseas distributors to get into their export assistance networks and stay on the lookout for information that can help you in other markets.

Chapter **11**

The Future of
International Business

The future of international business will mirror what is happening today in the United States and reinforce the concept that the competitive advantage for the United States lies in our willingness to use technological and marketing innovations to flatten traditional distribution systems. The growth of mail order and direct marketing, together with the appearance of large wholesale outlets, bodes poorly for the future of traditional distribution methods.

International acceptance of direct marketing channels is growing faster than expected, especially in Europe. In fact, a number of companies are already direct marketing through international mail order sales.

ROOTS OF INNOVATION

The business innovations that will spur this continuing evolution over the next twenty years have roots in a number of areas.

Third-Party Service Firms

Firms increasingly find themselves in a multivendor environment, often selling to a number of VARs (value-added retailers) and other sorts of resellers in the same market. In part, this trend is due to the "new value-added" discussed earlier and to the increasing number of applications found for the same sort of technology.

Let's look at the example of a floppy disk manufacturer or a chip producer. These products are sold for a number of applications and are used by any number of manufacturers in their products. When the OEM (original equipment manufacturer) producer has no marketing channel aside from that of customers who use the components in their equipment, how does that producer support the product? Traditionally, this has been done through the distribution system of the customer, but two resulting problems are common. The first is that the general level of service expertise tends to be lower with the customer than the producer. The second is that most producers prefer to have one service provider, for ease of operation and to achieve lower costs.

As a result of all these factors, we have witnessed the growth of a number of third-party service providers who service equipment worldwide, usually under contract with the producers. We have seen such companies as TRW, countless subsidiaries of large manufacturers, and even start-up service companies enter this arena. In fact, this service industry is expected to grow at around 19 percent a year for the foreseeable future.

The result of the emergence of this industry is that the international marketing function for companies that require service and support has been greatly simplified. They no longer have to slow the pace of product introduction due to not having service capability in place. They can engage in more direct marketing as the role of the distributor declines due to the availability of these service providers and decrease prices to end users, which will translate to higher market penetration with little or no requirement for activities that detract from the marketing effort.

Should you get tied to the wrong provider, the service may not be delivered with the quality that you would like, damaging your reputation in the international marketplace.

Fulfillment Services

Companies like TNT Fulfillment Services will stock your product in other countries, forward the order to the warehouse, and deliver the product to the end user. This service allows the U.S. company to shorten deliveries and use sea freight (saving the expense of more costly air freight) or consolidated air freight services offered by the company. It also gives the U.S. firm the flexibility of leasing the space from the fulfillment company rather than purchasing warehousing.

These services may offer "remail" facilities as well. This service allows you to mail catalogs and other promotional pieces in bulk, with a reply card to a post box in the foreign country that is rented by the remail service. As the responses come in, the remail service forwards the reply cards to your company, not only saving a great deal in postage but offering the client the convenience of responding to a domestic address. This service is valuable as a direct marketing tool and can be used as well to conduct surveys and poll client groups.

Credit Cards

The growing international use of credit cards has led to the emergence of an entirely new payment method. Much in the same way you pay for a hotel by use of a credit card and are billed later, foreign customers can bill their international purchases to these cards and gain several advantages thereby: (1) there are no letter of credit fees to pay, (2) they receive automatic terms by using the card rather than having to pay cash in advance and, in many cases have the ability to finance the transaction over longer periods of time, and (3) may avoid the need to have freight insurance by virtue of the programs many card companies have in place to insure purchases.

The advantages to the exporter are just as impressive. Payment barriers are usually avoided, and you do not have to convert foreign currencies; the conversions are done within the card company's system. Risk of nonpayment can be minimized by verifying the legitimacy of the account before shipment.

The Fax Machine

Both U.S. and foreign executives generally agree that the fax machine has revolutionized international business. In the early 1980s there were approximately 400,000 fax machines worldwide. Today, there are 8 million, and counting. Two of the finest features are the "mail merge" and "send later" options available with these machines. We have created databases with which we can, from a fax modem on our computer, send hundreds of faxes every evening (while we are home watching television) at a cost of 11 cents per page to most European countries. In fact, many companies now use the fax to do "signatures on file" for their international sales.

The fax machine has implications for both direct marketing and the search for new customers and distributors. We will become less dependent on traditional distributors for many products, and for products that will continue to require traditional distribution, we will become less research oriented. Why would I do exhaustive market research for potential markets and distributors when I can essentially "poll" the entire world at a cost and time investment that is much smaller than that needed to conduct the research?

Put another way, marketing Darwinism is just around the corner. Many functions that currently require a great degree of international savvy and high-cost talent will shortly be reduced to a clerical function. The challenge of the rest of the 1990s for American business will be building the right sort of databases to meet the needs of U.S. firms for this sort of information. I do not mean that the fax machine will take the place of personal contact in a sales situation, but it will reduce the need for this contact to take place.

Translations

You will eventually need to translate your company literature into other languages. One of the best, cheapest, and most user-friendly services available is the Massachusetts-based WordNet. It accepts documents for translation via fax at any time and passes them on to one of the 400 translators who freelance for comparatively reasonable fees. WordNet will also review the quality of the translation if the topic is sufficiently complicated.

Prices vary, but most translations cost $25 to $50 per 100 words, and WordNet will typeset and print the documents as well. Technical and difficult language translations will be extra. Contact WordNet at (508) 264-0600.

Several commercially developed software programs automatically translate in and out of English from several European languages. However, these programs are not sufficiently well developed yet for good business usage. An added problem is that most of these programs are currently available only in European languages.

If you simply need to communicate with an existing customer or distributor and complete accuracy is not required, these programs can probably do the job. However, you must be careful not to use slang or idiomatic expression in English when you input the document. These programs are quite inexpensive (around $100), but can run easily into the thousands for the more sophisticated versions. They are quite user friendly.

Videoconferencing

Buying videoconferencing equipment may be a sizable initial investment, but rates have dropped to $2.60 a minute with AT&T. MCI now offers its Mail Global Access at $.50 a minute. This service is not really videoconferencing, but it can offer a cheap alternative if you don't mind not seeing a face on the other end.

Interpreters

AT&T offers a service that allows you to speak, via an interpreter from AT&T (and with a toll-free line if you choose), to other businesspeople around the world. Because of time differences, this service is available twenty-four hours a day, and AT&T has the ability to deliver over 140 languages to you instantly. The service is not cheap, but is not out of line for the value offered.

Greater Levels of Available Information

The Yellow Pages from all over the world are the best possible database available to any international marketer, and free of charge. It is current and updated yearly; you can easily identify candidates or end users by broad heading; and it contains anyone in that industry who has a telephone.

Private organizations that sell international mailing lists have emerged. This service, combined with the increasing use of international catalogs and delivery and payment services, strongly indicates that all of the necessary components are in place for a radically different future.

Postal Services

The 170 postal administrations throughout the world, which make up the Universal Postal Union (UPU), can assist international direct marketers to function effectively in the global market. Postal service is theoretically available worldwide but works best in the developed world, where postal services are marked by efficiency and a spirit of cooperation between countries.

Both public and private postal services offer plans for shipping a number of mail pieces to a particular country in a large container. Upon arrival, this container is opened and the individual mail pieces sent along. The result is greatly reduced postal costs.

The case in the developing world is less clear. But consistent with the tenets of capitalism, rapid mail services, parcel delivery services, and other private companies have jumped into the breach and now have service to most of the world. Moreover, delivery services often get the product to the customer much more cheaply than normal commercial shipments.

In many cases, air express companies offer competitive rates, especially for high value-to-weight ratio products that are time sensitive. This is particularly true for companies that can achieve reasonable volume, where deep discounts will be offered. For companies with infrequent international air express delivery needs, similar rates can be achieved through one of many consolidators that have appeared.

I have had nothing but good experiences with these services and highly recommend them for export shipments, mostly for small shipments of high dollar value. Obviously this sort of service is not useful to heavy equipment manufacturers and the like.

DIRECT MARKETING

Several companies have already begun direct marketing operations using two different methods. The first, used where good direct marketing infrastructure is in place, is for the firm to handle everything from advertising to order fulfillment from their U.S. base. They place advertisements in foreign publications or develop foreign language catalogs and direct mail them, often using credit cards as payment methods, or electronic transfers. The second method is to license a foreign firm to do the mail order or, conversely, open a wholly owned or joint venture mail order operation in the foreign market where the goods are warehoused and fulfillment occurs through the organization in the foreign country. This method is used in countries where the infrastructure does not exist for a direct fulfillment mechanism, or if economies of scale can be achieved by having a warehousing operation in country. This method has been used by several firms to get into the Japanese markets—in some cases, with minor adaptation in delivery methods.

For the most part, you can determine which markets will be good candidates for direct marketing by compiling the following information:

- Is the economy wealthy and stable?
- Is the infrastructure in place to allow for the logistics of direct marketing?
- Are good delivery services available?
- Is credit card use high?
- Do advertising media exist for you to target end users?
- Is the population density such that you can reach a large audience efficiently?

You can gather this information in a matter of minutes with a few telephone calls to private delivery services and the post office; credit card companies to find out if you can get paid and how you process that payment and at what cost; and the Direct Marketing Association to find out who to talk to about advertising or developing a direct mail piece for end users. You will find more complicated treatments of this subject in other publications. However, these calls and a little common sense will tell you what you need to know to get started. Remember: Perfect is the enemy of good enough.

For additional information, write:

Direct Marketing Association
West 42d Street, 25th Floor
Suite 900
New York, N.Y. 20036–4704

There are also direct marketing associations in the following countries:

Argentina	Netherlands
Australia	New Zealand
Belgium	Singapore
Canada	South Africa
Denmark	Spain
France	Sweden
Ireland	United Kingdom
Italy	Germany
Japan	Uruguay
Mexico	

MAIL ORDER LOGISTICS

Foreign countries require export documents to accompany most mail order shipments. The majority of these documents can be easily computerized. What is important is that you understand the documentary requirements and that you describe the package contents in a straightforward and easily understandable manner. The carrier can tell you what documents are required. The documents themselves are normally available through office supply houses or commercial printers. The key is to invoice correctly, and be descriptive with regard to what the box contains.

Mail order shipments, regardless of their means of delivery, normally are subject to customs duties and taxes. These additional charges are almost always paid by the overseas customer and need to be specified in your quotations and literature.

Before the overseas customer receives the order, the package must be cleared by the local customs authorities. A customs official will examine the shipper's invoice to determine the amount of duty (if any) and taxes that are due. Normally after inspection, the items are given to the local postal system for delivery to the addressee. The postal service, in most cases, collects the amount of duty and tax that is payable. The recipient then pays the amount due, usually by check or credit card.

CONCLUSION

The trend is definitely in the direction of a flatter and more efficient distribution system, but the traditional systems will not disappear. Certain products will always require distributors. Moreover, the rate of this change will differ among countries. The European countries and the United States will (and have) accepted these changes more quickly than the developing countries and Japan. In Europe, direct mail purchases grew at 4.2 percent in 1990. In England, direct mail is nearly as commonplace as in the United States. In France, one in every two families purchases $600 in mail order every year. Germany maintains a similar purchasing pattern.

The Pacific Rim countries lag behind North America and Europe, although several of the countries offer attractive conditions for mail order operations. For example, Singapore and Hong Kong have direct marketing industries that grew at rates between 20 percent and 40 percent in 1989 and 1990. Japan will adopt a flatter distribution system more slowly because of an entrenched and multilayered distribution system that is part of their business culture. Nevertheless, Japan's growth rate in direct marketing has remained at a steady 15 percent. Australia and New Zealand also offer interesting markets.

The underdeveloped world—the Middle East, Latin America, Africa, and parts of Asia—has yet to accept mail order operations broadly. At the same time, they are much less troublesome in the sense that customers are easily identified. In poorer nations, the best mailing list is the telephone book, because only the comparatively wealthy have telephones.

Before you enter mail order operations in a large way, use the following guidelines:

- Search for accurate and well-targeted mailing lists. Overseas lists are often not as specific as those in the United States and they may be more expensive (a list of 1,000 runs $300 in Japan, $170 in the United Kingdom, and $75 in the United States). Often the best consumer lists can be bought from U.S. magazines with foreign editions such as *Businessweek, Time,* and *Fortune.* Direct marketing associations in your target countries may be able to supply lists or refer you to brokers.
- Make sure you understand privacy laws in the countries you target, especially in Europe.
- Determine whether you can direct market in English.
- Understand foreign postal service requirements regarding outer marking on boxes. The U.S. Postal Service has a list of these requirements.
- Don't be automatic about pricing. Some companies charge 40 percent over U.S. pricing levels and still sell very well.

- Investigate the possibility of using a fulfillment service or courier deliveries for problematic markets.
- Free offers or giveaways don't work.
- Rely more on images and less on language with promotional pieces to keep costs down and generally allow for wider usage of the same piece.
- Check with both private carriers and the post office to determine if business reply mail is possible to your markets. Inquire about remail services.

C h a p t e r **12**

Beyond Exporting: Joint Ventures, Licensing and Subsidiary Operations

In almost all instances, U.S. firms export to a particular market before they establish foreign operations in that country. Trade leads to investment in almost all cases. It stands to reason that most companies will endeavor to finance the more costly methods of pursuing international sales only after a good marketing beachhead has been established, via export sales. There is no question that most firms prefer to grubstake their international expansion from cash flow. While this is a general rule, it is generally true. What is a bit lamentable is that fact that many U.S. firms have no qualms about borrowing for purposes of expanding their domestic efforts yet shy away from engaging in the same behavior internationally, when the returns are, in most cases, at least equivalent.

The exception most commonly found is with consumer goods, where the cost of getting finished product to market is such that there is often no choice in the matter. These kinds of goods tend to have a high weight-to-value computation and need to be produced in the market in order to remain competitive with other locally produced items. The fact that these companies were faced, in most countries, with an inability to market the product by any

167

means whatsoever, with the exception of some sort of local production, has led many U.S. consumer goods companies to develop good international skills.

This situation is responsible for the spawning of a highly professional cadre of international managers in such consumer industries as food production and processing and pharmaceutical manufacturing and distribution. These industries are fertile ground for recruiting well-trained, experienced executives for overseas operations. Most of these executives have spent the majority of their careers overseas, speak at least one foreign language (many are not U.S. citizens), and will have undertaken, at a very young age, profit and loss responsibility for their country operations. Usually they carry the title of country manager or president of the subsidiary operation. Many believe that they have little future in their current company because "international is not sufficiently recognized" or "there is nowhere to go but another country." The availability of these executives can make the decision to enter a particular market with an investment posture a much less ominous process.

Another reason to look at production overseas is that some countries prohibit the importation of certain items but encourage local manufacture. For the most part, these tend to be developing countries that have employed their domestic market potential to attract foreign investment via the assembly or other manufacture of goods in that country. The idea was the local markets could be held hostage to force foreign firms to manufacture in their nations, thus creating jobs, an industrial base, tax revenue, and technology transfer. This philosophy of economic development became known as the import substitution model.

Many of these economies are beginning to move away from this model, popular in the 1960s and 1970s, by opening their markets to foreign competition. Many remain essentially closed economies. To surmount these barriers, U.S. companies may need to consider manufacturing their products in those markets.

This calculation, however, is not sufficient to warrant a manufacturing decision. The wise businessperson will disregard, for the most part, the vagaries of government regulations and focus on the business issues. The market is either an attractive one from a profitability standpoint, or it is not. This should be the essential factor driving the decision.

Many companies that allowed government regulation to drive the manufacturing decision are now regretting the choice. In most cases, these closed economies used high duty rates to attract the manufacturers and thus created markets with very little competition. Eventually, the local manufacturing companies became corpulent and somewhat complacent, although many remained profitable. As time goes on and additional economies open to foreign competition, more of the protective duty rates have been slashed, and the local firms have found themselves entirely unable to compete. Almost overnight, many manufacturers have found themselves going from highly profitable operations to losers as competition takes advantage of lower duty rates by launching superior products at lower prices.

REGIONAL AGREEMENTS

Yet another consideration is the rapidly developing consolidation of markets. Led by the European Economic Community initiative, the Canada/U.S. Free Trade Initiative, and the Mexico/U.S. agreement, we are likely to witness many such agreements over the next few years as nations strive to band together to meet the competitive challenge of other alliances. There have been other trade agreements in the past such as ASEAN and LAFTA (Southeast Asian and Latin American trade agreements), but for the most part they have not achieved the degree of integration necessary to be truly effectual.

The EC initiative changed all of that, and we are now watching the inception of regional agreements that will have a dramatic impact on how companies structure their international manufacturing operations to derive benefit from trade incentives offered to the members of such agreements. A further benefit is that the European countries that are not currently members of the EC will likely be confirmed for membership in the near future or will be granted some sort of associate status.

In Europe, as a consequence of the EC agreements, we will probably see a consolidation of former manufacturing facilities in individual member countries into one member country in order to realize higher production efficiencies. Because the advantages of having manufacturing in each of the member countries will plunge as duty rates and other barriers are lowered between member states, this is a likely outcome for many firms.

169

For U.S. companies new to European operations, this trend will likely produce unprecedented opportunities in that one investment will allow greater access to the remainder of the EC countries. In addition many countries will experience a net decline in investment as production facilities are moved to EC countries with lower labor rates and the like. As a result, many existing facilities may be attractively priced for the newcomer.

ENTRY OPTIONS

The decision to increase your presence in a particular market is often the easy side of the equation. The next consideration is how to effect that entry. There are also options to handling the manufacture of your product in a foreign market alone.

Licensing

Licensing is a contractual arrangement in which the licenser's patents, trademarks, service marks, copyrights, or know-how may be transferred to foreign companies for production in another market or country. The compensation for the U.S. companies customarily takes place in the form of royalties, which can include both an initial payment and remuneration based upon production numbers. However, it is important to develop licensing agreements that afford additional sources of revenues. Examine the possibility of binding the agreement to the provisions of materials and/or component parts for the licensee.

Furthermore, you will need to explore both the local and U.S. laws concerning the rate of taxation with the use of a royalty, as opposed to the use of a management fee or a separate technical support fee. Consider using all of these possibilities to offset the generally lower levels of revenue you will generate from a licensing agreement, as opposed to a wholly owned subsidiary, and fully consider the tax exposure you take on with this sort of operation.

A licensing agreement usually enables a U.S. firm to enter a foreign market with fewer financial and legal risks than owning a foreign facility or entering a joint venture agreement. However, it is not a technique I recommend so long as my technology enjoys some competitive advantage and I can continue to export to the country in question.

The best way to view licensing—its legal structure and the possibilities for sources of revenue—is to examine franchising because there is little difference between the two. (International franchising has been around for some time, most notably in the food service industry.)

When considering licensing, remember that a licensee may attempt to use the technology in competition with you, most often in other foreign markets, although there a few extraordinary instances of their attempting to market in the United States. A good way to evade this difficulty is to restrict the use of licensing to older technologies and impose territorial restrictions on their sales of the product. You can also use patent, trademark, and copyright laws to protect against this sort of raid on your other export markets, providing you have adequate protection in place.

Licensing the manufacture of the product to an overseas firm is not always the answer—it tends to leave more profits in their pocket than yours—but you suffer only minimally from downturns, and it is a good method to prolong the life of old technology. Typically, old technology will not be of interest to the developed world and is licensed to Third World countries that still have import substitution policies in effect, which will protect the market, normally via a dramatic increase in import duties, against other foreign competition. Licensing is also a good means of turning back foreign competition from a market where it is beginning to secure market share from you.

A good example is the case of Brazil. During the 1970s, several companies licensed their personal computers for production by Brazilian companies. What ensued has effectively kept new technology from entering the country and provided a protective layer of duty rates for imported computers that exceeds, in some cases, 100 percent of landed value. Although there are ongoing efforts to pry open the Brazilian market, these companies have enjoyed almost two decades of unchallenged supremacy in that market. You can argue that this is undesirable from an economic standpoint. What is indisputable is the effect it has had on the profitability for the Brazilian manufacturers and their foreign technology suppliers.

Foreign licensees are bound by your licensing agreement to the extent that it benefits both parties. There are repeated examples of former licensees ceasing payment to the principal and attempting to abrogate their agreements with U.S. firms. The best means to ensure mutual dependence is to grant the licensee a judicious territory, ensure that the contract allows reasonable profit for both sides, and tie him or her to future technology so that his or her development costs for this technology exceed payment for yours.

I know of one case, in India, where a U.S. firm ceased receiving payments over four years ago and is still battling its way through the Indian court system to attempt to get the contract honored. Nevertheless, these sorts of stories are quite rare, and they are usually the result of the U.S. firm's relying too heavily on supposed legal protection and not enough on sound business principles.

SUBSIDIARY OPERATIONS

If you elect to open a wholly owned branch or subsidiary, you are in sole control of sales and production and can completely manage the operation. You will also be in full control of your intellectual property, and this sort of operation tends to allow you to maximize profits (and losses) from the operation. Additionally, the use of a wholly owned branch or subsidiary operation enables you to take advantage of any investment or tax incentives that may be tendered by the host country.

Be sure that you get these benefits, in writing, from the local government prior to laying your money on the table. Often, long and delicate negotiations will be required with the host government, and you would be wise to ensure that whatever concessions are gained are protected for a reasonable period of time.

Generally, these sorts of operations are best left to large companies because direct investment normally requires a great deal of capital and large investment in human resources. It can hold the specter of losses over a small company that can become very difficult to cope with from the standpoint of a small international department. In fact, most of these sorts of operations are undertaken by large corporations. The exception is companies that have such high requirements for service and support that they dare not entrust them to others.

Another important factor is the amount of investment required to establish a plant and the benefit to be gained by doing so. If you have a product that can reasonably expect to gain significant tariff advantage in a lucrative market by establishing a plant at small cost (usually this means an assembly operation), then the equation changes rapidly.

WAREHOUSING AND DISTRIBUTION COMPANIES

Another option, fitting somewhere between a wholly owned subsidiary and a straight export strategy, is that of having foreign warehousing or a distribution company. The capital requirements (and the associated risks) are much lower, and it offers many of the advantages of a direct presence. There are also many sound practical arguments that make this a viable entry strategy.

As time goes on, greater emphasis is being placed on logistical efficiency and better customer service. As a result, U.S. firms are looking to European locations as assembly and warehousing sites for their products. In many cases, the inputs for the product's final production come from suppliers throughout the world and are assembled in Europe. In other cases, the European hub serves as a warehousing site for finished goods from the United States.

In either case, great efficiencies can be achieved through a European operation. In addition to the obvious advantage of being closer to the customer, there are other good reasons to consider this sort of presence, assuming that Europe's market potential warrants the decisions:

- With a European hub, you can begin to lower freight costs by shipping less frequently and in higher volumes. In many cases, especially for commonly air-freighted products, you can begin to look at the cheaper ocean-freight alternative, although the cost of maintaining the inventory over longer cycles will have to be set against the savings in transportation costs.
- Regardless of the method of delivery to European operations, the ongoing shipment to the final customer will be quicker, assuming that the item is held in stock at your European warehouse.
- Technical and marketing support will be greatly enhanced, due not only to the proximity factors, which will allow for a greater degree of lower cost travel to European markets, but also because you will elim-

inate the time differences and hence provide support when it is needed, not when you happen to be in the office in the United States.

I favor the Netherlands as a center for European operations. The reasons are varied, some of them guided by personal preference. The Dutch are honest, hard-working, and astute businesspeople, and multilingual staff are easily located. The Netherlands is, however, somewhat more expensive than some other options.

The Netherlands has been favored with good location. It is a short distance from most major trading cities and has excellent transportation infrastructure—numerous airports, seaports, inland waterways, and a transportation industry—which, given its location, is marked by a high degree of efficiency and competition.

The Dutch customs service has a well-earned reputation for being the most efficient and reliable service in Europe and perhaps the world. So given the fact that, in principle, the import duty paid for your product will be the same in all EC countries, the real issue, with regard to the importation of your goods, becomes the ease with which you can deal with the customs service of a particular country.

An added consideration is the availability of customs-bonded warehouses, which will allow you to avoid payment of duty until the goods leave the warehouse. In many countries, these sites are warehousing facilities for companies that wish to avoid the payment of duty until the sale is made or the distributor calls for additional stock. These warehouses exist in some form or other through the world. In the Netherlands, many products may be stored in a *Fembac*, a customs-bonded warehouse in which the goods move out without the physical control of customs. Put another way, the distribution company has the authority to issue the customs documents, generally reporting the movement of goods monthly to the Dutch authorities.

JOINT VENTURES

Assuming that the decision to manufacture in the foreign market has been made, the joint venture can often be the preferred approach, for a number of reasons that have to do with both reduced capital requirements and increased overall profitability. The joint venture can sometimes cost your company nothing out of pocket, aside from the technology, and can be structured so that the local partner is responsible for all capital investment for the project. Additionally, the deal can be structured so that both sets of tax codes can be taken into account in which a way as to minimize the impact of the new revenues to the U.S. firm.

Some would argue that the disadvantage is that many countries require the foreign firm to take a minority stake in the venture, but you can generally get around these requirements by granting 2 percent of the venture to a third party. In Mexico, during the 1970s, we granted this 2 percent to an American attorney who had moved to Mexico and taken on Mexican citizenship by marrying a citizen of the country. However, he was also our attorney for the contractual work done and stayed on retainer for any legal requirements we had in the country. As a result, we were able to keep control of the joint venture, which proved to be valuable at a time when close control of the financial side of the operation resulted in our flourishing during a difficult period.

Joint ventures can provide needed local expertise quickly. There are many situations whereby foreign governments give preference to local firms, either informally or formally, on government procurements. Having a local partner, most often acting as president of the operation, can greatly assist you in keeping a national flavor to these operations. Many countries have central governments that produce the vast majority of the gross national product through government-owned companies and government purchases. It pays to have local staff in the forefront of the operation. In addition, it provides for better morale with the local staff, who can see a career progression with the company by virtue of the fact that the top position in the company is a local person. Many companies safeguard their interests by having the chief financial Officer or the director of manufacturing from the home office to keep tight control of the pursestrings and provide for good training and quality control in the plant.

Joint ventures can provide the flexibility for your company to grow into a multinational that can eventually become a global manufacturer, sourcing various components for final assembly in selected markets from your joint venture or wholly owned plants around the world. This allows you to take advantage of such variables, by markets, as availability of raw materials, labor rates and skills, tax incentives and codes, and shipping rates for various components to the assembly areas. The initial joint venture will provide the basis for this sort of expansion, the market expertise to manage it, and the capital base from which to launch it (all this, of course, assumes that you have control of the venture).

The joint venture seems like a sure thing, but 70 percent break up within three and a half years of their formation. So why am I a proponent of this seemingly doomed approach? The answer is that most fail because the parties entering the venture don't take the time to understand the nature of the partnership prior to forming the new company. The statistic is also misleading in that many of these ventures serve their purpose and are then disbanded. Following are guidelines that will help to ensure that joint ventures last as long as both parties want them to continue:

- One plus one does not equal three. Realistic expectations about the performance of the new company is critical. Many consultants love to speak of the synergy that develops from partnerships and often assume the new company will do better than the sum of the two separate partners' performance. There are a few cases where this has proved to be the case, but they are rare.
- Never enter a joint venture with a company that is losing money. Desperation may lead it to seek a partnership for short-term reasons, which will not survive any longer than the desperation.
- Meet at least ten times with the potential partner before signing on the line. Learn their corporate philosophy and approach. If it is not consistent with your own, walk on by.
- Do not think the joint venture is an easy way to buy into a foreign market. They often require more work than establishing a direct presence.
- Make sure you understand that accounting standards differ by country. Reading foreign financial statements can be tricky since net assets, consolidations, amortization, and the like vary widely. Use the services of local brokers and research firms, or restate the statements in terms compatible to U.S. standards.

BILATERAL INVESTMENT TREATY

The host country's dispositions toward protecting foreign investors and licensees can be discerned by ascertaining if a bilateral investment treaty is in force between the United States and the host country. The existence of these treaties is a good indicator that you will be able to get relief through the local legal system, if need be.

A bilateral investment treaty (BIT) is a bit like an insurance policy against the day that the host government decides to change the rules of the game. Although there is no guarantee that U.S. investors will never suffer from prejudicial treatment, the existence of a BIT will ensure, in general terms, that redress through the U.S. government, should the host country deviate from the terms of the agreement set out by the treaty, is available.

BITs not only protect you during the process of actually making the investment; they also provide for ongoing protection over the life of the investment. Several aspects of these treaties bear discussion.

First, U.S. model BITs provide for absolute protection, such as a general requirement of fair and equitable treatment. This generally means that the country must refrain from arbitrary and discriminatory measures directed against U.S. investors. It also provides the full protection and security (physical safety), and treatment for foreign investors that establishes provisions of international law as the minimum standard that can be applied.

Certain provisions concern immigration of investors and hiring practices. Generally the requirement is that the investor have basic freedom of action with regard to utilizing expatriate staff where necessary (often within specific limits). This is important in countries with a volatile labor force and unpredictable labor laws.

There is also a promise to publish all laws and regulations that could have an impact on the investors and to establish a method by which investors can make claims and enforce their rights under the treaty, if the need should arise. This point can be very important in ensuring that information concerning government regulations and procurement is presented fairly to all parties.

The treaties will require that host countries extend treatment to investors that is equal to national company treatment, or that which is afforded to investors from most-favored-nation countries. "National treatment" means that each country will treat investments by the U.S. company in the same manner as it treats its local companies. Most-favored-nation treatment means that the host country will treat U.S. firms at least as favorably as the most favorable treatment it extends to firms of any third country in the same circumstances.

The U.S. BIT also requires that the treaty country apply international standards should the host government expropriate or nationalize the investment. The treaty provides that the action be subject to prompt and fair compensation and guarantees the right to due process of law, including the right to a prompt review of the action. This is an important provision of the BITs because it provides the investor some assurance that, should disaster befall the investment, there are means at least to recover the fair value of that which was taken from the firm.

The U.S. model BIT also requires that currency transfers related to an investment are available out of the host country. Although some BITs vary from this principle, the general understanding is that this free transfer ability encompasses profits as well as proceeds from sale of the asset, payments under a contract (including a loan agreement), and any monies resulting from compensation for expropriation. The treaty provides further that the transfers are to be made in usable currency and at the prevailing market rate of exchange.

All U.S. BITs provide for arbitration between the investor and the host government. In all cases, both parties must agree to submit the dispute to an arbitration body within a specific period of time after the disagreement arose—normally six months although sometimes a year. However, arbitration is normally an alternative only if the case has not yet been brought before the courts or administrative bodies of that country.

The United States has bilateral investment treaties in force or is in some stage of negotiation with the following countries: Bangladesh, Cameroon, Grenada, Senegal, Turkey, Zaire, Panama, Egypt, Morocco, Poland, the Congo, Tunisia, Argentina, Bolivia, Bulgaria, Hungary, Jamaica, Nigeria, and Uruguay.

The number of these BITs is certain to increase, and the provisions will tend toward granting investors even higher levels of protection. Be sure to check for the existence of a BIT during the time that you are investigating investment in the target country.

For information on the U.S. bilateral investment treaty program, contact:

Office of Multilateral Affairs
International Trade Administration
U.S. Department of Commerce
Washington, D.C. 20230
(202) 377-3227

LEGAL ASSISTANCE

While I am not generally enamored with the need for attorneys with your in-ternational operations, an investment decision is certainly the exception. Two attorneys are needed: one in the United States and one in the country in question. The foreign attorney should be drafting an agreement intended to maximize the enforceability of your contract in that country (with the use of arbitration, if possible), and the U.S. attorney should be carefully reviewing the tax codes to minimize the effect of the new investment on your tax expo-sure. The difference between transferring an asset and transferring a technol-ogy, for example, can have an immense impact on the profitability of the transaction.

To take on the establishment of a direct presence in a foreign market, you need good legal and tax advice. The Price Waterhouse *Doing Business In* series, available free of charge, can help you avoid some expense in doing the initial research, so that consultants are needed only once the business decision to enter that market has been taken. These publications include a great deal of information about the business conditions in a country: the applicable tax and legal structures available to an investor, the incentive programs in place to attract investment, and the answers to a host of other questions you will have concerning the local environment, including its regulatory practices and procedures.

Some additional sources for help are "Licensing in Foreign and Domestic Operations," including volumes on joint-ventures by MacLaren and Marple (New York: Clark Boardman Company) and "Milgrim on Trade Secrets" (New York: Matthew Bender & Co).

OVERSEAS INVESTMENT FINANCE

A number of commercial banks, in both the United States and the recipient country, are interested in financing new ventures, especially if the venture is to be undertaken by an existing company with a strong balance sheet and a firm operating base in the United States. But what about when the country in which the investment is being contemplated is not a developed nation and the risk factors are somewhat higher? These commercial banks tend to disappear quickly in this case. However, there is an option.

The Overseas Private Investment Corporation (OPIC) has supported U.S. investment in more than 100 countries and in 1990 assisted in financing over $7 billion worth of projects. Many of these projects would not have gone forward without this support from OPIC. Moreover, OPIC, a quasi-governmental agency, made $143 million in 1990, and it has had a low default and loss rate over the years.

OPIC is structured like a private company and operates on income it earns in each year of operation. Its mission is to assist U.S. companies with their investments in underdeveloped nations. OPIC received its initial funding from the government in 1970, repaid the initial amount it was given, and has not looked back since.

There are essentially five OPIC programs designed to assist U.S. companies with overseas operations:

> *Financing.* OPIC offers medium- and long-term loan guarantees and/or direct loans for overseas investment projects. OPIC will consider all aspects of the project based on sound business principles. It will consider joint ventures as well as wholly owned investments, so long as the joint venture is at least 25 percent U.S. owned. Typically, and especially for large projects, OPIC is one of several players in the financing of the venture. Thus, OPIC support is critical for gaining the interest of other entities, and it will assist the U.S. investor in locating the remainder of the funding needed from both private and public sources.
>
> *Political Risk Insurance.* This insurance is intended to take the uncertainty out of foreign investment by covering against the risk of political and economic turmoil. It is a key component in many commercially fi-

nanced ventures since the banks will not touch projects in many countries unless this coverage is present. The insurance is also key for many projects, such as licensing, contracting, and leasing transactions.

Investment Missions. These missions are intended to assist U.S. businesspeople contact potential partners in other countries.

Opportunity Bank. Another "matching" service, this is a data bank that attempts to match U.S. companies interested in joint ventures with foreign firms.

Investor Information. Informational kits, developed by OPIC, about foreign markets and opportunities.

The World Bank has created an organization that mirrors OPIC's operations and will provide additional sources of finance and insurance for U.S. and other member country firms. It is known as MIGA (Multilateral Investment Guarantee Agency) and is open for business in a number of countries.

Glossary

absorption Investment and consumption purchases by households, businesses, and governments, both domestic and imported. When absorption exceeds production, the excess is the country's current account deficit.

accession The process by which a country becomes a member of an international agreement, such as the General Agreement on Tariffs and Trade (GATT) or the European Community. Accession to the GATT involves negotiations to determine the specific obligations a nonmember country must undertake before it will be entitled to full GATT membership benefits.

account party Party who applies to the issuing or opening bank for the issuance of a letter of credit.

administration protective order (APO) Used to protect proprietary data obtained during an administrative proceeding. Within the Department of Commerce, APO is most frequently used in connection with antidumping and countervailing duty investigations to prohibit opposing counsel from releasing data. The term is also applied in connection with civil enforcement of export control laws to protect against the disclosure of information provided by companies being investigated for violations.

ad valorem "According to value." Any charge, tax, or duty applied as a percentage of value.

advance against documents A loan made on the security of the documents covering the shipment.

advising bank A bank operating in the exporter's country that handles letters of credit for a foreign bank by notifying the exporter that the credit has been opened in his or her favor. The advising bank fully informs the exporter of the conditions of the letter of credit without necessarily bearing responsibility for payment.

Advisory Committee on Trade Policy and Negotiations (ACTPN) A group (membership of 45; two-year terms) appointed by the U.S. president to provide advice on matters of trade policy and related issues, including trade agreements. The 1974 Trade Act requires the ACTPN's establishment and broad representation of key economic sectors affected by trade. Below the ACTPN are seven policy committees: SPAC (Services Policy Advisory Committee), INPAC (Investment), IGPAC (Intergovernmental), IPAC (Industry), APAC (Agriculture), LAC (Labor), and DPAC (Defense). Below the policy committees are sectoral, technical, and functional advisory committees.

affiliate A business enterprise located in one country that is directly or indirectly owned or controlled by a person of another country to the extent of 10 percent or more of its voting securities for an incorporated business enterprise or an equivalent interest for an unincorporated business enterprise, including a branch. For outward investment, the affiliate is referred to as a *foreign affiliate*; for inward investment, it is referred to as a *U.S. affiliate*.

affiliated foreign group (1) The foreign parent. (2) Any foreign person, proceeding up the foreign parent's ownership chain, who owns more than 50 percent of the person below it up to and including that person who is not owned more than 50 percent by another foreign person. (3) Any foreign person, proceeding down the ownership chain(s) of each of these members, who is owned more than 50 percent by the person above it.

African Development Bank (ACB) Established in 1963, with headquarters in Abidjan, Cote d'Ivoire. The AFDB provides financing through direct loans to African member states to cover the foreign exchange costs incurred in bank-approved development projects in those countries. Fifty-one African countries are members and ordinarily receive loans. The Republic of South Africa is the only African country not a member.

African Development Foundation (ADF) An independent, nonprofit government corporation established to provide financial assistance to grass-roots organizations in Africa. ADF became operational in 1984.

Agency for International Development (AID) Created in 1961 to administer foreign economic assistance programs of the U.S. government. AID has field missions and representatives in approximately 70 developing countries in Africa, Latin America, the Caribbean, and the Near East.

agent distributor service (ADS) An International Trade Administration (ITA) fee-based service that locates foreign import agents and distributors. ADS provides a customized search overseas for interested and qualified foreign representatives on behalf of a U.S. exporter. Officers abroad conduct the search and prepare a report identifying up to six foreign prospects that have examined the U.S. firm's product literature and have expressed interest in representing the U.S. firm's products.

air waybill A bill of lading that covers domestic and international flights transporting goods to a specified destination. Technically, it is a nonnegotiable instrument of air transport that serves as a receipt for the shipper, indicating that the carrier has accepted the goods listed therein and obligates itself to carry the consignment to the airport of destination according to specified conditions.

alongside A phrase referring to the side of a ship. Goods to be delivered alongside are to be placed on the dock or within reach of the transport ship's tackle so that they can be loaded aboard the ship. Goods are delivered to the port of embarkation but without loading fees.

American Business Initiative (ABI) Also known as the American Business and Private Sector Development Initiative for Eastern Europe. Emphasizes the export of American telecommunications, energy, environment, housing, and agriculture products and services to Eastern European countries.

American Institute in Taiwan (ATI) A nonprofit corporation that represents U.S. interests in Taiwan in lieu of an embassy. In 1979, the United States terminated formal diplomatic relations with Taiwan when it recognized the People's Republic of China as the sole legal government of China. AIT was authorized to continue commercial, cultural, and other relations between the United States and Taiwan.

Andean Group A group of Latin American countries formed in 1969 to promote regional economic integration among medium-sized countries. Members are Bolivia, Colombia, Ecuador, Peru, and Venezuela.

Andean Trade Initiative (ATI) The trade element of the U.S. administration's drug policy, which provides for assistance for alternative economic development to the drug-producing countries of Bolivia, Colombia, Ecuador, and Peru. The Andean Trade Preference Act of 1991 proposes the designation of ten years of duty-free treatment for most goods produced in one or a combination of these four countries. Currently, none of the four ATI countries has received formal designation as a beneficiary.

antidumping A reference to the system of laws to remedy dumping, defined as a converse of dumping.

Antidumping/Countervailing Duty System Part of Customs' Automated Commercial System; contains a case reference database and a statistical reporting system to capture data for International Trade Commission reports on antidumping and countervailing duties assessed and paid.

arbitrage The simultaneous buying and selling of the same commodity or foreign exchange in two or more markets in order to take advantage of price differentials. *See also* hedging.

assessment The imposition of antidumping duties on imported merchandise.

Asian Development Bank (ADB) Formed in 1966 to foster economic growth and cooperation in Asia and to help accelerate economic development of members. ADB headquarters are in the Philippines.

Asia Pacific Economic Cooperation (APEC) An informal grouping of Asia Pacific countries that provides a forum for ministerial-level discussion of a broad range of economic issues. APEC includes the six Association of Southeast Asian Nations countries (Brunei, Indonesia, Malaysia, Philippines, Singapore, and Thailand), plus Australia, Canada, China, Hong Kong, Japan, South Korea, Taiwan, and the United States.

Association of Southeast Asian Nations (ASEAN) Established in 1967 to promote political, economic, and social cooperation among its six member countries: Indonesia, Malaysia, Philippines, Singapore, Thailand, and Brunei.

at sight Indicates that payment on a negotiable instrument is due upon presentation or demand.

Automated Broker Interface (ABI) A part of Customs' Automated Commercial System that permits transmission of data pertaining to merchandise being imported into the United States. Qualified participants include brokers, importers, carriers, port authorities, and independent data processing companies referred to as service centers.

Automated Clearinghouse (ACH) A feature of the Automated Broker Interface, which is a part of Customs' Automated Commercial System. Combines elements of bank lock box arrangements with electronic funds transfer services to replace cash or check for payment of estimated duties, taxes, and fees on imported merchandise.

Automated Manifest Systems (AMS) A part of Customs' Automated Commercial System (ACS) that controls imported merchandise from the time a carrier's cargo manifest is electronically transmitted to customs until control is relinquished to another segment of the ACS.

balance of payments A statistical summary of international transactions. These transactions are defined as the transfer of ownership of something that has an economic value measurable in monetary terms from residents of one country to residents of another. The transfer may involve (1) goods, which consist of tangible and visible commodities or products; (2) services, which consist of intangible economic outputs, which usually must be produced, transferred, and consumed at the same time and in the same place; (3) income on investments; and (4) financial claims on, and liabilities to, the rest of the world, including changes in a country's reserve assets held by the central monetary authorities. Generally, a transaction is the exchange of one asset for another—or one asset for several assets—but it may also involve a gift, which is the provision by one party of something of economic value to another party without something of economic value being received in return.

International transactions are recorded in the balance of payments on the basis of the double-entry principle used in business accounting, in which each transaction gives rise to two offsetting entries of equal value so that, in principle, the resulting credit and debit entries always balance.

Transactions are generally valued at market prices and are, to the extent possible, recorded when a change of ownership occurs. Transactions in goods, services, income, and unilateral transfers constitute the current account, and transactions in financial assets and liabilities constitute the capital account.

The International Monetary Fund, which strives for international comparability, defines the balance of payments as "a statistical statement for a given period showing (1) transactions in goods, services, and income between an economy and the rest of the world, (2) changes of ownership and other changes in that economy's monetary gold, special drawing rights (SDRs), and claims on and liabilities to the rest of the world, and (3) unrequited transfers and counterpart entries that are needed to balance, in the accounting sense, any entries for the foregoing transactions and changes which are not mutually offsetting."

The U.S. balance of payments presentation does not contain a specific number that indicates an overall balance, although partial balances are published. In an accounting sense, an overall balance is not possible, because the net sum of credit and debit entries in the balance of payments accounts is conceptually zero, in accordance with the principles of double-entry accounting. If the entries do not balance exactly, the net amount of missing credits or debits is entered as a statistical discrepancy in order to bring the two parts of the statement into equilibrium.

Six balances are published quarterly:

1. The balance on merchandise trade, which measures the net transfer of merchandise exports and imports (which differs in some ways from the trade balance published monthly by the Bureau of the Census).
2. The balance on services, which measures the net transfer of services, such as travel, other transportation, and business, professional, and other technical services (this balance was redefined in 1990 to exclude investment income).
3. The balance on investment income, which measures the net transfer income on direct and portfolio investments.
4. The balance on goods, services, and income, which measures the net transfer of merchandise plus services and income on direct and portfolio investment. (This balance is equivalent to the pre-1990 balance

on goods and services; it is also conceptually comparable to net exports of goods and services included in GNP.)

5. The balance on unilateral transfers (net), which measures the net value of gifts, contributions, government grants to foreign countries, and other unrequited transfers.

6. The balance on current account (widely used for analysis and forecasting) which measures transactions in goods, services, income, and unilateral transfers between residents and nonresidents.

bank affiliate export trading company An export trading company partially or wholly owned by a banking institution, as provided under the U.S. Export Trading Company Act. A bank that is established by mutual consent by independent and unaffiliated banks to provide a clearinghouse for financial transactions.

bank guarantee An assurance, obtained from a bank by a foreign purchaser, that the bank will pay an exporter up to a given amount for goods shipped if the foreign purchaser defaults. *See also* letter of credit.

bank holding company Any company that directly or indirectly owns or controls, with power to vote, more than 5 percent of voting shares of each of one or more other banks.

bank release Negotiable time draft drawn on and accepted by a bank, which adds its credit to that of an importer of merchandise.

banker's acceptance A draft drawn on and accepted by the importer's bank. Depending on the bank's creditworthiness, the acceptance becomes a financial instrument, which can be discounted.

banker's draft Draft payable on demand and drawn by or on behalf of the bank itself; it is regarded as cash and cannot be returned unpaid.

barter Trade in which merchandise is exchanged directly for other merchandise or services without use of money.

beneficiary The person in whose favor a letter of credit is issued or a draft is drawn. The word *accepted* and the date and place of payment must be written on the face of the draft.

bilateral investment treaty (BIT) Ensures U.S. investments abroad of national or most-favored-nation treatment, prohibits the imposition of performance requirements, and allows the American investor to engage top management in a foreign country without regard to nationality. BITs ensure the right to make investment-related transfers and guarantee that expropriation takes place only in accordance with accepted international law. BITs also guarantee access by an investing party to impartial and binding international arbitration for dispute settlement.

bill of lading Contract between the owner of the goods and the carrier. There are two types. A straight bill of lading is nonnegotiable. A negotiable or shipper's order bill of lading can be bought, sold, or traded while goods are in transit and is used for letter of credit transaction. The customer usually needs the original or a copy as proof of ownership to take possession of the goods.

Bond System Part of Customs' Automated Commercial System that provides information on bond coverage. A customs bond is a contract between a principal, usually an importer, and a surety, which is obtained to insure performance of an obligation imposed by law or regulation. The bond covers potential loss of duties, taxes, and penalties for specific types of transactions. Customs is the contract beneficiary.

bonded exchange Exchange that cannot be freely converted into other currencies.

bonded warehouses Warehouses authorized by the U.S. Customs Service for storage or manufacture of goods on which payment of duties is deferred until the goods enter the customs territory. The goods are not subject to duties if reshipped to foreign points.

Brussels Tariff Nomenclature A once widely used international tariff classification system that preceded the Customs Cooperation Council Nomenclature (CCCN) and the Harmonized System Nomenclature (HS).

Bureau of International Expositions (BIE) An international organization established by the Paris Convention of 1928 to regulate the conduct and scheduling of international expositions in which foreign nations are officially invited to participate. The BIE divides international expositions into different categories and types and requires each member nation to observe specified minimum time intervals in scheduling each of these categories and types of operations. Under BIE rules, member nations may not ordinarily participate in an international exposition unless the exposition has been approved by the BIE. The United States became a member of the BIE in April 1968. Federal participation in a recognized international exposition requires specific authorization by the Congress, based on the president's finding that participation is in the national interest.

business facilitation office Usually a booth with a reference desk with product catalogs staffed by the commercial section of the American Embassy or a qualified contractor to assist fair visitors or buyers searching for U.S. products or services at an international trade fair.

business information office A post or contract-staffed commercial reference facility, usually at a scheduled international trade exhibition.

Cairns Group Established in August 1986, an informal association of agricultural exporting countries. Members are Argentina, Australia, Brazil, Canada, Chile, Colombia, Hungary, Indonesia, Malaysia, New Zealand, Philippines, Thailand, and Uruguay.

Calvo Doctrine (or **Principle**) Holds that jurisdiction in international investment disputes lies with the country in which the investment is located; thus, the investor has no recourse but to use the local courts. The principle, named after an Argentinean jurist, has been applied throughout Latin America and other areas of the world, but its use appears to now be on the decline in many countries.

Caribbean Basin Economic Recovery Act Affords nonreciprocal tariff preferences to developing countries in the Caribbean Basin area to aid their economic development and to diversify and expand their production and exports. Applies to merchandise entered or withdrawn from warehouse for consumption, on or after January 1, 1984. This tariff preference program has no expiration date.

Caribbean Basin Initiative (CBI) An inter-American program to increase economic aid and trade preferences for 23 states of the Caribbean region. The Caribbean Basin Economic Recovery Act of 1983 provided for 12 years of duty-free treatment of most goods produced in the Caribbean region. The initiative was extended permanently (CBI II) by the Customs and Trade Act of August 1990. The twenty-three countries are Antigua and Barbuda, the Bahamas, Barbados, Belize, the British Virgin Islands, Costa Rica, Dominica, the Dominican Republic, El Salvador, Grenada, Guatemala, Guyana, Honduras, Jamaica, Montserrat, the Netherlands Antilles, Nicaragua, Panama, St. Christopher–Nevis, St. Lucia, St. Vincent and the Grenadines, and Trinidad and Tobago. The following countries may be eligible for CBI benefits but have not formally requested designation: Anguilla, Cayman Islands, Suriname, and the Turks and Caicos Islands.

Caribbean Common Market (CARICOM) Composed of 13 English-speaking Caribbean nations: Antigua and Barbuda, the Bahamas, Barbados, Belize, Dominica, Grenada, Guyana, Jamaica, Montserrat, St. Kitts-Nevis, St. Lucia, St. Vincent/Grenadines, and Trinidad and Tobago.

carnets Customs documents permitting the holder to carry or send sample merchandise temporarily into certain foreign countries without payment duties or posting bonds.

carriage paid to (CPT) Carriage paid to (CPT) and carriage and insurance paid to (CIP) a named place of destination. Used in place of CFR (cost and freight) and CIF (cost, insurance, and freight), respectively, for shipment by modes other than water, usually for the inland portion of a shipment.

cartel An organization of independent producers formed to regulate the production, pricing, or marketing practices of its members in order to limit competition and maximize their market power.

cash against documents (CAD) Payment for goods in which a commission house or other intermediary transfers title documents to the buyer upon payment in cash.

cash in advance (CIA) Payment for goods in which the price is paid in full before shipment is made. This method is usually used only for small purchases or when the goods are built to order.

cash with order (CWO) Payment for goods in which the buyer pays when ordering and in which the transaction is binding on both parties.

catalog and video/catalog exhibitions Low-cost exhibits of U.S. firms' catalogs and videos that offer small, less-experienced companies an opportunity to test overseas markets for their products without travel. The International Trade Administration promotes exhibitions, provides staff fluent in the local language to answer questions, and forwards all trade leads to participating firms.

Central American Common Market In July 1991, the governments of Honduras, Guatemala, El Salvador, Nicaragua, and Costa Rica agreed to establish a new common market in Central America. The common market will cover all products traded within the region by the end of 1992. A second step toward regional integration will be the establishment of a common external tariff. Panama is becoming progressively more involved in the regional integration discussions.

certificate of inspection A document certifying that merchandise (such as perishable goods) was in good condition immediately prior to shipment. Preshipment inspection is a requirement for importation of goods into many developing countries.

certificate of manufacture A document (often notarized) in which a producer of goods certifies that the manufacturing has been completed and the goods are now at the disposal of the buyer.

certificate of origin A signed statement as to the origin of the export item. Such certificates, required by some nations, are usually obtained through a semiofficial organization such as a local chamber of commerce. A certificate may be required even though the commercial invoice contains the information.

Certified Trade Fair Program A Department of Commerce program designed to encourage private organizations to recruit new-to-market and new-to-export U.S. firms to exhibit in trade fairs overseas. In addition to the services the organizer provides, the Department of Commerce will assign a Washington coordinator and operate a business information office, which provides meeting space, translators, hospitality, and assistance from U.S. exhibitors and foreign customers.

Chaebol Republic of Korea conglomerates characterized by strong family control, authoritarian management, and centralized decision making. *Chaebol* dominate the Korean economy. Korean government tax breaks and financial incentives emphasizing industrial reconstruction and exports provided continuing support to the growth of *chaebols* during the 1970s and 1980s. In 1988, the output of the thirty largest *chaebol* represented almost 95% of Korea's gross national product.

charter party A written contract, usually on a special form, between the owner of a vessel and a "charterer" who rents use of the vessel or a part of its freight space. The contract generally includes the freight rates and the ports involved in the transportation.

"class or kind" of merchandise A term used in defining the scope of an antidumping investigation. Included is merchandise sold in the home market that is "such or similar" to the petitioned product. "Such or similar" merchandise is identical to or like the petitioned product in physical characteristics.

clean bill of lading A receipt for goods issued by a carrier with an indication that the goods were received in "apparent good order and condition," without damages or other irregularities.

clean draft A draft to which no documents have been attached.

collection papers All documents (invoices, bills of lading, etc.) submitted to a buyer for the purpose of receiving payment for a shipment.

Collections System A part of Customs' Automated Commercial System, which controls and accounts for the billions of dollars in payments collected by customs each year and the millions in refunds processed each year. Daily statements are prepared for the automated brokers who select this service. The system permits electronic payments of the related duties and taxes through the automated clearinghouse capability. Automated collections also meet the needs of the importing community through acceptance of electronic funds transfers for deferred tax bills and receipt of electronic payments from lockbox operations for customs bills and fees.

Commerce Business Daily The Commerce Department's daily newspaper, which lists government procurement invitations and contract awards, including foreign business opportunities and foreign government procurements.

Commerce Control List (CCL) A list published by the Bureau of Export Administration (BXA) that includes all items—commodities, software, and technical data—subject to BXA export controls and incorporates not only the national security-controlled items, but also items controlled for foreign policy and other reasons. The list adopts a totally new method of categorizing commodities and is divided into 10 general categories: materials, materials processing, electronics, computers, telecommunications and cryptography, sensors, avionics and navigation, marine technology, propulsion systems and transportation equipment, and miscellaneous.

commercial invoice A bill for the goods from the seller to the buyer. These invoices are often used by governments to determine the true value of goods for the assessment of customs duties and to prepare consular documentation. Governments using the commercial invoice to control imports often specify its form, content, number of copies, language to be used, and other characteristics.

Commercial News USA (CNUSA) An International Trade Administration fee-based magazine, published 10 times per year. CNUSA provides exposure for U.S. products and services through an illustrated catalog and electronic bulletin boards. The catalog is distributed through U.S. embassies and consulates to business readers in 140 countries. Copies are provided to international visitors at trade events around the world.

The CNUSA program covers about 30 industry categories and focuses on products that have been on the U.S. market for no longer than three years. To be eligible, products must be at least 51 percent U.S. parts and 51 percent U.S. labor. The service helps U.S. firms identify potential export markets and make contacts leading to representation, distributorships, joint venture or licensing agreements, or direct sales.

commercial officers Embassy officials who assist U.S. business through arranging appointments with local business and government officials, providing counsel on local trade regulations, laws, and customs; identifying importers, buyers, agents, distributors, and joint venture partners for U.S. firms; and other business assistance. At larger posts, International Trade Administration staff perform these functions. At small posts, commercial interests are represented by economic officers in the Department of State.

commercial treaty An agreement between two or more countries setting forth the conditions under which business between the countries may be transacted. May outline tariff privileges, terms on which property may be owned, the manner in which claims may be settled, etc.

Committee on Trade and Development (CTD) Established in 1965 to consider how the General Agreement on Tariffs and Trade (GATT) can aid the economic development of less developed country (LDC) contracting parties (that is, LDC members).

Commodity Credit Corporation (CCC) A government corporation controlled by the Department of Agriculture, which provides financing and stability to the marketing and exporting of agricultural commodities.

Common Agricultural Policy (CAP) A set of regulations by which member states of the European Community (EC) seek to merge their individual agricultural programs into a unified effort to promote regional agricultural development, fair and rising standards of living for the farm population, stable agricultural markets, increased agricultural productivity, and methods of dealing with food supply security. Two of the principal elements of the CAP are the variable levy (an import duty amounting to the difference between EC target farm prices and the lowest available market prices of imported agricultural commodities) and export restitutions, or subsidies, to promote exports of farm goods that cannot be sold within the EC at the target prices.

common external tariff (CET or CXT) A uniform tariff adopted by a customs union to be assessed on imports entering the union territory from counties outside the union.

common market A group with a common external tariff; may allow for labor mobility and common economic policies among the participating nations. The European Community is the most notable example of a common market.

Common Monetary Agreement (CMA) An agreement among South Africa, Lesotho, and Swaziland under which they apply uniform exchange control regulations to ensure monetary order in the region. Funds are freely transferable among the three countries, and Lesotho and Swaziland have free access to South African capital markets. Lesotho also uses the South African currency, the rand. The CMA was formed in 1986 as a result of the renegotiation of the Rand Monetary Agreement (RMA), which was formed in 1974 by the same member countries.

commonwealth A free association of sovereign independent states that has no charter, treaty, or constitution. The association promotes cooperation, consultation, and mutual assistance among members. The British Commonwealth, the most notable example, included 50 states at the beginning of 1991.

Commonwealth of Independent States (CIS) Established in December 1991 as an association of 11 republics of the former Soviet Union: Russia, Ukraine, Belarus (formerly Belorussia), Moldova (formerly Moldavia), Armenia, Azerbaijan, Uzbekistan, Turkmenistan, Tajikistan, Kazakhstan, and Kirgizstan (formerly Kirghiziya).

Conference on Security and Cooperation in Europe (CSCE) Established in 1991 as a successor to the Eastern bloc's Council for Mutual Economic Assistance (CMEA or COMECON). CSCE administers residual tariffs and quotas and relations with other organizations.

confirmed letter of credit A letter of credit, issued by a foreign bank, whose validity has been confirmed by an American bank. An exporter whose payment terms are a confirmed letter of credit is assured of payment even if the foreign buyer or the foreign bank defaults.

confirming A financial service in which an independent company confirms an export order in the seller's country and makes payment for the goods in the currency of that country. Among the items eligible for confirmation are the goods; inland, air, and ocean transportation costs; forwarding fees; custom brokerage fees; and duties. Confirming permits the entire export transaction from plant to end user to be fully coordinated and paid for over time.

consignee The person or firm named in a freight contract to whom goods have been consigned or turned over.

consignment Delivery of merchandise from an exporter (the consignor) to an agent (the consignee) under agreement that the agent sell the merchandise for the account of the exporter. The consignor retains title to the goods until sold. The consignee sells the goods for commission and remits the net proceeds to the consignor.

constructed value A means of determining fair or foreign market value when sales of such or similar merchandise do not exist or, for various reasons, cannot be used for comparison purposes. The constructed value consists of the cost of materials and fabrication or other processing employed in producing the merchandise, general expenses of not less than 10 percent of material and fabrication costs, and profit of not less than 8 percent of the sum of the production costs and general expenses. To this amount is added the cost of packing for exportation to the United States.

consular declaration A formal statement, made to the consul of a foreign country, describing goods to be shipped.

consular invoice A document, required by some foreign countries, describing a shipment of goods and showing information such as the consignor, consignee, and value of the shipment. Certified by a consular official of the foreign country, it is used by the country's customs officials to verify the value, quantity, and nature of the shipment.

container A uniform, sealed, reusable metal box in which merchandise is shipped by vessel, truck, or rail. Standard lengths are 10, 20, 30, and 40 feet (40-foot lengths are generally able to hold about 40,000 pounds). Containers of 45 and 48 feet are also used, as well as containers for shipment by air.

contracting parties The signatory countries to the General Agreement on Tariffs and Trade (GATT). These countries have accepted the specified obligations and privileges of the GATT agreement.

Convention on Contracts for the International Sale of Goods (CISG) A U.N. convention that became the law of the United States in January 1988. CISG establishes uniform legal rules governing formation of international sales contracts and the rights and obligations of the buyer and seller. The CISG applies automatically to all contracts for the sale of goods between traders from two different countries that have both ratified the CISG, unless the parties to the contract expressly exclude all or part of the CISG or expressly stipulate a law other than the CISG.

convertible currency A currency that can be bought and sold for other currencies at will.

Coordinating Committee on Multilateral Export Controls (CoCom) An informal organization that cooperatively restricts strategic exports to controlled countries. CoCom controls three lists: (1) the international industrial list (synonymous with the "dual-use" or "core" list), (2) the international munitions list, and (3) the atomic energy list. The 17 CoCom members are Australia, Belgium, Canada, Denmark, France, the Federal Republic of Germany, Greece, Italy, Japan, Luxembourg, the Netherlands, Norway, Portugal, Spain, Turkey, the United Kingdom, and the United States.

CoCom controls exports at three levels, depending on the item and the proposed destination. At the highest or "general exception" level, unanimous approval by CoCom members is necessary. At the next level, "favorable consideration," there is a presumption of approval; the export may be made if no CoCom member objects within 30 days of submission to CoCom. At the lowest level, "national discretion" (also called "administrative exception"), a member nation may approve the export on its own, but CoCom must be notified after the fact.

correspondent bank A bank that, in its own country, handles the business of a foreign bank.

cost and freight (CFR) The seller quotes a price for the goods that includes the cost of transportation to the named point of debarkation. The cost of insurance is left to the buyer's account. (Typically used for ocean shipments only. CPT, or carriage paid to, is a term used for shipment by modes other than water.)

cost, insurance, and freight (CIF) Under this term, the seller quotes a price for the goods (including insurance), all transportation, and miscellaneous charges to the point of debarkation for the vessel. (Typically used for ocean shipments only. CIP, or carriage and insurance paid to, is a term used for shipment by modes other than water.)

cost of production (COP) A term used to refer to the sum of the cost of materials, fabrication, and/or other processing employed in producing the merchandise sold in a home market or to a third country together with appropriate allocations of general administrative and selling expenses. COP is based on the producer's actual experience and does not include any mandatory minimum general expense or profit.

costs of manufacture (COM) In the context of dumping investigations, the costs of manufacture is equal to the sum of the materials, labor, and both direct and indirect factory overhead expenses required to produce the merchandise under investigation.

Council of Europe (COE) Established in May 1949 to encourage unity and social and economic growth among members, which currently are Austria, Belgium, Cyprus, Denmark, Finland, France, Germany, Greece, Hungary, Iceland, Ireland, Italy, Lichtenstein, Luxembourg, Malta, the Netherlands, Norway, Portugal, San Marino, Spain, Sweden, Switzerland, Turkey, and the United Kingdom.

Council for Mutual Economic Assistance (CMEA, COMECOM) Established in 1949, ostensibly to create a common market. CMEA was a Soviet initiative with Bulgaria, Czechoslovakia, Hungary, Poland, and Rumania as founder members. The council was later joined by the German Democratic Republic, Mongolia, Cuba, and Vietnam; Yugoslavia held associate status. CMEA was succeeded in 1991 by the Organization for Economic Cooperation (OIEC).

countertrade An umbrella term for several sorts of trade in which the seller is required to accept goods or other instruments or trade, in partial or whole payment for its products. Forms include barter, buy-back or compensation, counterpurchase, offset requirements, swap, switch, or triangular trade, evidence or clearing accounts.

In counterpurchase (one of the most common forms of countertrade), exporters agree to purchase a quantity of goods from a country in exchange for that country's purchase of the exporter's product. The goods being sold by each party are typically unrelated but are equivalent in value.

In offset, the exporter agrees to use goods and services from the buyer's country in the product being sold. Offsets may be direct or indirect, depending on whether the goods and services are integral parts of the product. In a direct offset, a U.S. manufacturer selling a product uses a component that is made in the purchasing country. In an indirect offset, the exporter would buy products that are peripheral to the manufacture of its product.

In a compensation or buy-back deal, exporters of heavy equipment, technology, or even entire facilities agree to purchase a certain percentage of the output of the facility.

Barter is a simple swap of one good for another. Switch trading is a complicated form of barter, involving a chain of buyers and sellers in different markets.

countervailing duty An extra charge that a country places on imported goods to counter the subsidies or bounties granted to the exporters of the goods by their home governments. The duty is allowed by the Code on Subsidies and Countervailing Duties negotiated at the Tokyo Round, if the importing country can prove that the subsidy would cause injury to domestic industry. U.S. countervailing duties can be only imposed after the International Trade Commission has determined that the imports are causing or threatening to cause material injury to a U.S. industry.

country of export destination The country where the goods are to be consumed, further processed, or manufactured, as known to the shipper at the time of exportation. If the shipper does not know the country of ultimate destination, the shipment is credited to the last country to which the shipper knows the merchandise will be shipped in the same form as when exported.

country groups For export control purposes, the Bureau of Export Administration of the U.S. Commerce Department separates countries into seven country groups designated by the symbols Q, S, T, V, W, Y, Z.

country of origin The country where the merchandise was grown, mined, or manufactured, in accordance with U.S. Customs regulations. When the country of origin cannot be determined, transactions are credited to the country of shipment. Certain foreign trade reports show country subcodes to indicate special tariff treatment afforded some imported articles.

credit risk insurance Insurance designed to cover risks of nonpayment for delivered goods.

critical circumstances A determination made by the assistant secretary for import administration as to whether there is a reasonable basis to believe or suspect that there is a history of dumping in the United States or elsewhere of the merchandise under consideration, or that the importer knew or should have known that the exporter was selling this merchandise at less than fair value, and there have been massive imports of this merchandise over a relatively short period. This determination is made if an allegation of critical circumstances is received from the petitioner.

Customs Cooperation Council Nomenclature A customs tariff nomenclature formerly used by many countries, including most European nations but not the United States. It has been superseded by the Harmonized System Nomenclature, to which most major trading nations, including the United States, adhere.

customshouse broker An individual or firm licensed to enter and clear goods through customs.

customs import value The U.S. Customs Service appraisal value of merchandise. Methodologically, the customs value is similar to FAS (free alongside) value since it is based on the value of the product in the foreign country of origin and excludes charges incurred in bringing the merchandise to the United States (import duties, ocean freight, insurance, and so forth); but it differs in that the U.S. Customs Service, not the importer or exporter, has the final authority to determine the value of the good.

customs union An agreement between two or more countries to remove trade barriers with each other and to establish common tariff and nontariff policies with respect to imports from countries outside of the agreement. The European Community is the best-known example.

date draft A draft that matures a specified number of days after the date it is issued, without regard to the date of acceptance.

deferred payment credit Type of letter of credit providing for payment some time after presentation of shipping documents by exporter.

delivered/duty paid Denotes the seller's maximum obligation. "Delivered/ Duty Paid" may be used irrespective of the mode of transport. If the parties wish that the seller should clear the goods for import but that some of the cost payable upon the import of the goods should be excluded—such as value-added tax (VAT) and/or other similar taxes—this should be made clear by adding words to this effect (e.g., "exclusive of VAT and/or taxes").

delivered at frontier The seller's obligations are fulfilled when the goods have arrived at the frontier—but before "the customs border" of the country named in the sales contract. The term is primarily intended to apply to goods by rail or road but is also used irrespective of the mode of transport.

delivery instructions Specific information provided to the inland carrier concerning the arrangement made by the forwarder to deliver the merchandise to the particular pier or steamship line. Not to be confused with delivery order, which is used for import cargo.

demurrage Excess time taken for loading or unloading a vessel. Refers only to situations in which the charter or shipper, rather than the vessel's operator, is at fault.

deposit of estimated duties Refers to antidumping duties that must be deposited upon entry of merchandise that is the subject of an antidumping duty order for each manufacturer, producer, or exporter. Such duties are equal to the amount by which the foreign entity is found to be in violation of dumping regulations.

devaluation The official lowering of the value of one country's currency in market value terms against one or more foreign currencies. (E.g., if the U.S. dollar is devalued in relation to the French franc, one dollar will "buy" fewer francs than before.)

direct investment Defined in the International Monetary Fund's *Balance of Payments Manual* as "investment that is made to acquire a lasting interest in an enterprise operating in an economy other than that of the investor, the investor's purpose being to have an effective voice in the management of the enterprise."

In the United States, direct investment is defined for statistical purposes as the ownership or control, directly or indirectly, by one person of 10 percent of more of the voting securities of an incorporated business enterprise or an equivalent interest in an unincorporated business enterprise. Direct investment transactions are not limited to transactions in voting securities. The percentage ownership of voting securities is used to determine if direct investment exists, but once it is determined that it does, all parent-affiliate transactions, including those not involving voting securities, are recorded under direct investment.

disclosure meeting An informal meeting at which the International Trade Administration methodology used in determining the results of an antidumping investigation or administrative review.

dismissal of petition A determination made by the International Trade Administration that the petition does not properly allege the basis on which antidumping duties may be imposed, does not contain information deemed reasonably available to the petitioner supporting the allegations, or is not filed by an appropriate interested party.

dispatch An amount paid by a vessel's operator to a charter if loading or unloading is completed in less time than stipulated in the charter agreement.

distribution license A bulk license that allows the holder to make multiple exports of authorized commodities to foreign consignees who are approved in advance by the Bureau of Export Administration. The procedure also authorizes approved foreign consignees to reexport among themselves and to certain approved countries.

distributor A foreign agent who sells directly for a supplier and maintains an inventory of the supplier's products.

diversionary dumping Occurs when foreign producers sell to a third-country market at less than fair value and the product is then further processed and shipped to another country.

dock receipt Used to transfer accountability when the export item is moved by the domestic carrier to the port of embarkation and left with the international carrier for export.

document collections, documents against payment Stipulations that the exporter ships goods to the importer without a letter of credit or another form of guaranteed payment. The importer must sign a sight draft before receiving the necessary documents to pick up the goods. Documents against acceptance (D/A) are instructions given by a shipper to a bank stating that the documents transferring title to goods should be delivered to the buyer only upon the signing of a time draft. In this manner, an exporter extends credit to the importer and agrees to accept payment at a readily determined future date.

documentary draft A draft to which documents are attached.

documents against acceptance Instructions given by a shipper to a bank indicating that documents transferring title to goods should be delivered to the buyer (or drawee) only upon the buyer's payment of the attached draft.

domestic exports Includes commodities that are grown, produced, or manufactured in the United States, and commodities of foreign origin that have been changed in the United States, including U.S. Foreign Trade Zones, from the form in which they were imported, or which have been enhanced in value by further manufacture in the United States.

Domestic International Sales Corporation (DISC) The predecessor of the Foreign Sales Corporation,which took on a new definition as a result of the 1984 Tax Reform Act. DISCs can now provide a tax deferral on up to $10 million of exports so long as the funds remain in export-related investments.

downstream dumping Occurs when foreign producers sell at below cost to a producer in its domestic market and the product is then further processed and shipped to another country.

draft bill of exchange A written, unconditional order for payment from one person (the drawer) to another (the drawee). It directs the drawee to pay a specified sum of money, in a given currency, at a specific date to the drawer. A sight draft calls for immediate payment (on sight); a time draft calls for payments at a readily determined future date.

drawback Repayment by a government, in whole or in part, of customs duties assessed on imported merchandise that is subsequently manufactured into a different article or reexported in the same service, or the refund, upon the exportation of an article, or a domestic tax to which it has been subjected.

drawback system Provides the means for processing and tracking of drawback claims. Part of Customs' Automated Commercial System.

drawee The individual or firm on whom a draft is drawn and who owes the indicated amount.

drawer The individual or firm that issues or signs a draft and thus stands to receive payment of the indicated amount from the drawee.

dual pricing The selling of identical products in different markets for different prices. This often reflects dumping practices.

dumping The sale of a commodity in a foreign market at less than fair value. Dumping is generally recognized as unfair, because the practice can disrupt markets and injure producers of competitive products in an importing country. Article VI of the General Agreement on Tariffs and Trade permits imposition of antidumping duties equal to the difference between the price sought in the importing country and the normal value of the product in the exporting country.

With price-price dumping, the foreign producer can use its sales in the high-priced market (usually the home market) to subsidize its sales in the low-priced export market. The price difference is often due to protection in the high-priced market.

Price-cost dumping indicates that the foreign supplier has a special advantage. Sustained sales below cost are normally possible only if the sales are somehow subsidized.

dumping margin The amount by which the imported merchandise is sold in the United States below the home market or third-country price or the constructed value (that is, at less than its "fair value"). For example, if the U.S. "purchase price" is $200 and the fair value is $220, the dumping margin is $20. This margin is expressed as a percentage of the U.S. price. In this example, the margin is 10 percent.

duty A tax imposed on imports by the customs authority of a country. Duties are generally based on the value of the goods (ad valorem duties), some other factors such as weight or quantity (specific duties), or a combination of value and other factors (compound duties).

Eastern Europe Business Information Center (EEBIC) A U.S. Department of Commerce facility that was opened in January 1990 to provide information on trade and investment opportunities in Eastern Europe. EEBIC may be reached at (202) 377-2645 (telephone) and (202) 377-4473 (fax).

Economic Bulletin Board (EBB) A personal computer-based economic bulletin board operated by the U.S. Department of Commerce in Washington, D.C. The EBB is an online source for trade leads and statistical releases from the Bureau of Economic Analysis, the Census Bureau, the International Trade Administration, the Bureau of Labor Statistics, the Federal Reserve Board, Department of the Treasury, and other federal agencies. The EBB may be reached 24 hours each day, 7 days each week, (202) 377-3870.

Economic Community of West African States (ECOWAS) Established in May 1975 by the Treaty of Lagos to bring together 16 West African countries in an economic association aimed at creating a full customs union (not yet achieved). Members are Benin, Burkina Faso, Cape Verde, Cote d'Ivoire, Gambia, Ghana, Guinea, Guinea-Bissau, Liberia, Mali, Mauritania, Niger, Nigeria, Senegal, Sierra Leone, and Togo.

Edge Act corporations Banks that are subsidiaries to bank holding companies or other banks established to engage in foreign business transactions.

enabling clause Part I of the General Agreement on Tariffs and Trade (GATT) framework, which permits developed country members to give more favorable treatment to developing countries and special treatment to the least developed countries, notwithstanding the most-favored-nation provisions of the GATT.

Enterprise for the Americas Initiative (EAI) Launched in June 1990 to develop a new economic relationship of the United States with Latin America. The EAI has trade investment, debt, and environment aspects. With regard to trade, the EAI involves an effort to move toward free trade agreements with markets in Latin America and the Caribbean, particularly with groups of countries that have associated for purposes of trade liberalization.

To begin the process of creating a hemispheric free trade system, the United States seeks to enter into framework agreements on trade and investment with interested countries or groups of countries. These agreements set up intergovernmental councils to discuss and, where appropriate, to negotiate the removal of trade and investment barriers.

entrepot An intermediary storage facility where goods are kept temporarily for distribution within a country or for reexport.

entry summary system An entry is the minimum amount of documentation needed to secure the release of imported merchandise. The Entry Summary System, a part of Customs' Automated Commercial System, contains data on release, summary, rejection, collection, liquidation, and extension or suspension.

escape clause Allows countries temporarily to violate their obligations under the General Agreement on Tariffs and Trade (GATT) to the degree and time necessary to protect a domestic industry from serious injury. Countries taking such actions, however, must consult with affected contracting parties to determine appropriate compensation for the violation of GATT rights, or be subject to retaliatory trade actions.

Section 201 of the Trade Act of 1974 requires the U.S. International Trade Commission to investigate complaints filed by domestic industries or workers claiming that they are injured or threatened by rapidly rising imports.

Section 203 of the act provides that if the ensuing investigation establishes that the complaint is valid, relief may be granted in the form of adjustment assistance, which may be training, technical, and financial assistance, or temporary import restrictions in the form of tariffs, quotas, tariff rate quotas, and/or orderly marketing agreements. Import restrictions imposed under the escape clause authority are limited in duration. They may last no longer than five years but can be extended by the president for a three-year period.

Eurodollars U.S. dollar-denominated deposits in banks and other financial institutions outside the United States. Originating from, but not limited to, the large quantity of U.S. dollar deposits held in Western Europe.

European Bank for Reconstruction and Development (EBRD) Provides assistance through direct loans designed to facilitate the development of market-oriented economies and to promote private and entrepreneurial initiatives. EBRD began financing operations in June 1991. Headquarters are in London.

European Commission One of the five major institutions of the European Community (EC). The commission is responsible for ensuring the implementation of the Treaty of Rome and Community rules and obligations; submission of proposals to the Council of Ministers; execution of the council's decisions; reconciliation of disagreements among council members; administration of EC policies, such as the Common Agricultural Policy and coal and steel policies; taking necessary legal action against firms or member governments; and representing the Community in trade negotiations with nonmember countries.

European Committee for Electrotechnical Standardization A non-profit-making international organization under Belgian law that seeks to harmonize electrotechnical standards published by the national organizations and to remove technical barriers to trade that may be caused by differences in standards. Members are Austria, Belgium, Denmark, Finland, France, Germany, Greece, Iceland, Ireland, Italy, Luxembourg, Netherlands, Norway, Portugal, Spain, Sweden, Switzerland, and the United Kingdom.

European Committee for Standardization (or **Comité européen de normalisation, CEN**) An association of the national standards organizations of 18 countries of the European Economic Communities (EEC) and of the European Free Trade Association (EFTA). CEN membership is open to the national standards organization of any European country that is, or is capable of becoming, a member of the EEC or EFTA. CEN develops voluntary standards in building, machine tools, information technology, and in all sectors including the electrical ones covered by the European Committee for Electrotechnical Standardization. CEN is involved in accreditation of laboratories and certification bodies as well as quality assurance.

European Community A regional organization created in 1958 providing for gradual elimination of intraregional customs duties and other trade barriers, applying a common external tariff against other countries, and providing for gradual adoption of other integrating measures, including a Common Agricultural Policy and guarantees of free movement of labor and capital. The original six members were Belgium, France, West Germany, Italy, Luxembourg, and the Netherlands. Denmark, Ireland, and the United Kingdom became members in 1973, Greece acceded in 1981, and Spain and Portugal in 1986.

European Currency Unit (ecu) A "basket" of specified amounts of each

European Community (EC) currency. Amounts are determined according to the economic size of the EC member and are revised every five years. The value of the ecu is determined by using the current exchange rate of each member currency. All the member states' currencies participate in the ecu basket. The ecu is the community's accounting unit and is a popular private financial instrument.

European Economic Area (EEA) An organization that has been partially implemented to join the member nations of the European Community (EC) and the European Free Trade Association (EFTA). It would comprise 19 nations, nearly 380 million people, and approximately 40 percent of world trade. The EEA is considered a major step toward eventually encompassing all nineteen countries in the EC.

European Free Trade Association (EFTA) A regional organization established in December 1959 by the Stockholm Convention as an alternative to the Common Market, designed to provide a free trade area for industrial products among member countries. Unlike the EC, however, EFTA members did not set up a common external tariff and did not include agricultural trade. The original members were the United Kingdom, Austria, Denmark, Norway, Portugal, Sweden, and Switzerland. The United Kingdom, Denmark, and Portugal left EFTA when they joined the EC. EFTA currently has seven members: Austria, Finland, Iceland, Lichtenstein, Norway, Sweden, and Switzerland. Austria and Sweden have applied for EC membership.

European Investment Bank (EIB) An independent public institution set up by the Treaty of Rome to contribute to balanced and steady development in the European Community. It provides loans and guarantees to companies and public institutions to finance regional development and structural development and achieve cross-border objectives. The EIB has emphasized regional development and energy, with Italy, Greece, and Ireland receiving major support.

European Monetary System A monetary system intended to move Europe toward closer economic integration and avoid the disruptions in trade that can result from fluctuations in currency exchange rates. The EMS member countries deposit gold and dollar reserves with the European Monetary Cooperation Fund in exchange for the issuance of European currency units. Established in 1979. All EC members except Greece and the United Kingdom participate in the exchange rate mechanism of the EMS.

European Organization for Testing and Certification (EOTC) An organization created in October 1990 by the European Community Commission under a memorandum of agreement with member nations and the European Free Trade Association countries. EOTC promotes mutual recognition of tests, test and certification procedures, and quality systems within the European private sector for product areas of characteristics not covered by EC legislative requirements.

European Patent Convention (EPC) An agreement between European nations to centralize and standardize patent law and procedure. The EPC, which took effect in 1977, established a single European patent through application to the European Patent Office in Munich. Once granted, the patent matures into a bundle of individual patents—one in each member country.

exchange permit A government permit sometimes required by the importer's government to enable the importer to convert his or her own country's currency into foreign currency with which to pay a seller in another country.

ex- When used in pricing terms, such as "Ex Factory" or "Ex Dock," it signifies that the price quoted applies only at the point of origin (in the two examples, at the seller's factory or a dock at the import point). In practice, this kind of quotation indicates that the seller agrees to place the goods at the disposal of the buyer at the specific place within a fixed period of time.

Export Administration Act (EAA) As amended in 1979, authorizes the president to control exports of U.S. goods and technology to all foreign destinations, as necessary for the purpose of national security, foreign policy, and short supply. As the basic export administration statute, the EAA is the first big revision of export control law since enactment of the Export Control Act of 1949. The EAA is not a permanent legislation; it must be reauthorized, usually every three years. There were reauthorizations of the EAA in 1982, 1985 (the Export Administration Amendments Act), and 1988 (Omnibus Amendments of 1988), which changed provisions of the basic act. The Export Administration Act of 1990 was pocket vetoed by the president, charging that provisions involved micro management.

Export Administration Regulations Provide specific instructions on the use and types of licenses required and the types of commodities and technical data under control.

Export Administration Review Board (EAB) A cabinet-level export licensing dispute resolution group. The EARB was established in June 1970 under Executive Order 11533. Under Executive Order 12755 of March 1991, EARB membership includes Commerce (as chair), State, Defense, and Energy, and the Departments of the Arms Control and Disarmament Agency and, as nonvoting members the Joint Chiefs of Staff and the Central Intelligence Agency. The EARB is the final review body to resolve differences among agency views on the granting of an export license.

export broker An individual or firm that brings together buyers and sellers for a fee but does not take part in actual sales transactions.

Export Contact List Service (ECLS) A service of the International Trade Association that provides mailing lists of prospective overseas customers from its file of foreign firms (the Foreign Traders Index). The ECLS identifies manufacturers, distributors, retailers, service firms, and government agencies. A summary of the information on the company includes contact information, product and service interests, and other data.

export control classification number A number assigned to every product within the Commerce Control List. The ECCN consists of a five-character number that identifies categories, product groups, strategic level of control, and country groups.

Export Credit Enhanced Leverage (EXCEL) A program developed in 1990 by the World Bank in conjunction with a working group of the International Union of Credit and Investment Insurers (the Berne Union). The objective is to provide export credits at consensus rates for private sector borrowers in highly indebted countries, which would previously have been too great a risk for most agencies to cover.

export declaration Also known as the shipper's export declaration (SED), this form includes complete particulars on an individual shipment and is required by the Department of Commerce to control exports and act as a source document for export statistics.

exporter's sales price A statutory term used to refer to the U.S. sales prices of merchandise that is sold or likely to be sold in the United States, before or after the time of importation, by or for the account of the exporter. Certain statutory adjustments are made to permit a meaningful comparison with the foreign market value of such or similar merchandise; e.g., import duties, U.S. selling and administrative expenses, and freight are deducted from the U.S. price.

Export-Import Bank of the United States (Eximbank) An independent agency chartered in 1934 to finance the export of U.S. goods and services. Eximbank offers four major export finance support programs: loans, guarantees, working capital guarantees, and insurance. Eximbank undertakes some of the risk associated with financing the production and sale of American-made goods; provides financing to overseas customers for American goods when lenders are not prepared to finance the transactions; and enhances a U.S. exporter's ability to match foreign government subsidies by helping lenders meet lower rates or by giving financing incentives directly to foreign buyers.

Export Legal Assistance Network (ELAN) A nationwide group of attorneys with experience in international trade who provide free initial consultations to small businesses on export-related matters. Telephone: (202) 778-3080.

export license A government document authorizing exports of specific goods in specific quantities to a particular destination. This document may be required in some countries for most or all exports and in other countries only under special circumstances.

export management company (EMC) A private firm that serves as the export department for several manufacturers, soliciting and transacting export business on behalf of its clients in return for a commission, salary, or retainer plus commission.

export merchant A company that buys products directly from manufacturers and then packages and marks the merchandise for resale under its own name.

export processing zone Industrial parks designated by a government to provide tax and other incentives to export firms.

export quotas Specific restrictions or target objectives on the value or volume of exports of specified goods imposed by the government of the exporting country. These restraints may be intended to protect domestic producers and consumers from temporary shortages of certain materials or as a means to moderate world prices of specified commodities. Commodity agreements sometimes contain explicit provisions to indicate when export quotas should go into effect among producers. Export quotas are also used in connection with orderly marketing agreements and voluntary restraint agreements.

export revolving line of credit (ERLC) A form of financial assistance provided by the Small Business Administration (SBA). The ERLC guarantees loans to U.S. firms to help bridge the working capital gap between the time inventory and production costs are disbursed until payment is received from a foreign buyer. SBA guarantees 85 percent of the ERLC subject to a $750,000 guarantee limit. The ERLC is granted on the likelihood of a company's satisfactorily completing its export transaction. The guarantee covers default by the exporter but not by a foreign buyer; failure on the buyer's side is expected to be covered by letters of credit or export credit insurance.

export statistics Measurements of the total physical quantity or value of merchandise (except for shipments to U.S. military forces overseas) moving out of the United States to foreign countries, whether such merchandise is exported from within the U.S. Customs territory or from a U.S. Customs bonded warehouse or a U.S. Foreign Trade Zone.

export subsidies Generally, direct government payments or other economic inducements given to domestic producers of goods that are sold in foreign markets. The General Agreement on Tariffs and Trade (GATT) recognizes the export subsidies may distort trade, unduly disturb normal commercial competition, and hinder the achievement of GATT fair trade objectives, but it does not clearly define what practices constitute export subsidies.

export trade certificate of review A certification of partial immunity from U.S. antitrust laws that can be granted based on the Export Trading Company Act legislation by the Department of Commerce with Department of Justice concurrence. Any prospective or present U.S.-based exporter with antitrust concerns may apply for certification.

export trading company (ETC) A company doing business in the United States principally to export goods or services produced in the United States or to facilitate such exports by unaffiliated persons. The ETC can be owned by foreigners and can import, barter, and arrange sales between third countries, as well as export.

Export Trading Company Act (1982) Initiates the Export Trade Certificate of Review program that provides antitrust preclearance for export activities; permits bankers' banks and bank holding companies to invest in export trading companies; and establishes a Contact Facilitation Service within the Commerce Department designed to facilitate contact between firms that produce exportable goods and services and firms that provide export trade services.

ex quay The seller makes the goods available to the buyer on the quay (wharf) at the destination named in the sales contract. The seller has to bear the full cost and risk involved in bringing the goods there. There are two ex quay contracts in use: (1) ex quay duty paid and (2) ex quay duties on buyer's account, in which the liability to clear goods for import is to be met by the buyer instead of by the seller.

ex ship The seller will make the goods available to the buyer on board the ship at the destination named in the sales contract. The seller bears all costs and risks involved in bringing the goods to the destination.

ex works (EXW) At a named point of origin (e.g., ex factory, ex mill, ex warehouse). Under this term, the price quoted applies only at the point of origin, and the seller agrees to place the goods at the disposal of the buyer at a specified place on the date or within the period fixed. All other charges are for the account of the buyer.

factoring The discounting of a foreign account receivable that does not involve a draft. The exporter transfers title to its foreign accounts receivable to a factoring house (an organization that specializes in the financing of accounts receivable) for cash at a discount from the face value. Factoring is often done without recourse to the exporter. Factoring of foreign accounts receivable is less common than with domestic receivables.

factoring houses Companies that purchase export receivables (e.g., the invoices to foreign buyers) at a discounted price, usually about 2–4 percent less than their face value.

fair value The reference against which U.S. purchase prices of imported merchandise are compared during an antidumping investigation. Generally expressed as the weighted average of the exporter's domestic market prices, or prices of exports to third countries during the period of investigation.

In some cases fair value is the constructed value. Constructed value is used if there are no, or virtually no, home market or third-country sales or if the number of such sales made at prices below the cost of production is so great that remaining sales above the cost of production provide an inadequate basis for comparison.

fast track Procedures for approval of trade agreements included by Congress in trade legislation in 1974, in 1979, and again in the 1988 Trade Act. Fast track provides two guarantees essential to the successful negotiation of trade agreements: (1) a vote on implementing legislation within a fixed period of time and (2) a vote, up or down, with no amendments to that legislation.

Provisions in the Omnibus Trade and Competitiveness Act of 1988 include that the foreign country request negotiation of an FTA (Fast Track Authority) and that the president give the Congress a 60-legislative-day notice of intent to negotiate an FTA. During the 60-day period, either committee can disapprove fast track authority by a majority vote. Disapproval would likely end the possibility of FTA negotiations. The 60 legislative days can translate into five to ten months of calendar time, depending on the congressional schedule. Formal negotiations would begin following this 60-day congressional consideration period.

final determination the International Trade Administration makes a final determination after the investigation of sales at "less than fair value" and the receipt of comments from interested parties. This determination usually is made within 75 days after the date a preliminary determination is made. However, if the preliminary determination was affirmative, the exporters who account for a significant proportion of the merchandise under consideration may request, in writing, a postponement of this determination. If the preliminary determination was negative, the petitioner may request a postponement.

In neither case can this postponement be more than 135 days after the date of the preliminary determination. If the final determination is affirmative and follows a negative preliminary determination, the matter is referred to the International Trade Commission (ITC) for a determination of the injury caused or threatened by the sales at less than fair value. (Had the preliminary determination been affirmative, the ITC would have begun its investigation at that time.) Not later than 45 days after the date the International Trade Administration makes an affirmative final determination, in a case where the preliminary determination also was affirmative, the ITC must render its decision on injury. Where the preliminary determination was negative, the ITC must render a decision not later than 75 days after the affirmative final determination. A negative final determination by the assistant secretary for import administration terminates an antidumping investigation.

fines, penalties, and forfeitures system (FPFS) A part of Customs' Automated Commercial System, used to assess, control, and process penalties resulting from violations of law or customs regulations. FPFS provides retrieval of case information for monitoring case status.

force majeure The title of a standard clause in marine contract exempting the parties for nonfulfillment of their obligations as a result of conditions beyond their control, such as earthquakes, floods, or war.

foreign affiliate of a foreign parent With reference to a given U.S. affiliate, any member of the affiliated foreign group owning the U.S. affiliate that is not a foreign parent of the U.S. affiliate.

foreign assets control Sanctions programs involving specific countries and restricting the involvement of U.S. persons in third-country strategic exports, administered by the Treasury Department's Office of Foreign Assets.

foreign availability The Bureau of Export Administration conducts reviews to determine the foreign availability of selected commodities or technology subject to export control. The reviews use four criteria to determine foreign availability: comparable quality, availability-in-fact, foreign source, and adequacy of available quantities that would render continuation of the U.S. control ineffective in meeting its intended purpose. A positive determination of foreign availability means that a non-U.S.-origin item of comparable quality may be obtained by one or more proscribed countries in quantities sufficient to satisfy their needs so that U.S. exports of such item would not make a significant contribution to the military potential of such countries. A positive determination may result in the decontrol of a U.S. product that has been under export control or the approval of an export license. However, the control may be maintained if the president invokes the national security override provision of the act.

Beginning with the 1977 amendments to the Export Administration Act, the Congress directed that products with foreign availability be identified and decontrolled unless essential to national security. In January 1983, a program to assess the foreign availability of specific products was established within the Office of Export Administration, now the Bureau of Export Administration. Amendments to the act in 1985 directed that an Office of Foreign Availability be created.

Foreign Buyer Program (FBP) A joint industry–International Trade Administration (ITA) program to assist exporters in meeting qualified foreign purchasers for their product or service at trade shows held in the United States. ITA selects leading U.S. trade shows in industries with high export potential. Each show selected for the FBP receives promotion through overseas mailings, U.S. embassy and regional commercial newsletters, and other promotional techniques. ITA trade specialists counsel participating U.S. exhibitors.

Foreign Corrupt Practices Act Prohibits U.S. individuals, companies, and direct foreign subsidiaries of U.S. companies from offering, promising, or paying anything of value to any foreign government official in order to obtain or retain business.

Foreign Credit Insurance Association (FCIA) An agency of the Export-Import Bank (Eximbank) that offers insurance covering political and commercial risks on export receivables. FCIA was founded in 1961 as a partnership of Eximbank and a group of private insurance companies. Eximbank is responsible for the political risk and may underwrite or reinsure the commercial risk. FCIA acts as an agent responsible for the marketing and daily administration of the program.

foreign direct investment in the United States The ownership or control, directly or indirectly, by a single foreign person (an individual, or related group of individuals, company, or government) of 10 percent or more of the voting securities of an incorporated U.S. business enterprise or an equivalent interest in an unincorporated U.S. business enterprise, including real property. Such a business is referred to as a U.S. affiliate of a foreign direct investor.

foreign exports Commodities of foreign origin that have entered the United States for consumption or into customs-bonded warehouses or U.S. foreign trade zones, and that, at the time of exportation, are in substantially the same condition as when imported.

foreign flag A reference to a carrier not registered in the United States that flies the American flag. Applies to air and sea transportation.

foreign market value The price at which merchandise is sold, or offered for sale, in the principal markets of the country from which it is exported. If information on foreign home market sales is not useful, the foreign market value is based on prices of exports to third countries or constructed value. Adjustments for quantities sold, circumstances of sales, and differences in the merchandise can be made to those prices to ensure a proper comparison with the prices of goods exported to the United States.

foreign-owned affiliate in the United States A business in the United States in which there is sufficient foreign investment to be classified as direct foreign investment. To determine fully the foreign owners of a U.S. affiliate, three entities must be identified: the foreign parent, the ultimate beneficial owner, and the foreign parent group. All these entities are persons in the broad sense; thus, they may be individuals; business enterprises; governments; religious, charitable, and other nonprofit organizations; estates and trusts; and associated groups.

foreign parent The first foreign person or entity outside the United States in an affiliate's ownership chain that has direct investment in the affiliate. The foreign parent consists only of the first person or entity outside the United States in the affiliate's ownership chain; all other affiliated foreign persons are excluded.

foreign parent group (FPG) Consists of: (1) the foreign parent, (2) any foreign person or entity, proceeding up the foreign parent's ownership chain, that owns more than 50 percent of the party below it, up to and including the ultimate beneficial owner (UBO), and (3) any foreign person or entity, proceeding down the ownership chain(s) of each of these members, that is owned more than 50 percent by the party above it. A particular U.S. affiliate may have several ownership chains above it, if it is owned at least 10 percent by more than one foreign party. In such cases, the affiliate may have more than one foreign parent, UBO, and/or foreign parent group.

foreign person Any person resident outside the United States or subject to the jurisdiction of a country other than the United States. "Person" is any individual, branch, partnership, association, associated group, estate, trust, corporation, or other organization (whether or not organized under the laws of any state), and any government (including a foreign government, the U.S. government, a state or local government, and any agency, corporation, financial institution, or other entity or instrumentality thereof, including a government-sponsored agency).

A U.S. affiliate may have an ultimate beneficial owner (UBO) that is not the immediate foreign parent; moreover, the affiliate may have several ownership chains above it, if it is owned at least 10 percent by more than one foreign person. In such cases, the affiliate may have more than one foreign parent, UBO, and/or foreign parent group.

foreign sales agent An individual or firm that serves as the foreign representative of a domestic supplier and seeks sales abroad for the supplier.

foreign sales corporation A corporation created to secure U.S. tax exemption on a portion of earnings derived from the sale of U.S. products in foreign markets. To qualify for special tax treatment, a FSC must be a foreign corporation, maintain an office outside U.S. territory, maintain a summary of its permanent books of account at the foreign office, and have at least one director resident outside of the United States.

foreign trade zones (FTZs) Special commercial and industrial areas in or near ports of entry where foreign and domestic merchandise, including raw materials, components, and finished goods, may be brought in without being subject to payment of customs duties. Merchandise brought into these zones (also known as free zones, free ports, or bonded warehouses) may be stored, sold, exhibited, repacked, assembled, sorted, graded, cleaned, or otherwise manipulated prior to reexport or entry into the national customs territory.

FTZs are restricted-access sites in or near ports of entry, which are licensed by the Foreign Trade Zones Board and operated under the supervision of the Customs Service. Zones are operated under public utility principles to create and maintain employment by encouraging operations in the United States that might otherwise have been carried on abroad.

Quota restrictions do not normally apply to foreign goods stored in zones, but the board can limit or deny zone use in specific cases on public interest grounds. Domestic goods moved into a zone for export may be considered exported upon entering the zone for purposes of excise tax rebates and drawback.

Subzones are a special-purpose type of ancillary zone authorized by the board, through grantees of public zone, when it can be demonstrated that the activity will result in significant public benefit and is in the public interest. Goods in a zone for a bonafide Customs reason are exempt from state and local ad valorem tax.

Foreign Traders Index The U.S. and Foreign Commercial Service headquarters compilation of overseas contact files, intended for use by domestic businesses. Includes background information on foreign companies, address, contact person, sales figures, size of company, and products by SIC (standardized industrial classification) code.

forfaiting The selling, at a discount, of longer term accounts receivable or promissory notes of the foreign buyer. These instruments may also carry the guarantee of the foreign government. Forfaiting emerged after the Second World War to expedite finance transactions between Eastern and Western European countries, and, more recently, it has become popular in Asian and Third World countries. Both U.S. and European forfaiting houses, which purchase the instruments at a discount from the exporters, are active in the U.S. market.

foul bill of lading A receipt for goods issued by a carrier with an indication that the goods were damaged when received.

free alongside ship (FAS) The seller quotes a price for the goods that includes charges for delivery of the goods alongside a vessel at the port of departure. The seller handles the cost of unloading and wharfage; loading, ocean transportation, and insurance are left to the buyer. Also a method of export and import valuation.

Free Carrier (named point) Designates the seller's responsibility for the cost of loading goods at the named shipping point. It may be used for multimodal transport, container stations, and any mode of transport, including air.

free in A pricing term indicating that the charterer of a vessel is responsible for the cost of loading goods onto the vessel.

free in and out A pricing term indicating that the charterer of a vessel is responsible for the cost of loading and unloading goods from the vessel.

free on board (FOB) The seller quotes the buyer a price that covers all costs up to and including delivery of goods aboard a vessel at a port. Also a method of export valuation.

FOB airport A term based on the same principle as the ordinary free-on-board (FOB) term. The seller's obligations include delivering the goods to the air carrier at the airport of departure. The risk of loss of or damage to the goods is transferred from the seller to the buyer when the goods have been so delivered.

free on rail/free on truck Used when the goods are to be carried by rail. ("Truck" relates to the railway wagons.)

free out A pricing term indicating that the quoted prices include the cost of unloading the goods from the vessel.

free port An area, such as a port city, into which merchandise may legally be moved without payment of duties.

free trade agreement (FTA) An arrangement that establishes unimpeded exchange and flow of goods and services between trading partners regardless of national borders. An FTA does not (as opposed to a common market) address labor mobility across borders or other common policies, such as taxes. Member countries of a free trade area apply their individual tariff rates to countries outside the free trade area.

free trade area A cooperative arrangement by a group of nations whereby trade barriers are removed among the members, but each may maintain its own trade regime with nonmember nations. Allows member countries to maintain individually separate tariff schedules for external countries; members of a customs union employ a common external tariff.

freight Carriage . . . paid to The seller pays the freight for the carriage of the goods to the named destination. However, the risk of loss of or damage to the goods, as well as of any cost increases, is transferred from the seller to the buyer when the goods have been delivered into the custody of the first carrier and not at the ship's rail. The term can be used for all modes of transport, including multimodal operations and container or "roll on–roll off" traffic by trailer and ferries. When the seller has to furnish a bill of lading, waybill, or carrier's receipt, he duly fulfills this obligation by presenting such a document issued by the person with whom he has contracted for carriage to the named destination.

freight Carriage . . . and insurance paid to Same as "Freight/Carriage Paid to . . ." but with the addition that the seller has to procure transport insurance against the risk of loss of damage to the goods during the carriage. The seller contracts with the insurer and pays the insurance premium.

freight forwarder An independent business that handles export shipments for compensation.

GATT Panel A panel of neutral representatives that may be established by the Secretariat of the General Agreement on Tariffs and Trade (GATT) under the dispute settlement provisions of the GATT to review the facts of a dispute and render findings of GATT law and recommend action.

General Agreement on Tariffs and Trade (GATT) A binding contract among 103 governments. GATT was established in 1947 as an interim measure pending the establishment of the International Trade Organization, under the Havana Charter. The International Trade Organization (ITO) was never ratified by Congress. Operating in the absence of an explicit international organization, GATT has provided the legal framework for international trade, with its primary mission being the reduction of trade barriers.

general imports A measure of the total physical arrivals of merchandise from foreign countries, whether such merchandise enters consumption channels immediately or is entered into bonded warehouses or foreign trade zones under customs custody.

general license Licenses, authorized by the Bureau of Export Administration, that permit the export of nonstrategic goods to specified countries without the need for a validated license. No prior written authorization is required, and no individual license is issued.

There are over 20 different types of general licenses, each represented by a symbol. The reason so many general licenses exist is to accommodate the various exporting situations that the Bureau of Export Administration has determined should not require an individual validated license. These licenses include:

General License-BAGGAGE: Authorizes individuals leaving the United States for any destination to take with them as personal baggage the following: personal effects, household effects (including personal computers), vehicles, and tools of the trade (including highly technical ones), provided certain conditions concerning these items pertain.

General License CREW: Authorizes a member of the crew on an exporting carrier to export personal and household items among his or her effects. With some limitations.

General License GATS (Aircraft on Temporary Sojourn): Authorizes the departure from the United States of foreign registry civil aircraft on temporary sojourn in the United States and of U.S. civil aircraft for temporary sojourn abroad.

General License GCG (Shipments to Agencies of Cooperating Governments): Authorizes the export of commodities for official use of any agency of a cooperating government within the territory of the cooperating government.

General License G-COCOM: Authorizes exports to CoCom participating countries, Austria, Finland, Ireland, and Switzerland, for use or consumption therein, of commodities that the United States may approve for export to controlled countries with only notification to the CoCom governments, as well as commodities that may be shipped to China.

General License GCT: Authorizes exports to eligible countries of all "A" level commodities except those specifically excluded by the "Commodities Not Eligible for GCT" paragraphs in certain Export Control Commodity Numbers on the Commodity Control List. Exports may be made under GCT only when intended for use or consumption within the importing country, reexport among and consumption within eligible countries, or reexport in accordance with other provisions of the Export Administration Regulations.

General License G-DEST: Shipments of commodities to destinations not requiring a validated license. The majority of all items exported fall under the provisions of General License G-DEST.

General License–Free World: Authorizes exports of certain low-level commodities subject to national security controls. In most cases, these commodities have performance characteristics that permit the United States to approve exports to controlled countries with only notification to other CoCom governments.

General License GIFT: Authorizes the export of gift parcels by an individual in the United States. Subject to various provisions and limitations.

General License GIT (intransit shipments): Authorizes the export from the United States of commodities that originate in one foreign country and are destined to another foreign country. With limitations.

General License GLR (return or replacement of certain commodities): Authorizes the return or repair of commodities and the replacement of parts. Subject to various provisions.

General License GLV (shipments of limited value): Authorizes a "single shipment" of a commodity when the shipment does not exceed the value limit specified in the GLV paragraph of the ECCN.

General License GTDA (technical data): Available to all destinations. Authorizes exports to all destinations of technical data that are in the public domain and generally available.

General License GTDR: When exporting technical data to free world destinations and the information does not qualify under GTDA and an IVL (individual validated license) is not required, an exporter may use GTDR. GTDR shipments must be accompanied by a written assurance from the foreign consignee stating that neither the technical data nor the direct product thereof will be shipped to Country Groups Q, S, W, Y, or Z, the People's Republic of China, or Afghanistan.

General License G-TEMP: Authorizes the temporary export of commodities and software for temporary use abroad for a period generally not to exceed 12 months. Subject to conditions and exceptions.

General License GTF-U.S. (goods imported for display at U.S. exhibitions or trade fairs): Authorizes the export of commodities that were imported into the United States for display at an exhibition or trade fair; and either entered under bond or permitted temporary free importation under bond providing for their export and are being exported in accordance with the terms of such bond.

General License GUS (shipments to personnel and agencies of the U.S. government): Authorizes the export of commodities and software for personal or official use to any destination. With limitations.

General License Plane Stores: Authorizes the export on aircraft of U.S. or foreign registry departing from the United States of usual and reasonable kinds and quantities of commodities necessary to support the operation of an aircraft, provided the commodities are not intended for unloading in a foreign country and are not exported under a bill of lading as cargo.

General License Ship Stores: Authorizes the export of usual and reasonable kinds and quantities of the commodities to support the operations of a vessel, provided the commodities are not intended for unloading in a foreign country and are not exported under a bill of lading as cargo. With limitations.

general tariff A tariff that applies to countries that do not enjoy preferential or most-favored-nation tariff treatment. Where the general tariff rate differs from the most-favored-nation rate, the general tariff rate is usually the higher rate.

Generalized System of Preferences (GSP) A framework under which developed countries give preferential tariff treatment to manufactured goods imported from certain developing countries. GSP is one element of a coordinated effort by the industrial trading nations to bring developing countries more fully into the international trading system. The U.S. GSP scheme is a system of nonreciprocal tariff preferences for the benefit of these countries. The United States conducts annual GSP reviews to consider petitions requesting modification of product coverage and/or country eligibility. U.S. GSP law requires that a beneficiary country's laws and practices relating to market access, intellectual property rights protection, investment, export practices, and workers' rights be considered in all GSP decisions.

Global Export Manager (GEM) An electronic system for collecting and disseminating trade leads and business opportunities. GEM is maintained by the National Association of State Development Agencies.

global quota A quota on the total imports of a product from all countries.

government procurement policies and practices A nontariff barrier to trade involving the discriminatory purchase by official government agencies of goods and services from domestic suppliers, despite their higher prices or inferior quality, as compared with competitive goods that could be imported.

grandfather clause The General Agreement on Tariffs and Trade (GATT) provision that allows the original contracting parties to exempt from general GATT obligations mandatory domestic legislation that is inconsistent with GATT provisions but existed before the GATT was signed. Newer members may also "grandfather" domestic legislation if that is agreed to in negotiating the terms of accession.

grey list A list of disreputable end users in nations of concern for missile proliferation from the intelligence community. Licensing officials in the Departments of Commerce and State use this list as a cross-reference when reviewing export license applications for sensitive commodities.

gross weight The full weight of a shipment, including goods and packaging. *Compare* tare weight.

Group of . . .

>   Five: Similar to the Group of Seven (G-7), with the exception of Canada and Italy.
>   Seven: This term refers to seven major economic powers (Canada, France, Germany, Great Britain, Italy, Japan, and the United States) whose fi-

nance ministers seek to promote balanced economic growth and stability among exchange rates.

Ten: Under the International Monetary Fund's General Agreements to Borrow (GAB), established in 1962, ten of the wealthiest industrial members of the IMF "stand ready to lend their currencies to the IMF up to specified amounts when supplementary resources are needed." The finance ministers of these countries comprise the Group of 10 (also called the Paris Club).

Fifteen: The G-15, established in 1990, consists of relatively prosperous or large developing countries. The G-15 discusses the benefits of mutual cooperation in improving their international economic positions. Members are Algeria, Argentina, Brazil, Egypt, India, Indonesia, Jamaica, Malaysia (a very active member), Mexico, Nigeria, Peru, Senegal, Venezuela, and Zimbabwe.

Twenty-four: A grouping of finance ministers from 24 developing country members of the International Monetary Fund. The group, representing eight countries from each of the African, Asian, and Latin American country groupings in the Group of 77, was formed in 1971 to counterbalance the influence of the Group of 10.

Seventy-Seven: A grouping of developing countries that had its origins in the early 1960s. This numerical designation persists. The G-77 functions as a caucus for the developing countries on economic matters in many forums, including the United Nations.

Harmonized System (HS) A system for classifying goods in international trade, developed under the auspices of the Customs Cooperation Council. The full title is Harmonized Commodity Description and Coding System. Beginning on January 1, 1989, the new HS numbers replaced previously adhered-to schedules in over 50 countries, including the United States. For the United States, the HS numbers are the numbers that are entered on the actual export and import documents. Any other commodity code classification number (SIC, SITC, end-use, etc.) is a rearrangement and transformation of the original HS numbers.

horizontal export trading company An export trading company that exports a range of similar or identical products supplied by a number of manufacturers or other producers. Webb-Pomerene Organizations, trade-grouped organized export trading companies, and an export trading company formed by an association of agricultural cooperatives are the prime examples of horizontally organized export trading companies.

import certificate A means by which the government of the country of ultimate destination exercises legal control over the internal channeling of the commodities covered by the import certificate.

import license A document required and issued by some national governments authorizing the importation of goods.

import quota A means of restricting imports by the issuance of licenses to importers, assigning each a quota, after determination of the total amount of any commodity to be imported during a period. Import licenses may also specify the country from which the importer must purchase the goods.

import quota auctioning The process of auctioning the right to import specified quantities of quota-restricted goods.

import restrictions Restrictions applied by a country with an adverse trade balance (or for other reasons), reflecting a desire to control the volume of goods coming into the country from other countries. May include the imposition of tariffs or import quotas, restrictions on the amount of foreign currency available to cover imports, a requirement for import deposits, the imposition of import surcharges, or the prohibition of various categories of imports.

import substitution A strategy that emphasizes the replacement of imports with domestically produced goods, rather than the production of goods for export, to encourage the development of domestic industry.

imports Include commodities of foreign origin as well as goods of domestic origin returned to the United States with no change in condition or after having been processed and/or assembled in other countries. For statistical purposes, imports are classified by type of transaction: (1) merchandise entered for immediate consumption ("duty free" merchandise and merchandise on which duty is paid on arrival); (2) merchandise withdrawn for consumption from customs-bonded warehouses, and U.S. foreign trade zones; and (3) merchandise entered into customs-bonded warehouses and U.S. foreign trade zones from foreign countries.

imports for consumption A measurement of the total of merchandise that has physically cleared through U.S. Customs, either entering consumption channels immediately or entering after withdrawal for consumption from bonded warehouses under customs custody or from foreign trade zones. Many countries use the term *special imports* to designate statistics compiled on this basis.

in-bond system A part of Customs' Automated Commercial System, designed to control merchandise from the point of unloading at the port of entry or exportation. The system works with the input of departures (from the port of unlading), arrivals, and closures (accountability of arrivals).

incoterms A codification of terms, maintained by the International Chamber of Commerce (ICC), that is used in foreign trade contracts to define which parties incur the costs and at what specific point the costs are incurred.

Independent European Program Group (IEPG) An intergovernmental organization that is not formally part of the North Atlantic Treaty Organization but whose membership includes all the EC members of the alliance, plus Norway and Turkey. Established in 1976, IEPG's objectives are to promote European cooperation in research, development, and production of defense equipment; improve transatlantic armaments cooperation; and maintain a healthy European defense industrial base.

individual validated license Written approval by the U.S. Department of Commerce granting permission, which is valid for two years, for the export of a specified quantity of products or technical data to a single recipient. Individual validated licenses also are required, under certain circumstances, as authorization for reexport of U.S.-origin commodities to new destinations abroad.

inherent vice An insurance term referring to any defect or other characteristics of a product that could result in damage to the product without external cause. Insurance policies may specifically exclude losses caused by inherent vice.

initial negotiating right (INR) A right held by one member country of the

General Agreement on Tariffs and Trade (GATT) to seek compensation for an impairment of a given bound tariff rate by another GATT country. INRs stem from past negotiating concessions and allow the INR holder to seek compensation for an impairment of tariff concessions regardless of its status as a supplier of the product in question.

injury In U.S. law, a finding by the International Trade Commission that imports are causing, or are likely to cause, harm to a U.S. industry. An injury determination is the basis for a Section 201 case. It is also a requirement in all antidumping and most countervailing duty cases, in conjunction with Commerce Department determinations on dumping and subsidization.

inland bill of lading A bill of lading used in transporting goods overland to the exporter's international carrier. Although a through bill of lading can sometimes be used, it is usually necessary to prepare both an inland bill of lading and an ocean bill of lading for export shipments.

inspection certification A certificate of inspection, required by some purchasers and countries, attesting to the specifications of the goods shipped, usually performed by a third party. Inspection certificates are often obtained from independent testing organizations.

insurance certificate A certificate used to assure the consignee that insurance is provided to cover loss of or damage to the cargo while in transit.

integrated carriers Carriers that have both air and ground fleets or other combinations, such as sea, rail, and truck. Since they usually handle thousands of small parcels an hour, they are less expensive and offer more diverse services than regular carriers.

intellectual property rights The ownership of the right to possess or otherwise use or dispose of products created by human ingenuity.

Inter-American Development Bank (IADB) A regional financial institution established in 1959 to advance the economic and social development of 27 Latin American member countries. Headquarters are in Washington, D.C.

intermediate consignee The bank, forwarding agent, or other intermediary (if any) that acts in a foreign country as an agent for the exporter, the purchaser, or the ultimate consignee, for the purpose of effecting delivery of the export to the ultimate consignee.

International Air Transport Association (IATA) A trade association serving airlines, passengers, shippers, travel agents, and governments. Headquarters are in Geneva, Switzerland.

International Anticounterfeiting Coalition (IACC) A nonprofit organization, founded in 1978, located in Washington, D.C. The IACC seeks to advance intellectual property rights (IPR) protection on a worldwide basis by promoting laws, regulations, and directives designed to render theft of IPR unattractive and unprofitable.

International Bank for Reconstruction and Development (IBRD) Popularly known as the World Bank. Established in 1944 to help countries reconstruct their economies after World War II. IBRD now assists developing member countries by lending to government agencies or by guaranteeing private loans for such projects as agricultural modernization or infrastructural development.

international banking facility (IBF) One of four categories of foreign banking in the United States. An IBF is a set of asset and liability accounts that is segregated and limited to financing international trade.

International Centre for Settlement of Investment Disputes (ICSID) A separate organization of the World Bank, was established in October 1966. The ICSID encourages greater flows of investment capital by providing facilities for the conciliation and arbitration of disputes between governments and foreign investors. The ICSID also conducts and publishes research in foreign investment law.

international commodity agreement (ICA) An international understanding, usually reflected in a legal instrument, relating to trade in a particular basic commodity, and based on terms negotiated and accepted by most of the countries that export and import commercially significant quantities of the commodity. Some commodity agreements (such as exist for coffee, cocoa, natural rubber, sugar, and tin) center on economic provisions intended to defend a price range for the commodity through use of buffer stocks or export quotas or both. Other commodity agreements (such as existing agreements for jute and jute products, olive oil, and wheat) promote cooperation among producers and consumers through improved consultation, exchange of information, research and development, and export promotion.

International Development Association (IDA) An affiliate of the World Bank Group that was created in 1959 to lend money to developing countries at no interest and for a long repayment period. By providing development assistance through soft loans, IDA meets the needs of many developing countries that cannot afford development loans at ordinary rates of interest and in the time span of conventional loans.

International Development Cooperation Agency (IDCA) Coordinating body of all aspects of U.S. economic assistance and cooperation with less developed countries. IDCA consists of three parts: AID (Agency for International Development), TDP (Trade and Development Program), and the Overseas Private Investment Corporation (OPIC). The administrator of AID currently serves as the acting director of IDCA.

International Electrotechnical Commission (IEC) Established in 1906 to deal with questions related to international standardization in the electrical and electronic engineering fields. The members of the IEC are the national committees, one for each country, which are required to be as representative as possible of all electrical interests in the country concerned: manufacturers, users, governmental authorities, teaching, and professional bodies. They are composed of representatives of the various organizations that deal with questions of electrical standardization at the national level. Most of them are recognized and supported by their governments.

International Emergency Economic Powers Act (IEEPA) Enacted in 1977 to extend emergency powers previously granted to the president by the Trading with the Enemy Act of 1917 (which still authorized the president to exercise extraordinary powers when the United States is at war). IEEPA enables the president, after declaring that a national emergency exists because of a threat from a source outside the United States, to investigate, regulate, compel, or prohibit virtually any economic transaction involving property in which a foreign country or national has an interest.

International Finance Corporation (IFC) Established in 1956 as a member of the World Bank Group to promote capital flow into private investment in developing countries.

International Maritime Organization (IMO) Established as a specialized agency of the United Nations in 1948 to facilitate cooperation on technical matters affecting merchant shipping and traffic.

International Monetary Fund (IMF) Established in 1946 to act as the banker of last resort for countries experiencing foreign exchange deficiencies and to monitor currency exchange relationships among nations.

International Standards Organization (ISO) Established in 1947 as a worldwide federation of national bodies, representing approximately 90 member countries. The scope covers standardization in all fields except electrical and electronic engineering standards, which are the responsibility of the International Electrotechnical Commission (IEC). Together, the ISO and IEC form the specialized system for worldwide standardization—the world's largest nongovernmental system for voluntary industrial and technical collaboration at the international level.

The result of ISO technical work is published as International Standards. There are, for example, ISO standards for the quality grading of steel; for testing the strength of woven textiles; for storage of citrus fruits; for magnetic codes on credit cards; for automobile safety belts; and for ensuring the quality and performance of such diverse products as surgical implants, ski bindings, wire ropes, and photographic lenses.

International Trade Commission An independent U.S. government fact-finding agency with six commissioners who review and make recommendations concerning countervailing duty and antidumping petitions submitted by U.S. industries seeking relief from imports that benefit unfair trade practices. Known as the U.S. Tariff Commission before its mandate was broadened by the Trade Act of 1974.

International Telecommunication Union (ITU) A specialized agency of the United Nations with responsibilities for developing operational procedures and technical standards for the use of the radio frequency spectrum, the satellite orbit, and the international public telephone and telegraph network. There are over 160 member nations. The radio regulations that result from ITU conferences have treaty status and provide the principal guidelines for world telecommunications. In the case of the United States, they are the framework for development of the U.S. national frequency allocations and regulations. The ITU has four permanent organs: the General Secretariat, the International Frequency Registration Board (IFRB), the International Radio Consultative Committee (CCIR), and the International Telegraph and Telephone and Consultative Committee ITTCC).

invisibles Areas of nonmerchandise "invisible trade" that include expenses such as freight and insurance and most types of services and investment.

irrevocable letter of credit A letter of credit in which the specified payment is guaranteed by the bank if all terms and conditions are met by the drawee.

J curve and real exchange rates Accounts for the phenomenon that the current account may initially worsen before improving in response to real depreciation in exchange rates, because it takes time for the growth of import volumes to decline in response to higher import prices. So called because the downward movement followed by an upward movement in the current account resembles the letter J.

Japan Corporate Program Initiated by the U.S. Department of Commerce to help increase U.S. exports to Japan. The program was initiated in January 1991, following selection of 20 companies to participate in a five-year pilot project to improve U.S. knowledge of, and access to, the Japanese market. As part of the five-year commitment to the program, the companies arrange four visits a year to Japan, including two by their chief executives; publish product literature in Japanese; participate in at least one trade promotion event in Japan each year; and modify products to enhance consumer acceptance and promote sales in Japan. The Department of Commerce supports the 20 firms with market data, arranges introductory meetings with prospective Japanese buyers, and recommends market development strategies.

Japan Export Information Center Provides information on doing business in Japan, market entry alternatives, market information and research, product standards and testing requirements, tariffs, and nontariff barriers. The center maintains a commercial library and participates in private- and government-sponsored seminars on doing business in Japan. JEIC is operated by the International Trade Administration of the Department of Commerce. Telephone: (202) 377-2425 and (202) 377-4524; fax: (202) 377-0469.

Japan External Trade Organization (JETRO) Although legally under the aegis of the Ministry of International Trade and Industry (MITI), JETRO administers the export programs of the Japanese government independently. MITI subsidizes about 60 percent of JETRO's total annual expenditures and, technically, has final decision-making authority over JETRO management and programs. Originally established to help Japanese firms export, JETRO also assists American companies seeking to export to Japan and promotes Japanese direct investment in the United States and U.S. direct investment in Japan.

Joint Committee for Investment and Trade (JCIT) Established in October 1990 to demonstrate U.S. and Mexican commitment to greater economic cooperation. The committee identifies trade and investment opportunities and coordinates trade promotion events.

joint venture A business undertaking in which more than one firm shares ownership and control of production and/or marketing.

keiretsu The horizontally and vertically linked industrial structure of postwar Japan. The horizontally linked groups include a broad range of industries linked by banks and general trading firms. There are eight major industrial groups, sometimes referred to as *Kigyo Shudan*: Mitsubishi, Mitsui, Sumitomo, Fuyo, DKB, Sanwa, Tokai, and IBJ. The vertically linked groups (such as Toyota, Matshushita, and Sony) are centered around parent companies, with subsidiaries frequently serving as suppliers, distributors, and retail outlets. Common characteristics among the groups include crossholding of company shares, intragroup financing, joint investment, mutual appointment of officers, and other joint business activities. The *keiretsu* system emphasizes mutual cooperation and protects affiliates from mergers and acquisitions. Ties within groups became looser after the oil shocks of the 1970s as a result of decreasing dependence on banks for capital.

Latin American Integration Association (LAIA) Created by the 1980 Montevideo Treaty as a replacement to the Latin American Free Trade Association (LAFTA). LAFTA was rejected because members felt its rules governing integration trends were too rigid. LAIA, an association involving Argentina, Bolivia, Brazil, Chile, Colombia, Ecuador, Mexico, Paraguay, Peru, Uruguay, and Venezuela, has since declined as a major Latin American integration effort in favor of regional efforts, such as Mercosur.

letter of credit A financial document issued by a bank at the request of the consignee guaranteeing payment to the shipper for cargo if certain terms and conditions are fulfilled. Normally it contains a brief description of the goods, documents required, a shipping date, and an expiration date after which payment will no longer be made.

- Irrevocable letter of credit. One that obligates the issuing bank to pay the exporter when all terms and conditions of the letter of credit have been met. None of the terms and conditions may be changed without the consent of all parties to the letter of credit.
- Revocable letter of credit. Subject to possible recall or amendment at the option of the applicant, without the approval of the beneficiary.
- Confirmed letter of credit. Issued by a foreign bank with its validity confirmed by a U.S. bank. An exporter who requires a confirmed letter of credit from the buyer is assured payment from the U.S. bank in case the foreign buyer or bank defaults.
- Documentary letter of credit. One for which the issuing bank stipulates that certain documents must accompany a draft. The documents assure the applicant (importer) that the merchandise has been shipped and that title to the goods has been transferred to the importer.

less developed country (LDC) A country with low per capita gross national product. Terms such as *Third World, poor, developing nations,* and *underdeveloped* have also been used to describe less developed countries.

lesser developed countries (LLDC) A classification developed by the United Nations to give some guidance to donor agencies and countries about an equitable allocation of foreign assistance. The criteria for designating a country an LLDC, originally adopted by the U.N. Committee for Development Planning in 1971, have been modified several times. Criteria have included low per capita income, literacy, and manufacturing share of the country's total gross domestic product. There is continuing concern that the criteria should be more robust and less subject to the possibility of easy fluctuation of a country between less developed and least developed status.

licensing A business arrangement in which the manufacturer of a product (or a firm with proprietary rights over certain technology, trademarks, etc.) grants permission to some other group or individual to manufacture that product (or make use of that proprietary material) in return for specified royalties or other payment.

Line Release System A part of Customs' Automated Commercial System, designed for the release and tracking of shipments through the use of personal computers and bar code technology. To qualify for line release, a commodity must have a history of invoice accuracy and be selected by local customs districts on the basis of high volume. To release the merchandise, customs reads the bar code into a personal computer, verifies that the bar code matches the invoice data, and enters the quantity. The cargo release is transmitted to the Automated Commercial System, which establishes an entry and the requirement for an entry summary, and provides the Automated Broker Interface system participants with release information.

Lome Convention A 1975 agreement between the European Community (EC) and 62 African, Caribbean, and Pacific (ACP) states (mostly former colonies of the EC members). The agreement covers some aid provisions as well as trade and tariff preferences for the ACP countries when shipping to the EC. Lome grew out of the 1958 Treaty of Rome's association with the 18 African colonies/countries that had ties with Belgium and France. The ACP members are Angola, Bahamas, Barbados, Benin, Botswana, Burkina Faso, Burundi, Cameroon, Cape Verde, Central African Republic, Chad, Comoros, Congo, Cote d'Ivoire, Djibouti, Dominica, Equatorial Guinea, Ethiopia, Fiji, Gabon, Gambia, Ghana, Grenada, Guinea, Guinea-Bissau, Guyana, Jamaica, Kenya, Lesotho, Liberia, Madagascar, Malawi, Mali, Mauritius, Mauritania, Mozambique, Namibia, Niger, Nigeria, Papua New Guinea, Rwanda, Saint Lucia, Saint Vincent, Samoa, Sao Tome and Principe, Senegal, Seychelles, Sierra Leone, Solomon Islands, Somalia, Sudan, Suriname, Swaziland, Tanzania, Togo, Trinidad and Tobago, Uganda, Zaire, Zambia, and Zimbabwe.

London interbank offered rate (LIBOB) The interest rate that major international banks charge each other for large-volume loans of Eurodollars or dollars on deposit outside the United States.

maquiladora A program that allows foreign manufacturers to ship components into Mexico duty free for assembly and subsequent reexport. Industry established under the *maquiladora* program is Mexico's second largest source of foreign revenue (following oil exports).

In December 1989, the Mexican government liberalized the *maquiladora* program to make this a more attractive and dynamic sector of the economy. As a result, *maquiladora* operations may import, duty, and import, license free, products not directly involved in production, but that support production, including computers and other administrative materials and transportation equipment.

marine cargo insurance Broadly, insurance covering loss of or damage to goods at sea. Marine insurance typically compensates the owner of merchandise for losses in excess of those that can be legally recovered from the carrier that are sustained from fire, shipwreck, piracy, and various other causes.

market access Refers to the openness of a national market to foreign products. Market access reflects a government's willingness to permit imports to compete relatively unimpeded with similar domestically produced goods.

market disruption Refers to a situation created when a surge of imports in a given product line causes sales of domestically produced goods in a particular country to decline to an extent that the domestic producers and their employees suffer major economic hardship.

Market-Oriented Sector-Selective (MOSS) Talks begun in January 1985 as bilateral trade discussions between the United States and Japan in an effort to remove many trade barriers at once in a given sector. MOSS talks have focused on five sectors: telecommunications, medical equipment and pharmaceuticals, electronics, forest products, and auto parts. Overall, the talks focus high-level attention on reducing certain market obstacles and opening communication channels to resolve follow-up disputes.

markings Letters, numbers, and other symbols placed on cargo packages to facilitate identification.

marks of origin The physical markings on a product that indicate the country of origin where the article was produced. Customs rules require marks of origin of most countries.

matchmaker events Trade delegations organized and led by the International Trade Administration to help new-to-export and new-to-market firms meet prescreened prospects who are interested in their products or services in overseas markets. Matchmaker delegations usually target two major country markets in two countries and limit trips to a week or less. This approach is designed to permit U.S. firms to interview a maximum number of prospective overseas business partners with a minimum of time away from their home office. The program includes U.S. embassy support, briefings on market requirements and business practices, and interpreters' services. Matchmaker events, based on specific product themes and end users, are scheduled for a limited number of countries each year.

Mercosur (Mercosul; Southern Common Market) Comprising Argentina, Brazil, Paraguay, and Uruguay and scheduled to enter into force in December 1994 for Argentina and Brazil and December 1995 for Paraguay and Uruguay. Mercosur, modeled similarly to the European Community's Treaty of Rome, will establish a common external tariff and eliminate barriers to trade in services. In the Southern Cone, Chile has not sought entry to Mercosur but does have an agreement with Argentina that will provide for some similar benefits.

Military Critical Technologies List (MCTL) A document listing technologies that the U.S. Defense Department considers to have current or future utility in military systems. The MCTL describes arrays of design and manufacturing know-how; keystone manufacturing, inspection, and test equipment; and goods accompanied by sophisticated operation, application, and maintenance know-how. Military justification for each entry is included in a classified version of the list.

Ministry of International Trade and Industry (MITI) One of the three most powerful and prestigious ministries of Japan's central government (along with the Ministry of Finance and the Ministry of Foreign Affairs). In formulating and implementing Japan's trade and industrial policies, MITI is responsible for funding most of Japan's export promotion programs (although operation of these programs is left to JETRO). The ministry also supervises the export financing programs of Japan's Export-Import Bank, operates several types of export insurance programs, supports research organizations, and facilitates various types of overseas technical and cooperation training programs. Lately, MITI has assumed a role in encouraging imports of foreign products into Japan.

mixed credit The practice of combining concessional and market-rate export credit as an export promotion mechanism.

most-favored-nation (MFN) treatment A commitment that a country will extend to another country the lowest tariff rates it applies to any other country. All contracting parties undertake to apply such treatment to one another under Article I of the General Agreement on Tariffs and Trade (GATT). When a country agrees to cut tariffs on a particular product imported from one country, the tariff reduction automatically applies to imports of this product from any other country eligible for most-favored-nation treatment. This principle of nondiscriminatory treatment of imports appeared in numerous bilateral trade agreements prior to establishment of GATT. A country is under no obligation to extent MFN treatment to another country unless both are bilateral contracting parties of the GATT or MFN treatment is specified in a bilateral agreement.

Multilateral Investment Fund Provides program and project grants to advance specific, market-oriented investment policy initiatives and reforms and encourages domestic and foreign investment in Latin America and the Caribbean. Under the Enterprise for the Americas Initiative, the fund complements the Inter-American Development Bank.

Multilateral Investment Guarantee Agency (MIGA) Established in 1988 as a part of the World Bank Group to encourage equity investment and other direct investment flows to developing countries through the mitigation of noncommercial investment barriers. The agency offers investors guarantees against noncommercial risks; advises developing member governments on the design and implementation of policies, programs, and procedures related to foreign investments; and sponsors a dialogue between the international business community and host governments on investments issues.

multilateral trade negotiations The eight multilateral rounds of negotiations held under the auspices of the General Agreement on Tariffs and Trade since 1947.

National Association of State Development Agencies (NASDA) Formed in 1946 to provide a forum for directors of state economic development agencies to exchange information, compare programs, and deal with issues of mutual interest. NASDA's organization includes international trade and foreign investment components. Trade activities include maintenance of a state export program database.

national security controls Restrictions on exports of U.S. goods and technology that would make a significant contribution to the military potential of another country and thus be detrimental to the national security of Western countries.

National Trade Estimates Report An annual report by the U.S. Trade Representative that identifies significant foreign barriers to and distortions of trade.

national treatment Affords individuals and firms of foreign countries the same competitive opportunities, including market access, as are available to domestic parties.

net foreign investment The sum of U.S. exports of goods and services, receipts of factor income, and capital grants received by the United States (net), less the sum of imports of goods and services by the United States, payments of factor income, and transfer payments to foreigners (net). It may also be viewed as the acquisition of foreign assets by U.S. residents, less the acquisition of U.S. assets by foreign residents.

newly industrializing countries (NICs) A term, originated by the Organization for Economic Cooperation and Development, describing nations of the Third World that have enjoyed rapid economic growth and can be described as middle-income countries (such as Singapore and the Republic of Korea).

nontariff barriers (NTBs) Market access barriers that result from prohibitions, restrictions, conditions, or specific requirements and make exporting products difficult and/or costly. The term covers any restriction or quota, charge, or policy, other than traditional customs duties, domestic support programs, discriminatory labeling and health standards, and exclusive business practices which limit the access of imported goods. NTBs may result from government or private sector actions.

nontariff measures (NTMs) Includes import quotas or other quantitative restrictions, nonautomatic import licensing, customs surcharges or other fees and charges, customs procedures, export subsidies, unreasonable standards or standards-setting procedures, government procurement restrictions, inadequate intellectual property protection, and investment restrictions.

Participants in the Tokyo Round attempted to address these barriers through the negotiations of a number of General Agreement on Tariffs and Trade (GATT) codes, open for signature to all GATT members. Seven codes were negotiated during the Tokyo Round, covering customs valuations, import licensing, subsidies and countervailing duties, antidumping duties, standards, government procurement, and trade in civil aircraft.

Although the Tokyo Round codes alleviated some of the problems caused by nontariff measures, overall use of NTMs has increased since conclusion of the Tokyo Round.

North American Free Trade Agreement (NAFTA) A proposed free trade agreement that would comprise Canada, the United States, and Mexico, exceeding 360 million consumers and a combined output of $6 trillion—20 percent larger than the European Community.

North Atlantic Treaty Organization (NATO) A defense-oriented organization. NATO members are Belgium, Canada, Denmark, France (which was only partial membership), Greece, Iceland, Italy, Luxembourg, Netherlands, Norway, Portugal, Spain, Turkey, United Kingdom, and Germany. With the end of the cold war, NATO's role is being redefined.

ocean bill of lading A receipt for the cargo and a contract for transportation between a shipper and the ocean carrier. It may also be used as an instrument of ownership that can be bought, sold, or traded while the goods are in transit. To be used in this manner, it must be a negotiable "order" bill of lading.

- Clean bill of lading. Issued when the shipment is received in good order. If damaged or a shortage is noted, a clean bill of lading will not be issued.
- On board bill of lading. Certifies that the cargo has been placed aboard the named vessel and is signed by the master of the vessel or representative. On letter of credit transactions, an on board bill of lading is usually necessary for the shipper to obtain payment from the bank. When all bills of lading are processed, a ship's manifest is prepared by the steamship line. This summarizes all cargo aboard the vessel by port of loading and discharge.
- Inland bill of lading (a waybill on rail or the "pro forma" bill-of-lading in trucking). Used to document the transportation of the goods between the port and the point of origin or destination. It should contain information such as marks, numbers, steamship line, and similar information to match with a dock receipt.

official development assistance Financial flows to developing countries and multilateral institutions provided by official agencies of national, state, or local governments. Each transaction must be administered with the promotion of the economic development and welfare of developing countries as its main objective and concessional in character and contain a grant element of at least 25 percent.

offsets Industrial compensation practices mandated by many foreign governments when purchasing U.S. defense systems. Types of offsets include mandatory coproduction, subcontractor production, technology transfer, countertrade, and foreign investment. Countries require offsets for a variety of reasons: to ease (or "offset") the burden of large defense purchases on their economies, to increase domestic employment, to obtain desired technology, or to promote targeted industrial sectors.

In nondefense trade, governments sometimes impose offset requirements on foreign exporters as a condition for approval of major sales agreements in an effort to reduce the adverse trade impact of a major sale or to gain specified industrial benefits for the importing country. In these circumstances, offset requirements generally take one of two forms. In one formulation, an exporter may be required to purchase a specified amount of locally produced goods or services from the importing country. For example, a commercial aircraft manufacturer seeking sales to an airline in another country might be required to purchase products as different from airplanes as canned hams. In other instances, an exporter might be required to establish manufacturing facilities in the importing country or to secure a specified percentage of the components used in manufacturing the product from established local manufacturers.

open account A trade arrangement in which goods are shipped to a foreign buyer before, and without written guarantee of, payment. Because this method poses an obvious risk to the supplier, it is essential that the buyer's integrity be unquestionable.

open insurance policy A marine insurance policy that applies to all of the shipments made by an exporter over a period of time rather than to a single shipment.

orderly marketing agreement A bilateral agreement between governments by which one government limits exports to the other. Similar to a voluntary export restriction agreement or a voluntary restraint agreement. Used to address injury to a domestic industry.

Contracts negotiated between two or more governments, in which the exporting nation undertakes to ensure that international trade in specified "sensitive" products will not disrupt, threaten, or impair competitive industries or workers in importing countries.

Organization of African Unity (OAU) Founded in May 1963 with 32 African countries as original members; it had 51 members in 1990. The organization aims to further African unity and solidarity, to coordinate political, economic, cultural, scientific, and defense policies; and to eliminate colonialism in Africa. Members are Algeria, Angola, Benin, Botswana, Burkina Faso, Burundi, Cameroon, Cape Verde, Central Africa Republic, Chad, Comoros, Congo, Cote d'Ivoire, Egypt, Equatorial Guinea, Ethiopia, Gabon, the Gambia, Ghana, Guinea, Guinea-Bissau, Kenya, Lesotho, Liberia, Libya, Madagascar, Malawi, Mali, Mauritania, Mauritius, Morocco, Mozambique, Namibia, Niger, Nigeria, Rwanda, São Tome and Principe, Senegal, Seychelles, Sierra Leone, Somalia, Sudan, Swaziland, Tanzania, Togo, Tunisia, Uganda, Zaire, Zambia, and Zimbabwe.

Organization of American States (OAS) A regional organization established in April 1948 to promote Latin American economic and social development. Members are the United States, Mexico, and most Central American, South American, and Caribbean nations: Antigua and Barbuda, Argentina, the Bahamas, Barbados, Belize, Bolivia, Brazil, Canada, Chile, Colombia, Costa Rica, Cuba (participation suspended), Dominica, Dominican Republic, Ecuador, El Salvador, Grenada, Guatemala, Guyana, Haiti, Honduras, Jamaica, Mexico, Nicaragua, Panama, Paraguay, Peru, St. Christopher–Nevis, St. Lucia, St. Vincent and the Grenadines, Surinam, Trinidad and Tobago, the United States, Uruguay, and Venezuela.

Organization for Economic Cooperation and Development (OECD) The primary forum for the discussion of common economic and social issues confronting the United States, Canada, Western Europe, Japan, Australia, and New Zealand. It was founded in 1960 as the successor to the Organization for European Economic Cooperation, which oversaw European participation in the Marshall Plan. The OECD's fundamental objective is "to achieve the highest sustainable economic growth and employment and a rising standard of living in member countries while maintaining financial stability and thus contribute to the world economy." Members are Australia, Austria, Belgium-Luxembourg, Canada, Denmark, Finland, France, Germany, Greece, Iceland, Ireland, Italy, Japan, the Netherlands, New Zealand, Norway, Portugal, Spain, Sweden, Switzerland, Turkey, the United Kingdom, and the United States.

Organization of the Islamic Conference (OIC) Established in May 1971 to promote cooperation in cultural, economic, scientific, and social areas among Islamic nations. Headquarters are located in Jeddah, Saudi Arabia. Members are Afghanistan, Algeria, Bahrain, Bangladesh, Benin, Brunei, Burkina Faso, Cameroon, Chad, Comoros, Cyprus, Djibouti, Egypt, Gabon, the Gambia, Guinea, Guinea-Bissau, Indonesia, Iran, Iraq, Jordan, Kuwait, Lebanon, Libya, Malaysia, Maldives, Mali, Mauritania, Morocco, Niger, Nigeria, Oman, Pakistan, Qatar, Saudi Arabia, Senegal, Sierra Leone, Somalia, Sudan, Syria, Tunisia, Turkey, Uganda, the United Arab Emirates, and Yemen.

Organization of Petroleum Exporting Countries (OPEC) An association of the world's oil-producing countries, formed in 1960. The chief purpose of

OPEC is to coordinate the petroleum policies of its members: Algeria, Ecuador, Gabon, Indonesia, Iran, Iraq, Kuwait, Libya, Nigeria, Qatar, Saudi Arabia, the United Arab Emirates, and Venezuela.

overseas business reports Marketing studies of the major U.S. trading partners that provide updated export and economic outlooks, industrial trends, trade regulations, distribution and sales channels, transportation, and credit situation in individual countries. Available through ITA offices.

Overseas Private Investment Corporation (OPIC) A government corporation that assists U.S. private investments in less developed nations. These investments may include distributorships owned by U.S. manufacturers that are consistent with the economic interests of both the United States and the developing country involved. Telephone: (800) 424-6742.

Paris Club Under the International Monetary Fund's General Agreements to Borrow (GAB), established in 1962, ten of the wealthiest industrial members of the IMF agreed to lend funds to the IMF, up to specified amounts when supplementary resources are needed. The finance ministers of these countries comprise the Paris Club (also called the Group of 10).

The Paris Club has become a popular designation for meetings between representatives of a developing country that wishes to renegotiate its "official" debt (normally excluding debts owed by and to the private sector without official guarantees) and representatives of the relevant creditor governments and international institutions. These meetings usually occur at the request of a debtor country that wishes to consolidate all or part of its debt service payments falling due over a specified period. Meetings are traditionally chaired by a senior official of the French Treasury Department. Comparable meetings occasionally take place in London and in New York for countries that wish to renegotiate repayment terms for their debts to private banks. These meetings are sometimes called "creditor clubs."

Paris Convention for the Protection of Industrial Property The major international agreement providing basic rights for protecting industrial property. It covers patents, industrial designs, service marks, trade names, indications of source, and unfair competition. The U.S. ratified this treaty in 1903. The treaty, adopted in 1883, provides two fundamental rights.

The principle of national treatment provides that nationals of any signatory nation shall enjoy in all other countries of the union the advantages that each nation's laws grant to its own nationals. The right of priority enables any resident or national of a member country to, first, file a patent application in any member country and, thereafter, file a patent application for the same invention in any of the other member countries within 12 months of the original filing and receive benefit of the original filing date.

Patent Cooperation Treaty (PCT) A worldwide convention open to the member of any Paris Convention country. The PCT entered into force in 1978. Unlike the Paris Convention, which addresses substantive intellectual property rights, the PCT addresses procedural requirements, aiming to simplify the filing, searching, and publication of international patent applications.

Phytosanitary Inspection Certificate A certificate issued by the U.S. Department of Agriculture to satisfy import regulations of foreign countries, indicating that a U.S. shipment has been inspected and is free from harmful pests and plant diseases.

portfolio investment Any foreign investment that is not direct investment. Foreign portfolio investment includes the purchase of voting securities (stocks) at less than a 10 percent level, bonds, trade finance, and government lending or borrowing, excluding transactions in official reserves.

postshipment verifications (PSVs) Conducted to determine that a commodity is being used for the purposes for which its export was licensed. Firms or individuals representing the end user, intermediate consignees, or the purchaser may be subject to inquiries pertaining to the post-shipment verification. As part of the PSV process, the Bureau of Export Administration forwards a cable to the U.S. embassy or consulate in the respective geographical location to conduct an on-site inspection to ensure that the commodity is physically present and used as stated in the application. Postshipment verifications are usually conducted six to eight months subsequent to export of the commodity.

Preferential Trade Agreement for Eastern and Southern Africa (PTA) Established in 1981 with headquarters in Lusaka, Zambia. The PTA's 19 members are Burundia, Comoros, Djibouti, Ethiopia, Kenya, Lesotho, Malawi, Mauritius, Rwanda, Somalia, Swaziland, Tanzania, Uganda, Zambia, and Zimbabwe. It is essentially a regional trade group that oversees tariff reductions for member states.

prelicense checks Conducted to determine that a request for a license to export a controlled commodity represents a legitimate order. Firms or individuals representing the licensee (the applicant), a consignee, the purchaser, an intermediate consignee, or the end user may be subject to inquiries pertaining to the pre-license check. As part of the process, the Bureau of Export Administration (BXA) forwards a cable to the U.S. embassy or consulate in the respective geographical location to conduct an inspection or meet with company representatives to conduct inquiries on BXA's behalf.

preliminary determination The dumping determination by the International Trade Administration announcing the results of the investigation conducted within 160 days (or, in extraordinarily complicated cases, 210 days) after a petition is filed or an investigation is self-initiated by the International Trade Administration. If the International Trade Administration determines that there is a reasonable basis to believe or suspect that the merchandise under consideration is being sold or is likely to be sold at less than fair value, liquidation of all affected entries is suspended, and the matter is referred to the International Trade Commission (ITC). "Preliminary determination" also refers to the decision by the ITC where there is a reasonable indication that an industry in the United States is materially injured, or threatened with material injury, or the establishment of an industry in the United States is materially retarded by reason of the imports of the merchandise that is the subject of the petition. The ITC must make its decision within 45 days after the date on which the petition is filed or an investigation is self-initiated by the International Trade Administration. If this determination is negative, the investigation is terminated.

President's Export Council (PEC) An adviser to the president on government policies and programs that affect U.S. trade performance; promote export expansion; and provide a forum for discussing and resolving trade-related problems among the business, industrial, agricultural, labor, and government sectors.

The council was established by executive order of the president in 1973 and originally was composed only of business executives. The council was reconstituted in 1979 to include leaders of the labor and agricultural communities, Congress, and the executive branch.

Twenty-eight private sector members serve "at the pleasure of the president" with no set term of office. Other members include five U.S. senators and five members of the House; the secretaries of agriculture, commerce, labor, state, and treasury; the chairman of the Export-Import Bank; and the U.S. trade representative. The council reports to the president through the secretary of commerce.

Private Export Funding Corporation (PEFCO) Works with the Export-Import Bank in using private capital to finance U.S. exports. PEFCO acts as a supplemental lender to traditional commercial banking sources by making loans to public and private borrowers located outside the United States who require medium- and/or longer-term financing of their purchases of U.S. goods and services.

product groups Commodity groupings used for export control purposes.

profit For the purposes of constructed value in an antidumping duty investigation or review, the profit used is the profit normally earned by a producer, from the country of export, of the same or similar product as that under investigation. By statute, the amount of profit shall not be less than 8 percent of the sum of general expenses and cost.

pro forma invoice An invoice provided by a supplier prior to the shipment of merchandise, informing the buyer of the kinds and quantities of goods to be sent, their value, and important specifications (weight, size, and similar characteristics).

project license Used by the Bureau of Export Administration to authorize large-scale exports of a wide variety of commodities and technical data for specified activities. Those activities can include capital expansion, maintenance, repair or operating supplies, or the supply of materials to be used in the production of other commodities for sale.

protective order With regard to antidumping cases, a term for the order under which most business proprietary information is made available to an attorney or other representative of a party to the proceeding.

Protest System A part of Customs' Automated Commercial System that tracks protests from the date they are received through final action. A protest is the legal means by which an importer, consignee, or other designated part may challenge decisions made by a district director of customs.

purchase price A statutory term used in dumping investigations to refer to the U.S. sales price of merchandise that is sold or likely to be sold prior to the date of importation, by the producer or reseller of the merchandise for exportation to the United States. Certain statutory adjustments (e.g., import duties, commissions, freight) are made, if appropriate, to permit a meaningful comparison with the foreign market value of such or similar merchandise.

Quadrilateral Meetings Meetings involving trade ministers from the United States, the European Community, Canada, and Japan to discuss trade policy matters.

quantitative restrictions (QRs) Explicit limits, usually by volume, on the amount of a specified commodity that may be imported into a country, sometimes also indicating the amounts that may be imported from each supplying country. Compared to tariffs, the protection afforded by QRs tends to be more predictable, being less affected by changes in competitive factors. Quotas have been used at times to favor preferred sources of supply. The General Agreement on Tariff and Trade generally prohibits the use of quantitative restrictions, except in special cases, such as those cited in Articles XX (which permits exceptions to protect public health, national gold stocks, goods of archeological or historic interest, and a few other special categories of goods), or Article XXI (which permits exceptions in the interest of "national security"), or for safeguard purposes, when the appropriate procedures in Article XIX have been followed.

quotas, Quota System Absolute quotas permit a limited number of units of specified merchandise to be entered or withdrawn for consumption during specified periods. Tariff-rate quotas permit a specified quantity of merchandise to be entered or withdrawn at a reduced rate during a specified period. Quotas are established by presidential proclamations, executive orders, or other legislation.

The Quota System, part of Customs' Automated Commercial System, controls quota levels (quantities authorized) and quantities entered against those levels. Visas control exports from the country of origin. Visa authorizations are received from other countries, and quantities entered against those visas are transmitted back to them. Control of visas and quotas simplify reconciliation of other countries' exports and U.S. imports.

reciprocity The reduction of a country's import duties or other trade restraints in return for comparable trade concessions from another country. Reciprocity includes the lowering of customs duties on imports in return for tariff concessions from other countries; the negotiated reduction of a country's import duties or other trade restraints in return for similar concessions from another country. Reciprocity is a traditional principle of General Agreement on Tariffs and Trade trade negotiations that implies an approximate equality of concessions accorded and benefits received among or between participants in a negotiation. In practice this principle applies only in negotiations between developed countries. Because of the frequently wide disparity in their economic capacities and potential, the relationship between developed and developing countries is generally not one of equivalence. The concept of relative reciprocity has emerged to characterize the practice by developed countries to seek less than full reciprocity from developing countries in trade negotiations.

reexports For export control purposes, the shipment of U.S.-origin products from one foreign destination to another. For statistical reporting purposes, exports of foreign-origin merchandise that have previously entered the United States for consumption or into customs-bonded warehouses for U.S. foreign trade zones.

residual restrictions Quantitative restrictions that have been maintained by governments before they became contracting parties to the General Agreement on Tariffs and Trade and, hence, permissible under its grandfather clause. Most of the residual restrictions still in effect are maintained by developed countries against the imports of agricultural products.

restrictive business practices Actions in the private sector, such as collusion among the largest international suppliers, designed to restrict competition so as to keep prices relatively high.

retaliation Action taken by a country whose exports are adversely affected by the raising of tariffs or other trade-restricting measures by another country. The General Agreement on Tariffs and Trade permits an adversely affected contracting party (CP) to impose limited restraints on imports from another CP that has raised its trade barriers (after consultations with countries whose trade might be affected). In theory, the volume of trade affected by such retaliatory measures should approximate the value of trade affected by the precipitating change in import protection.

reverse preferences Tariff advantages once offered by developing countries to imports from certain developed countries that granted them preferences. Reverse preferences characterized trading arrangements between the European Community and some developing countries prior to the advent of the Generalized System of Preferences and the signing of the Lome Convention.

revocable letter of credit A letter of credit that can be canceled or altered by the drawee (buyer) after it has been issued by the drawee's bank.

revocation of antidumping duty order and termination of suspended investigation An antidumping duty order may be revoked or a suspended investigation may be terminated upon application from a party to the proceeding. Ordinarily the application is considered only if there have been no sales at less than fair value for at least the two most recent years. However, the International Trade Administration may on its own initiative revoke an antidumping duty order or terminate a suspended investigation if there have not been sales at less than fair value for a period of three years.

Rollback An agreement among Uruguay Round participants to dismantle all trade-restrictive or distorting measures that are inconsistent with the provisions of the General Agreement on Tariffs and Trade. Measures subject to rollback would be phased out or brought into conformity within an agreed time frame, no later than by the formal completion of the negotiations. The rollback agreement is accompanied by a commitment to stand still on existing trade-restrictive measures. Rollback is also used to refer to the imposition of quantitative restrictions at levels less than those occurring in the present.

safeguards The General Agreement on Tariffs and Trade (GATT) permits two forms of multilateral safeguards: (1) a country's right to impose temporary import controls or other trade restrictions to prevent commercial injury to domestic industry, and (2) the corresponding right of exporters not to be deprived arbitrarily of access to markets.

Article XIX of the GATT permits a country whose domestic industries or workers are adversely affected by increased imports to withdraw or modify concessions the country had earlier granted, to impose, for a limited period, new import restrictions if the country can establish that a product is "being imported in such increased quantities as to cause or threaten serious injury to domestic producers," and to keep such restrictions in effect for a such time as may be necessary to prevent or remedy such injury.

sales representative An agent who distributes, represents, services, or sells goods on behalf of foreign sellers.

Section 201 (Trade Act of 1974) An "escape clause" provision that permits temporary import relief, not to exceed a maximum of eight years, to a domestic industry seriously injured, or threatened with serious injury, due to increased imports. Import relief, granted at the president's discretion, generally takes the form of increased tariffs or quantitative restrictions. To be eligible for Section 201 relief, the International Trade Commission (ITC) must determine that the industry has been seriously injured or threatened to be injured and imports have been a substantial cause (not less than any other cause) of that injury. Industries need not prove that an unfair trade practice exists, as is necessary under the antidumping and countervailing duty laws. However, under Section 201, a greater degree of injury—"serious" injury—must be found to exist, and imports must be a "substantial" cause (defined as not less than any other cause) of that injury.

If the ITC finding is affirmative, the president's remedy may be a tariff increase, quantitative restrictions, or orderly marketing agreements. At the conclusion of any relief action, the commission must report on the effectiveness of the relief action, the commission must report on the effectiveness of the relief action in facilitating the positive adjustment of the domestic industry to import competition. If the decision is made not to grant relief, the president must provide an explanation to the Congress.

Section 232 (Trade Expansion Act of 1962, as amended) To determine whether articles are being imported into the United States in quantities or circumstances that threaten national security. Based on the investigation report, the president can adjust imports of the article(s) in question.

The Department of Commerce must report on the effects these imports have on national security and make recommendations for action or inaction within 270 days after starting an investigation. Within 90 days of the report, the president decides whether to take action to adjust imports on the basis of national security. The president must notify Congress of his decision within 30 days.

Section 301 Under Section 301 of the Trade Act, firms can complain about a foreign country's trade policies or practices that are harmful to U.S. commerce. The section empowers the U.S. trade representative to investigate the allegations and to negotiate the removal of any trade barriers. The section requires that the dispute resolution process of the General Agreement on Tariffs and Trade be invoked where applicable and, if negotiations fail, to retaliate within 180 days from the date that discovery of a trade agreement violation took place.

Section 337 (Tariff Act of 1930) Requires investigations of unfair practices in import trade. Under this authority, the International Trade Commission applies U.S. statutory and common law of unfair competition to the importation of products into the United States and their sale. Section 337 prohibits unfair competition and unfair importing practices and sales of products in the United States, when these threaten to destroy or substantially injure a domestic industry, prevent the establishment of such an industry, or restrain or monopolize U.S. trade and commerce. Section 337 also prohibits infringement of U.S. patents, copyrights, registered trademarks, or mask works.

Semiconductor Trade Arrangement A bilateral agreement between the United States and Japan that came into effect on August 1, 1991, replacing the prior 1986 Semiconductor Trade Arrangement. The new arrangement contains provisions to increase foreign access to the Japanese semiconductor market and deter dumping of semiconductors by Japanese suppliers into the U.S. market, as well as in third-country markets. In evaluating market access improvement, both governments agreed to pay particular attention to market share. The expectation of a 20 percent foreign market share by the end of 1992 is included in the arrangement. The arrangement explicitly states, however, that the 20 percent figure is not a guarantee, a ceiling, or a floor on the foreign market share.

senior commercial officer (SCO) The senior U.S. and foreign commercial officer at an embassy, who reports in-country to the ambassador. At major posts, this position carries the title of commercial counselor; in key posts, minister counselor. Usually reporting to the SCO are a commercial attaché and commercial officers. The latter are sometimes assigned to subordinate posts throughout the country.

shared foreign sales corporation A foreign sales corporation consisting of more than 1 and fewer than 25 unrelated exporters.

shipper's export declaration (SED) A declaration used to control exports and compile trade statistics; must be prepared and submitted to the customs agent for shipments by mail valued at more than $500 and for shipments by means other than mail valued at more than $2,500. An SED must be prepared for all shipments covered by an individual validated license, regardless of value.

shipping weight The gross weight in kilograms of shipments, including the weight of moisture content, wrappings, crates, boxes, and containers (other than cargo vans and similar substantial outer containers).

ship's manifest A list, signed by the captain of a ship, of the individual shipments constituting the ship's cargo.

short supply Commodities subject to export controls to protect the domestic economy from the excessive drain of scarce materials and to reduce the serious inflationary impact of satisfying foreign demand. Two commodities the U.S. controls for short supply purposes are crude oil and unprocessed western red cedar.

Single Internal Market Information Service (SIMS) Run by the International Trade Administration, a clearinghouse for information on EC 1992 activities. Telephone: (202) 377–5276.

soft loan A no-interest loan granted to developing countries by the International Development Association. It carries no interest (although there is a small annual service charge), is payable in 50 years, and has an amortization rate of 1 percent repayable annually for the 10 years following an initial 10-year grace period, followed by 3 percent repayable annually for the remaining 30 years.

Southern Africa Development Coordination Conference (SADCC) A regional economic pact comprising Angola, Botswana, Lesotho, Malawi, Mozambique, Namibia, Swaziland, Tanzania, Zambia, and Zimbabwe.

Southern African Customs Union (SACU) Established in 1910 to provide for its members—Botswana, Lesotho, Namibia, South Africa, and Swazilan—the free exchange of goods within the area, a common external tariff, and a sharing of custom revenues. External tariffs, excise duties, and several rebate and refund provisions are the same for all SACU members. SACU's revenues are apportioned among its members according to a formula. These funds constitute a significant contribution to each member's government revenues.

special and differential treatment A principle, enunciated in the Tokyo Declaration, that the Tokyo Round negotiations should seek to accord particular benefits to the exports of developing countries, consistent with their trade, financial, and development needs. Among proposals for special or differential treatment are reduction or elimination of tariffs applied to exports of developing countries under the Generalized System of Preferences (GSP), expansion of product and country coverage of the GSP, accelerated implementation of tariff cuts agreed to in the Tokyo Round for developing country exports, substantial reduction or elimination of tariff escalation, special provisions for developing country exports in any new codes of conduct covering nontariff measures, assurance that any new multilateral safeguard system will contain special provisions for developing country exports, and the principle that developed countries will expect less than full reciprocity for trade concessions they grant developing countries.

special drawing rights (SDRs) International reserve assets created by the International Monetary Fund (IMF) and allocated to individual member nations. Within conditions set by the IMF, SDRs can be used by a nation with a deficit in its balance of international payments to settle debts with another nation or with the IMF.

Special 301 Statute requiring the U.S. trade representative (USTR) to review annually the condition of intellectual property protection among U.S. trading partners. Submissions are accepted from industry, after which the USTR, weighing all relevant information, makes a determination as to whether a country presents excessive barriers to trade with the United States by virtue of its inadequate protection of intellectual property. If the USTR makes a positive determination, a country may be named to the list of Priority Foreign Countries (the most egregious), the Priority Watch List, or the Watch List.

Standard Industrial Classification (SIC) The classification standard underlying all establishment-based U.S. economic statistics classified by industry.

Standard International Trade Classification (SITC) Developed by the United Nations in 1950 and used solely by international organizations for reporting international trade. The SITC has been revised several times; the current version is Revision 3.

standards As defined by the Multilateral Trade Negotiations Agreement on Technical Barriers to Trade (Standards Code), technical specification contained in a document that lays down characteristics of a product, such as levels of quality, performance, safety, or dimensions. Standards may include, or deal exclusively with, terminology, symbols, testing and test methods, packaging, marking, or labeling requirements as they apply to a product.

standstill A commitment of the General Agreement on Tariffs and Trade contracting parties not to impose new trade-restrictive measures during the Uruguay Round negotiations.

State Export Program Database (SEPD) A trade lead system maintained by the National Association of State Development Agencies. Includes information on state-operated trade lead systems.

state/industry-organized, government approved Trade missions planned and organized by state development agencies, trade associations, chambers of commerce, and other export-oriented groups. To qualify for U.S. government sponsorship, organizers of this type of trade mission must agree to follow International Trade Administration criteria in planning and recruiting the mission.

258

state trading enterprises (STEs) Entities established by governments to import, export, and/or produce certain products. Examples include government-operated import/export monopolies, and marketing boards or private companies that receive special or exclusive privileges from their governments to engage in trading activities.

Structural Impediments Initiative (SII) Started in July 1989 to identify and solve structural problems that restrict bringing two-way trade between the United States and Japan into better balance. Both the U.S. and Japanese governments chose issues of concern in the other's economy as impediments to trade and current account imbalances. The areas the U.S. government chose as focus included Japanese savings and investment patterns, land use, distribution, *keiretsu*, exclusionary business practices, and pricing. Areas the Japanese government chose as focus included U.S. savings and investment patterns, corporate investment patterns and supply capacity, corporate behavior, government regulation, research and development, export promotion, and work force education and training.

In a June 1990 report, the United States and Japan agreed to seven meetings in the following three years to review progress, discuss problems, and produce annual joint reports.

subsidy A bounty or grant paid for the manufacture, production, or export of an article. Export subsidies are contingent on exports; domestic subsidies are conferred on production without reference to exports. While governments sometimes make outright payments to firms, subsidies usually take a less direct form (R&D support, tax breaks, loans on preferential terms, and provision of raw materials at below-market prices).

summary investigation A 20-day investigation conducted by the International Trade Administration immediately following filing of an antidumping petition to ascertain if the petition contains sufficient information with respect to sales at "less than fair value" and the injury or threat of material injury to a domestic industry caused by the alleged sales at "less than fair value" to warrant the initiation of an antidumping investigation.

Super 301 A provision enacted due to congressional concern that the regular Section 301 procedures narrowly limit U.S. attention to the market access problems of individual sectors or companies. Super 301 sets procedures to identify and address within three years certain "priority," systemic trade restriction policies of other nations. Super 301 authority expired May 30, 1990.

suspension of investigation A decision to suspend an antidumping investigation if the exporters who account for substantially all of the imported merchandise agree to stop exports to the United States or agree to revise their prices promptly to eliminate any dumping margin. An investigation may be suspended at any time before a final determination is made. No agreement to suspend an investigation may be made unless effective monitoring of the agreement is practicable and is determined to be in the public interest.

suspension of liquidation If affirmative, the preliminary determination of dumping or subsidization, or final determination after a negative preliminary determination, provides for suspension of liquidation of all entries of merchandise subject to the determination that are entered, or withdrawn from warehouse, for consumption, on or after the date of the publication of the notice in the Federal Register. Customs is directed to require a cash deposit, or the posting of a bond or other security, for each entry affected equal to the estimated amount of the subsidy or the amount by which the fair value exceeds the U.S. price. When an administrative review is completed, customs is directed to collect the final subsidy rate or amount by which the foreign market value exceeds the U.S. price, and to require for each entry thereafter a cash deposit that is equal to the newly determined subsidy rate or margin of dumping.

switch arrangements A form of countertrade in which the seller sells on credit and then transfers the credit to a third party.

Table of Denial Orders (TDO) A list of individuals and firms disbarred from shipping or receiving U.S. goods or technology. Firms and individuals on the list may be disbarred with respect to controlled commodities or general destination (across-the-board) exports.

tare weight The weight of a container and/or packing materials without the weight of the goods it contains.

tariff A tax assessed by a government in accordance with its tariff schedule on goods as they enter (or leave) a country. May be imposed to protect domestic industries from imported goods and/or to generate revenue. Types include ad valorem, specific, variable, or some combination.

tariff anomaly Exists when the tariff on raw materials or semimanufactured goods is higher than the tariff on the finished product.

tariff escalation A situation in which tariffs on manufactured goods are relatively high, tariffs on semiprocessed goods are moderate, and tariffs on raw materials are nonexistent or very low.

tariff quotas Application of a higher tariff rate to imported goods after a specified quantity of the item has entered the country at a lower prevailing rate.

tariff schedule A comprehensive list of the goods a country may import and the import duties applicable to each product.

Tax Information Exchange Agreement (TIEA) An agreement concluded between the United States and a beneficiary country designated pursuant to the Caribbean Basin Economic Recovery Act of 1983. This agreement generally involves an expanded version of the standard exchange of information article, usually included in a bilateral income tax treaty. The United States has similar agreements with most major trading partners. Like the standard tax treaty exchange of information article, a TIEA imposes on the agreeing countries a mutual and reciprocal obligation to exchange information relating to the enforcement of their respective tax laws.

technical barrier to trade According to the Standards Code, a specification that sets forth characteristics or standards a product must meet (such as levels of quality, performance, safety, or dimensions) in order to be imported.

technology transfer Used to characterize the transfer of knowledge generated and developed in one place to another, where it is used to achieve some practical end. Technology may be transferred by giving it away (technical journals, conferences, emigration of technical experts, technical assistance programs), by industrial espionage, or by sale (patents, blueprints, industrial processes, and the activities of multinational corporations).

through bill of lading A single bill of lading covering receipt of the cargo at the point of origin for delivery to the ultimate consignee, using two or more modes of transportation.

tied aid credit Refers to the practice of providing grants and/or concessional loans, either alone or combined with export credits, linked to procurement from the donor country.

tied loan A loan made by a government agency that requires a foreign borrower to spend the proceeds in the lender's country.

Tokyo Round Talks that called for consideration to be given "to improvements in the international framework for the conduct of world trade." Four separate agreements make up what is known as the "framework agreement." They concern (1) differential and more favorable treatment for, and reciprocity and fuller participation by, developing countries in the international framework for trade; (2) trade measures taken for balance of payments purposes; (3) safeguard actions for development purposes; and (4) an understanding on notification, consultation, dispute settlement, and surveillance in the General Agreement on Tariffs and Trade.

Trade Act of 1974 Legislation enacted late in 1974 and signed into law in January 1975, granting the president broad authority to enter into international agreements to reduce import barriers. Major purposes were to (1) stimulate U.S. economic growth and to maintain and enlarge foreign markets for the products of U.S. agriculture, industry, mining and commerce; (2) strengthen economic relations with other countries through open and nondiscriminatory trading practices; (3) protect American industry and workers against unfair or injurious import competition; and (4) provide "adjustment assistance" to industries, workers, and communities injured or threatened by increased imports. The act allowed the president to extend tariff preferences to certain imports from developing countries and set conditions under which most-favored-nation treatment could be extended to nonmarket economy countries and provided negotiating authority for the Tokyo Round or multilateral trade negotiations.

Trade Adjustment Assistance (TAA) Authorized for workers and firms by the 1974 Trade Act. TAA for firms is administered by the Department of Commerce; TAA for workers is administered by the Department of Labor.

Eligible firms must show that increased imports of articles like or directly competitive with those produced by the firm contributed importantly to declines in its sales and/or production and to the separation or threat of separation of a significant portion of the firm's workers. These firms receive help
through Trade Adjustment Assistance Centers (TAACs), primarily in implementing adjustment strategies in production, marketing, and management.

Eligible workers must be associated with a firm whose sales or production
have decreased absolutely due to increases in like or directly competitive imported products, resulting in total or partial separation of the employee and
the decline in the firm's sales or production. Assistance includes training, job
search and relocation allowances, plus reemployment services for workers adversely affected by the increased imports.

Trade Adjustment Assistance Centers (TAACs) Nonprofit, nongovernment
organizations established to help firms qualify for and receive assistance in
adjusting to import competition. Funded by the Commerce Department as a
primary source of technical assistance to certified firms.

Trade Agreements Act of 1979 Legislation authorizing the United States to
implement trade agreements dealing with nontariff barriers negotiated during
the Tokyo Round, including agreements that required changes in existing U.S.
laws, and certain concessions that had not been explicitly authorized by the
Trade Act of 1974. The act incorporated into U.S. law the Tokyo Round agreements on dumping, customs valuation, import licensing procedures, government procurement practices, product standards, civil aircraft, meat and dairy
products, and liquor duties. The act also extended the president's authority to
negotiate trade agreements with foreign countries to reduce or eliminate
nontariff barriers to trade.

trade barriers As classified by the U.S. trade representative, (1) import policies (tariffs and other import charges, quantitative restrictions, import licensing, and customs barriers); (2) standards, testing, labeling, and certification; (3)
government procurement; (4) export subsidies; (5) lack of intellectual property protection; (6) service barriers; (7) investment barriers; and (8) other barriers (e.g., barriers encompassing more than one category or barriers affecting a
single sector).

trade concordance Refers to the matching of Harmonized System (HS) codes to larger statistical definitions, such as the Standard Industrial Classification (SIC) code and the Standard International Trade Classification (SITC) system. The Bureau of the Census, the United Nations, as well as individual federal and private organizations maintain trade concordances for the purpose of relating trade and production data.

Trade and Development Program (TDP) Offers tied aid and resembles Japan's tied aid funding. The program provides project planning funding only for projects that are priorities of the host country and present a good opportunity for sales of U.S. goods and services. The TDP started within the Agency for International Development but was spun off as an independent agency in 1981.

trade event A promotional activity that may include a demonstration of products or services and brings together in one viewing area the principals in the purchase and sale of the products or services. As a generic term, trade events may include trade fairs, trade missions, trade shows, catalog shows, matchmaker events, foreign buyer missions, and similar functions.

trade fair A stage-setting event in which firms of several nationalities present their products or services to prospective customers in a preformatted setting (usually a booth of a certain size located adjacent to other potential suppliers). A distinguishing factor between trade fairs and trade shows is size. A trade fair is generally viewed as having a larger number of participants than other trade events or as an event bringing together related industries.

Trade Fair Certification Program A Commerce Department program started in 1983 to promote selected privately organized trade shows. The program helps private sector organizations in mounting certified international fairs. Commerce assistance includes promoting the fair among foreign customers and help exhibitors to make commercial contacts.

Trade Information Center (TIC) A one-stop source for information on Federal programs to assist U.S. exporters. Telephone 1 (800) USA-TRADE.

trade mission Individuals who are taken as a group to meet with prospective customers overseas. Missions visit specific individuals or places with no specific stage setting other than appointments. Appointments are made with government and/or commercial customers, or with individuals who may be a stepping stone to customers.

International Trade Association (ITA) trade missions are scheduled in selected countries to help participants find local agents, representatives, and distributors, to make direct sales, or to conduct market assessments. Some missions include technical seminars to support sales of sophisticated products and technology in specific markets. ITA missions include planning and publicity, appointments with qualified contacts and with government officials, market briefings and background information on contacts, as well as logistical support and interpreter service. Trade missions also are frequently organized by other federal, state, or local agencies.

Trade Negotiations Committee (TNC) The steering group that manages the Uruguay Round negotiations. The TNC comprises all countries participating in the current negotiations (that is, it is not limited simply to members of the General Agreement of Tariffs and Trade). Functioning at the nonministerial level, the TNC services as a vehicle for transparency.

Trade Opportunities Program (TOP) An International Trade Administration service that provides sales leads from overseas firms seeking to buy or represent U.S. products and services. Through overseas channels, U.S. foreign commercial officers gather leads and details, including specifications, quantities, end use, and delivery deadlines. TOPs are telexed to Washington, listed on the Commerce Department's Economic Bulletin Board, and redistributed by the private sector.

Trade Policy Committee (TPC) A cabinet-level, interagency trade committee established by the Trade Expansion Act of 1962 (chaired by the U.S. trade representative) to provide broad guidance on trade issues. The committee was renewed by an executive order at the end of the Carter administration. Toward the end of the first Reagan administration, with much dissention over Japan policy between the TPC, the Senior Interagency Group (chaired by Treasury), and the other groups, the White House created the Economic Policy Council (EPC) in 1985 as a single forum to reduce tensions.

The Trade Policy Review Group (TPRG) is a subcabinet group that meets about once a week. It is an ad hoc creation that was not established by law.

TPRG membership is fairly fluid, so that agencies that participate in a particular discussion can sit at the table.

The Trade Policy Staff Committee (TPSC) has met perhaps once a year since 1988. TPSC was established by law to obtain advice from the private sector on topics such as retaliation; it generally serves as a paper clearance structure.

Beneath the TPSC is a large number (60–100; exact counts are not maintained) of TPSC subcommittees. Subcommittees are not independent; they are established to deal with topics of interim interest and are sometimes no more than lists of interested parties on a given issue.

Trade Policy Information System (TPIS) Generally includes U.S. foreign trade data (detailed U.S. merchandise trade statistics), U.N. trade data, the International Monetary Fund and World Bank databases, and the Trade and Tariff Library project for use in the General Agreement on Tariffs and Trade.

Trade Policy Review Mechanism (TPRM) Created at the Uruguay Round midterm ministerial meeting in Montreal. Under the TPRM, the trade policies of any General Agreement on Tariffs and Trade (GATT) contracting party are subject to regularly scheduled review by the GATT Council. Reviews may lead to recommendations on ways to improve a contracting party's trade policies.

Trade Promotion Coordinating Committee (TPCC) Established by the president in May 1990 to unify and streamline the government's decentralized approach to export promotion. TPCC members include the Departments of Commerce (as chair), State, Treasury, Agriculture, Defense, Energy, and Transportation, the Office of Management and Budget, the U.S. trade representative, the Council of Economic Advisers, the Export-Import Bank, the Overseas Private Investment Corporation, the U.S. Information Agency, the Agency for International Development, the Trade and Development Program, and the Small Business Administration.

trade-related aspects of intellectual property rights (TRIPs) U.S. intellectual property rights objectives in the Uruguay Round. These objectives include achieving a comprehensive General Agreement on Tariffs and Trade agreement that would include substantive standards of protection for all areas of intellectual property (patents, trademarks, copyrights, etc.); effective enforcement measures (both at the border and internally); and effective dispute settlement provisions.

trade-related investment measures (TRIMs) Require the use of specified amounts of local inputs rather than imported goods, and requirements to export a certain amount of production. The developed countries (with the exception of Australia) favor prohibiting certain TRIMs; virtually all developing countries oppose prohibiting any TRIMs.

trade show A stage-setting event in which firms present their products or services to prospective customers in a preformatted setting (usually a booth of a certain size located adjacent to other potential suppliers). The firms are generally in the same industry but not necessarily of the same nationality since trade fairs are international. A distinguishing factor between trade fairs and trade shows is size. A trade show is generally viewed as a smaller assembly of participants.

transit zone A port of entry in a coastal country that is established as a storage and distribution center for the convenience of a neighboring country lacking adequate port facilities or access to the sea. A zone is administered so that goods in transit to and from the neighboring country are not subject to the customs duties, import controls, or many of the entry and exit formalities of the host country. A transit zone is a more limited facility than a free trade zone or a free port.

transmittal letter A list of the particulars of the shipment and a record of the documents being transmitted together with instructions for disposition of documents. Any special instructions are also included.

transparency The extent to which laws, regulations, agreements, and practices affecting international trade are open, clear, measurable, and verifiable.

travel mission A marketing activity carried out in foreign markets that usually involves trade information, presentations, and media activities.

Treaty of Rome (1957) Was intended to create a single market for the European Community, with free movement of goods, persons, services, and capital. Article 30 of the treaty prohibited not only quantitative restrictions on imports but also all measures having an equivalent effect.

trigger price mechanism (TPM) An antidumping mechanism designed to protect U.S. industries from underpriced imports. First used in 1978 to protect the steel industry, the TPM is the price of the lowest-cost foreign producer. Imports priced below the trigger price are assessed a duty equal to the difference between their price and the trigger price.

tropical products Traditionally, agricultural goods of export interest to developing countries in the tropical zones of Africa, Latin America, and East Asia (coffee, tea, spices, bananas, and tropical hardwoods).

trust receipt Release of merchandise by a bank to a buyer in which the bank retains title to the merchandise. The buyer, who obtains the goods for manufacturing or sales purposes, is obligated to maintain the goods (or the proceeds from their sale) distinct from the remainder of his or her assets and to hold them ready for repossession by the bank.

turnkey A method of construction whereby the contractor assumes total responsibility from design through completion of the project.

ultimate beneficial owner (UBO) The UBO of a U.S. affiliate is that person, proceeding up the affiliate's ownership chain beginning with and including the foreign parent, that is not owned more than 50 percent by another person. The UBO consists of only the ultimate owner; other affiliated persons are excluded. If the foreign parent is not owned more than 50 percent by another person, the foreign parent and the UBO are the same. A UBO, unlike a foreign parent, may be a U.S. person.

ultimate consignee The person located abroad who is the true party in interest, receiving the export for the designated end use.

unfair trade practice Any act, policy, or practice of a foreign government that violates, is inconsistent with, or otherwise denies benefits to the United States under any trade agreement to which the United States is a party; is unjustifiable, unreasonable, or discriminatory and burdens or restricts U.S. commerce; or is otherwise inconsistent with a favorable Section 301 determination by the U.S. trade representative.

United Nations Conference on Trade and Development (UNCTAD) Set up in December 1964 as a permanent organ of the U.N. General Assembly to promote international trade and increase trade between developing countries and countries with different social and economic systems. UNCTAD also examines problems of economic development within the context of principles and policies of international trade and seeks to harmonize trade, development, and regional economic policies.

United States Foreign and Commercial Service The State Department's Foreign Commercial Service was transferred to Commerce in April 1980. This group was merged with Commerce's domestic field operations in 1982, creating the U.S. and Foreign Commercial Service. It is responsible for assisting U.S. firms with the conduct of their international business operations.

United States price In the context of dumping investigations, refers to the price at which goods are sold in the United States compared to their foreign market value. The comparisons are used in the process of determining whether imported merchandise is sold at less than fair value.

United States trade representative (USTR) A cabinet-level official with the rank of ambassador who advises the president on trade policy. The USTR coordinates the development of U.S. trade policy initiatives; leads U.S. international trade negotiations; and seeks to expand U.S. exports by promoting removal or reduction of foreign trade barriers.

U.S. affiliate A U.S. business enterprise in which there is foreign direct investment—that is, a single foreign person owns or controls, directly or indirectly, 10 percent or more of its voting securities if the enterprise is incorporated or an equivalent interest if the enterprise is unincorporated. The affiliate is called a U.S. affiliate to denote that the affiliate is located in the United States (although it is owned by a foreign person).

validated export license A document issued by the U.S. government authorizing the export of commodities for which written export authorization is required by law.

value-added tax A European Community (EC) tax assessed on the increased value of goods as they pass from the raw material stage through the production process to final consumption. The tax on processors or merchants is levied on the amount by which they increase the value of items they purchase. The EC charges a tax equivalent to the value-added to imports and rebates value-added taxes on exports.

variable levy A tariff subject to alterations as world market prices change. The alterations are designed to ensure that the import price after payment of the duty will equal a predetermined "gate" price.

vertical export trading company An export trading company that integrates a range of functions, taking products from suppliers to consumers.

voluntary export restriction An understanding between trading partners in which the exporting nation, in order to reduce trade friction, agrees to limit its exports of a particular good. Also called voluntary restraint agreement.

voluntary restraint agreement Informal bilateral or multilateral understandings in which exporters voluntarily limit exports of certain products to a particular country destination in order to avoid economic dislocation in the importing country and the imposition of mandatory import restrictions. These arrangements do not involve an obligation on the part of the importing country to provide "compensation" to the exporting country, as would be the case if the importing country unilaterally imposed equivalent restraints on imports.

Webb-Pomerene Association Associations engaged in exporting that combine the products of similar producers for overseas sales. These associations have partial exemption from U.S. antitrust laws but may not engage in import, domestic, or third-country trade or combine to export services.

West Africa Economic Community (Fr. Communaute Economique de l'Afrique) Created in 1974, include Benin, Burkina Faso, Cote d'Ixvoire, Mali, Mauritania, Niger, and Senegal. (Togo has observer status). The CEAO operates as a free trade area for agricultural products and raw materials and as a preferential trading area for approved industrial products, with a regional cooperation tax replacing import duties and encouraging trade among member states. In order to ensure that benefits of the regional grouping flow to all members, especially the least developed ones (Mali, Mauritania, Niger, and Burkina Faso), the CEAO has established a fund to provide financial services and guarantees to development lenders in both public and private sectors for projects in member states. In addition, CEAO has the long-term objective of creating a customs union with extensive harmonization of fiscal policies among member states, though no concrete achievements in this direction have been recorded.

West African Monetary Union (WAMU; French: Union monetaire ouest africaine, UMOA) Created by treaty signed in May 1962. WAMU comprises seven French-speaking African countries: Benin, Burkina Faso, Cote d'Ivoire, Mali, Niger, Senegal, and Togo. Within WAMU, these countries share a common currency (CFA franc) freely convertible into the French franc at a fixed parity, and a common central bank (BCEAO) responsible for the conduct of the Union's monetary and credit policies. There is a common regional development bank, the Banque ouest africaine de développement (BOAD).

Wharfage A charge assessed by a pier or dock owner for handling incoming or outgoing cargo.

without reserve A term indicating that a shipper's agent or representative is empowered to make definitive decisions and adjustments abroad without approval of the group or individual represented.

World Bank Group An integrated group of international institutions that provides financial and technical assistance to developing countries. The group includes the International Bank for Reconstruction and Development, the International Development Association, and the International Finance Corporation.

World Intellectual Property Organization (WIPO) A specialized agency that is part of the United Nations system of organizations. Located in Geneva, WIPO promotes protection of intellectual property around the world through cooperation among states, and administers various "unions," each founded on a multilateral treaty and dealing with the legal and administrative aspects of intellectual property.

World Traders Data Reports (WTDRs) An International Trade Administration fee-based service that provides a background report on a specific foreign firm, prepared by commercial officers overseas. WTDRs provide information about the type of organization, year established, relative size, number of employees, general reputation, territory covered, language preferred, product lines handled, principal owners, financial references, and trade references. WTDRs include narrative information about the reliability of the foreign firm.

Index